SOUL DRINKER

Matthew Yard was born in Burlington, Wisconsin in 1978, and grew up in the small city of Delavan in the southeast of the state. He has always been an exceptional storyteller, whether he was telling stories while around a campfire with his family and friends or writing them down for others to read. When he was 22, he enlisted in the air force. After basic training and tech school, he was sent in 2001 to serve at an air base in Yokota, Japan. His time there was divided between two trips to Iraq. While based in Japan, he met his wife Mayumi. They have three young daughters, who all love listening to him tell them stories. He began writing when he was in high school, mostly short stories and poems, and had many of them published in newspapers and contests, even though he had a learning disability which made writing longer works very difficult. Reading horror books helped him work through his struggles, and has led to this supernatural thriller romance. *Soul Drinker* is his first novel.

SOUL DRINKER

A SUPERNATURAL THRILLER ROMANCE

Matthew Yard

Cp

Published in the United States by Capraro Press. www.
capraropress.com

Library of Congress Control Number: 2020913489

ISBN 978-1-943386-83-3 (pbk)

ISBN 978-1-943386-84-0 (ebook)

Want to get in the mood?

Praise for *Soul Drinker*

Reviewed by Rabia Tanveer for Readers' Favorite

Soul Drinker is the story of a man who is beset by evil and is just trying to survive. When Devin packed his bags and moved to Wisconsin, he had dreams of hitting it big and becoming a rock star. But that all changed when he witnessed something terrible. Devin saw something so evil that now he prefers to hide away inside his college than anywhere else, hoping that he will avoid the eyes of the evil being that invaded his life. His only salvation is Victoria. She is the one good thing in his life that is keeping him sane. As Devin's reality and nightmares blend into one, he relies on Victoria to keep him away from the dark. It is now them against an evil that is far more powerful than they could have anticipated. Is their love and need to survive strong enough to fight an evil that thrives on fear?

I was not expecting to like this story as much as I did. The execution of this supernatural thriller blew my mind. The narrative flows seamlessly, the transition between Devin's nightmares and reality was very well done and made me read on. I enjoyed how Victoria and Devin became a team; they understood each other and made sure the other was surviving. For me, Victoria was the true hero of the story; she kept Devin going, she made sure he remained safe and that he was ready to battle when it came knocking on his door. I don't know how the author did it, but he succeeded in offering genuine thriller fiction. He left little clues in the story; he made me look for them and completely surprised me at times. Soul Drinker is an incredible story; one that kept me up at night because I didn't want the story to end!

Reviewed by K.C. Finn for Readers' Favorite

Soul Drinker is a mix of horror, thriller and supernatural romance fiction. Combining these fascinating genres makes for a very compelling adult read, as we explore life through the eyes of protagonists Devin and Victoria. After witnessing ritualistic sights which he can't unsee, Devin finds himself swept up in a horrific supernatural battle with seemingly no way out. Victoria is the person capable of guiding him back towards the light, but to do so, they must face evil together and make an enemy of a powerful god. What follows is a wild and tempestuous adventure with truly dark moments of horror fiction and romantic snatches of a desperate love story in between.

Dark and light create wonderful contrasts all the way through this excellent supernatural novel, and that prevents the story from ever becoming 'one note' during the reading experience. Author Matthew Yard has a refreshing and modern take on the horror genre which allows him to expand into emotional storytelling, fantasy and supernatural layers, and this makes for a frighteningly realistic and well-grounded tale amid all Hell breaking loose. The plot is well-paced for excitement with some very unexpected twists. I particularly enjoyed Devin's internal struggle of good versus evil, which seemed entirely human and realistic of the trauma he's put through. Victoria too provides much more than the typical love interest with a power and strength of her own. Overall, I would certainly recommend *Soul Drinker* to readers seeking more depth in their horror fiction.

Reviewed by K.J. Simmill for Readers' Favorite

Soul Drinker is a supernatural thriller filled with suspense. I enjoyed how the melding of nightmare and reality was portrayed, allowing the reader to experience the same warped and fragmented sensations as Devin. Written in a combination of first and third person, the reader is privileged to have a deeper insight into Devin's psychological torment, fears and terror while also being given a glimpse of events from both other periods in time and other perspectives. The attention to detail allows readers to visualize every horrific moment fully. The love interest and developing romance give Devin hope, a way to combat the horrors and a place to put faith and draw strength. Horror, evil, torture and madness battle against hope, love and a will to survive in a dark and gruesome tale of ancient evil and a quest for power.

Reviewed by Ruffina Oserio for Readers' Favorite

Soul Drinker is a blend of horror and the supernatural, with extraordinary characters and strong plot points that are beautifully held together toward an explosive denouement. When Devin leaves Wisconsin with his best friend, it is in order to embrace their dream and become rock stars. But when he unwittingly witnesses a ritualistic sacrifice by an evil deity, his life becomes a perpetual nightmare. The deity that has been linked to a powerful Viking tribe will stop at nothing to get to Devin, and even the thick walls of the biggest college in the state can't protect him. He is haunted by nightmares and they come at him even while he is fully awake. But there is some hope: the love of a woman. With Victoria by his side, can he find what it takes to defeat the evil that comes at him incessantly?

This is well written and beautifully plotted; an engrossing story that arouses conflicting emotions in readers. At one point, the pathos is overwhelming, then the light of love dispels the darkness, and the reader wants it to stay on. But it hardly takes long before the horror returns. Sometimes it is chilling, at times it is like hell is opening up, and then there is the excitement of two souls in fusion. The suspense is powerful and it seems to be one of Matthew Yard's fortes. The reader wants to know what happens next to the characters, and the sense of the unexpected permeates the story and whets the reader's interest. *Soul Drinker* features compelling characters, a powerful theme and beautiful prose.

Reviewed by Lesley Jones for Readers' Favorite

This gripping thriller is a complete spine-chilling read. The graphic descriptions are superb and will draw you into this disturbing world of satanic rituals, evil forces and pure nightmares. I experienced many emotions while reading this novel. Although there are many tense, horrifying moments, they are interjected with the most endearing scenes between Devin and Victoria. I loved the two main characters; they were well developed and completely believable. I also thought the subplot of Victoria's parents really gave the plot an interesting dimension. The relationship dynamics between the characters are executed perfectly. I really could not foresee how this story would end. All seemed so hopeless. The ending, however, caught me completely by surprise. I greatly hope there is a sequel as I am interested to know more about these characters.

Contents

Prologue

A deity named the Destroyer found a way to break through the boundaries that separate realms and universes. He placed one of his children in that realm to destroy everything in that universe and realm. He did that so that the god of that universe would become weakened and would be easy prey for the Destroyer to feed upon. Before mankind was able to take its first breath, the Destroyer infiltrated this realm during the war of the angels. He mixed his son Luther in with the armies of Satan as they fell so as to hide him from God. Satan welcomed this being into his family with open arms because he saw Luther as a very powerful ally; a being whose power would rival God's.

Luther was aware of Satan's plan, but it didn't faze him or distract him from his goal. He was able to manipulate Satan and his army of demons to his will. Time after time, Luther built powerful cults in every empire and civilization on Earth. It didn't matter where he went or even what legend he twisted and used as his tool to gain strength and numbers. Everyone he interacted with became his puppet. Slowly, all the ancient pagan religions of the world began to be molded after Luther. He was their god and their devil.

In ancient Samaria, he built himself into a fearsome god king that had become too powerful for any single being to take on one on one. God, armed with his army of angels, fought alongside Satan and his demons to destroy Luther. But there were some angels and demons that knew this was a battle that was impossible to win. So they chose to stay loyal to Luther and fought with him. In the realm between life and death, they fought each other endlessly till they reached the point when Luther began to lose some ground. But knowing that there was no way for them to kill Luther and no way of locking him up in the bottomless pit, God and Satan found a way of binding him and separating Luther from the true source of his power. They locked it away in a book.

God and Satan created a sarcophagus out of clay and earth that were from the Garden of Eden. In it, they placed the book. But they had to make a lock, and to do so, both God and Satan had to sacrifice their most powerful and loyal angels and demons to become that lock. These angels and demons were melted into the inside of the sarcophagus. Their hands holding the book down were the only remnants of them.

Within this book, Luther's power was locked away for millennium after millennium. He spent that time searching for the perfect sacrifice that would finally release his book and allow him to be whole once more. Luther found a possible sacrifice among the Vikings. He loved the Vikings and their raw power. He grew a new cult with the help of a seer throughout most of their kingdoms. He gave the Vikings his army to use as they saw fit. No one could withstand an onslaught by them.

1

Devin's nightmare

The pale warmth of the sun bled through the frosted windows with an ease that seemed almost heavenly on that bitter morning in late January. It was a type of warmth that didn't merely brush over my skin, and pass by onto the next object or person. No, it was this warmth that penetrated past the few places of my body that were uncovered; through my depressed attire, which I always chose as my shell, and past my nightmares, which always hovered over me. In the same manner, alcohol stains the breath the day after a long night of drinking. The sight of the sun was truly breathtaking that day on its own. The warmth that the sun brought seemed to beckon me, almost enticing me to strip off my wintry clothes, leaving merely a T-shirt and pants on.

I watched that day's sun being born from my bedroom, as I was forcefully awakened from a shadow that had found its way into my life. In nothing but an empty blackness, I sat fully exposed to the wild woods below me. I sat there in the wake of a shadow. The house that was given to me by a stranger I had never met sat in a dense and wild set of woods, perfectly arranged and placed upon a high ridge so that my second-floor windows overlooked the tops of all the trees of the forest that surrounded it. The window was large enough to bring in a king-size bed easily. I sat clothed only in an old pair of gym shorts and longed to find a way to evacuate this tormented body and journey on to my next step.

Before the sun rose, there were no stars in the sky, only empty darkness. Quickly, the sunlight started to break into the overlaying sky, and it gave birth to the night's version of twilight. It is the moment before light blinds darkness, forcing it to retreat into the shadows once more. It was almost as if I could hear the evil that I just dreamt was trying to break free claw its way out of the pit that I also just dreamt about. The dream began to reverberate endlessly in my mind. Was this a dream, was it real, or was it merely the fear in it that was making it seem real? Then again, as an overpowered bouncing ball, the dream was thrown back at me. The memory of it was so vivid that I started reliving it again.

I wanted to watch the completion of the sunrise, but I was not permitted to. I felt as powerless as a vampire might be when it reaches the end of its first night. The mysteries and wonders that the night brought it were then ending. All that there was left for it to do was rest. Even as I fought to halt the process, sleep ambushed me during one of the moments my eyes blinked. The next thing I knew, I was completely aware again, standing on red, hollow-sounding stones. Words were written on the gate that I was standing before, and I knew those words. Even though they were in a foreign language that I could not read and could not understand, I somehow knew exactly what they meant. It was not because of the dream; just standing there made it possible for anyone who stood there to read those letters. Knowing what I knew still didn't stop my head and eyes from turning their gaze toward the engraved stone that hovered 20 feet above my head. "These are the gates to Hell."

I wondered if I was just reliving an echo of my previous dream. But I had no real control. Or was it a new experience with a similar outcome? All I could do was hope that that was not the case and that I could force myself awake so I could watch the sunrise as I had anticipated. I felt the same as a broken-down mourner left alone to sift through bodies on the lands of the ancient warlords after all the steam has left the blood-stained battlefield. Could it be that I had finally reached my destiny and that the place of torment I was in was my tomb?

With each step, my bare foot hammered down louder than any rock concert I have played in or attended. The depths of how hollow the ground was could be heard by how the sound of the impact was without structure, and felt by vibrations with each of those thundering steps. It shook the gate that looked sturdier and stronger than the thickest walls of castles still standing throughout the world. Those vibrations made the gate seem like something that a child might construct, not something built by God to house Satan and his legion.

Steam filled the air on the other side of the gate almost as rolling fog. It stopped at the edge of the gate. I assumed that it was from blood being boiled somewhere deep inside. But was it merely my mind running wild? Something from an unknown area within me was lusting for the blood that was being boiled. I craved it, but not in the same way that a starved vampire aches for it. No, I longed to see it being spilled.

It was just like in the dream before the whispers started singing in my ears, "Come in, Devin. It is sweeter than honey." I feared what might happen if I stepped across that threshold. I might never come back. Even so, the whispering became too tantalizing and overwhelming to resist. It was as if all sound was silenced with the suction of my foot releasing from the ground. Not even the ringing sound of silence could be heard, and for the first time, I truly heard nothing — not my breath or the beating of my heart or my own thoughts. There was only the complete focus on that step until the point when my foot finally breached the invisible line of no return. From there, I could feel a buildup of mass confusion to the point when everything became a blur. It wasn't just my foot that first contacted the threshold; as soon as one atom of my body or soul crossed, my entire body was thrown into the thick fog that was too dense even to see where my feet were walking. I couldn't feel or even hear that I was walking on the ground anymore. The only thing I could see was a door ahead of me clear as a midsummer day, but everything else seemed to have been erased.

The door was massively constructed, layering metal over metal, then riveting the layers together, much the same as how a large skyscraper would be. I couldn't believe I was able to open it, even in my dream state. But I knew it was more than a dream; the place was exactly what it said it was. The door was framed by chiseled rock, and when it opened, it revealed a cave that seemed to engulf the door to whoever dared enter. A lock had been on it, but it was broken off and thrown to the side, but that must have taken a tremendous force and speed. The ground that it landed on was cracked and left exposed like that of a crater made when a meteorite impacts the ground. The door reminded me somewhat of a door in an old movie; one for which a Greek god or an angel had the only key. On the other side, a Titan hid, just waiting for another chance to strike.

The cave reeked of burnt flesh. The smell wasn't in the air but was the air itself. As I breathed the smell, my lungs were attacked, as was the rest of my body. It went through my body, with each beat of my heart, like a drug that was injected into my veins. The words and screams inside the cave were very real. Some tried to talk to me, while others would curse me, because I was not facing their damnation. Others begged for me to take and share part of their pain. Many of them were having their flesh slowly burned or eaten away, but they could do nothing because their bodies lined the wall as part of the cave itself, unable to move. What kind of evil could keep them alive as their flesh was burned away? Yet they were still alive, and after their skin was burned off their bodies were tossed to the side for their flesh to regrow and then for it all to happen again.

Their screams were coming from everywhere but in a continual circle, one right after another. Some were calling for their master so he could punish me the same as them, but their master and tormenter was nowhere to be seen. Blood squirted violently from the bodies against the wall, but led nowhere. Their cries spun around me again, but this time, they were mixed with a stench so vile that it intoxicated me with a lust for their blood. Spinning among their screams and my blood lust, I began to see myself standing on top of a pile of bodies, bathed in their blood, and laughing hysterically at my lunacy. Then, in the next, I saw my own flesh being melted away, layer after layer, in a room with no fire. There was only a heat that seemed to come from nowhere. My laughing never stopped. In fact, it only increased.

Round and round I spun until it was only blackness I saw. I could not tell if I was standing, sitting, spinning, dying or dead. There was only blackness, and there was solitude in that. Slowly, the tips of my fingers and toes started to feel as though a cube of ice was kissing each of them, but all I saw was the blackness. I found peace as the cold grip had begun to engulf me, starting from my hand and working its way over the rest of me. But the darkness slowly gave way to a new thought. That thought was made up of dark blues, rather than blackness and hidden shadows.

Almost like a fresh mind coming out of a drug-induced trance, I looked at my surroundings as a new man in a new world. It was my world and the one I consumed every day, but nothing looked the same. I watched the dark-blue paradise slowly melting into a reddish-orange sunrise from my window. My nightmare was over, and the sun that I always cursed was what ended it. The sun was high above the point where it had risen. It awakened my mind, but instead of a nightmare, I found myself gazing out toward its warmth, while hoping for a dream to end the stalemate of the class. I sat on the far side of the science classroom.

My professor was a naturalist, who believed in using as much of nature as possible with very little help from things like lights, which made that side of the room easier to see. On that side of the room, windows made up most of the wall stretching down from the ceiling all the way down to three feet above the floor. The rest of the wall from the windows down was the typical offset, center-block style that most schools have. The color for some unknown reason always seemed to be an off white.

It was the lecture room, and it was set up in the same way as typical lecture halls. In the same design as a movie theater, the rows of seats descended down toward where the professor stood while giving his lectures. I often wondered if this room had been in the basement, without windows, whether this top corner where I always sat would be the black spot of the room rather than a shining note. The ground outside seemed to descend alongside the room, perfectly mirroring one another. This let the sunlight flow without any resistance and evenly from the top where I sat to the lower part where professors lectured. On mornings when the sun was more dominant and more passionate than a king who chose to fight a decade-long war before losing his greatest love, I would give in fully to whatever daydream chose to possess me.

The professor continually looked up at me from in front of the massive class as I drifted out into the world rather than listen to him, but I did not care. I chose the school to hide in, not to learn. The school was the largest state school, and that enabled me to hide more easily inside those walls than at an amusement park in peak season. The problems of my world would lie dormant while I sat up there sipping stale coffee and listening to people. I loved to listen to them talk about their lives. It was my way of existing in their world without having to leave mine. What a perfect hideaway! By being entrapped in a world filled with so many people, lost in their ideas, the miseries of my life were drowned out.

Each day, I would lose my grasp of what the studies of the day would bring as I gazed out into the snow-covered lawns and ice-gripped trees. Every so often, I could hear the crisp whistle of the wind trying hard to punch through the walls and windows to freeze me solid just as I sat. Yet it continued to wait outside like a shark in shallow water so that it may explode with rage as the layered bodies entered the frozen, naked world while exiting this prison cell of higher learning. The day was somehow bleeding into something bitterly different from the earlier sunrise that took the blackness from my dream away. That day held some of that darkness in every freckle of light.

My thoughts drifted back to the time of my best friend James's murder. Over and over, it was poured into me once again. I closed my eyes to block the memory, but it was no use. Glimpses of what his last moment must have been flashed thoroughly through me. Then powerful surges came with the flashes hitting me with an unknown force that sent swells up and down my body while paralyzing me. Visions came to me with each. Not only was each surge more powerful than the last, each was being sustained for longer periods of time. From every angle, they came, showing how his life was being spilled out of him. It was almost as if his body was repulsed by its own blood so that it was throwing it up like one might do after drinking month-old milk. His body couldn't rid itself of it quickly enough.

Around him stood a group of hooded men and women reciting a chant in different tones and octaves. Some had cups that looked to be dripping with my friend's blood, while others had knives that looked like they were made out of bone that was fused with metal for the blade. There were nine people standing around James, two by each leg, two by each arm and one by his head. One of the two people standing at each extremity was cutting into James's flesh, while the other was collecting whatever came off him or out of him.

It looked like they made sure that the areas that were being cut into were areas that wouldn't kill him. There were no major arteries involved. It seemed as if the people were trying to make his suffering last as long as possible before he finally died. One was cutting lightly on the outside of his lower leg, somewhere between his calf muscle and his shin on his right side. The cuts were made with surgical precision. That person was able to take a clumsy-looking blade and turn it into a scalpel, making such small cuts that they were barely visible to the naked eye. If not for the blood that started to cry out in tears one at a time, the cuts could easily be mistaken for paper cuts. His leg was plagued by all of those tiny cuts. They were all made vertically on his lower leg. The blood was collected right away in a bone cup by the person standing to the right of the surgeon.

The person standing by the other leg had an identical knife, but was cutting angrily at the top of my friend's left thigh. Even with the anger with which that person cut, he made sure to stay at the top and outside of the leg. He also made sure not to come close to the artery on the inside of James's leg. He was not making tiny, paper-thin cuts. No, he was taking inch-long pieces of flesh out of his leg. Then he let a woman to his left place it in the cup while using a different bone-shaped cup. The flesh collector would also lap up the blood that was oozing out of the holes in James's left thigh.

There were two woman cutters making long, straight incisions down his arms. Starting at the meaty part of James's shoulder, then moving down to each one of his fingers, there was one of those incisions for each of his fingers. Those cuts seemed to be the deepest of all the cuts. The blades were being forced deeply in until they hit bone. Eerily, I could hear the blades scratching against his bones. The blades dug into all of his arm and hand bones in the way a key would dig through the paint and into the sheet metal of a car when the car was keyed.

James's arms were hanging from the table, so the blood was allowed to roll down his arms, hands and off the tips of his fingers when friction could not beat the law of gravity any longer. The drops of blood fell as unguided missiles into two separate bone cups. Yet not a single drop of blood missed its target, nor did any blood splash out that was already in the cup.

There was one figure, who had a deep, almost inhuman voice, standing behind James's head. He was reading out of a book. His language was one I had never heard before. It wasn't even similar to anything that I had ever heard. In one hand, he held the book, and in the other, he held a bone that was sharpened into a rigid knife blade. There was no change in the tone of his voice as he read and chanted in a tone that sounded almost robotic or otherwise inhuman. The voice was cold and empty. When he read and chanted the last word, he simply placed the book beside James's right shoulder, and in one quick motion, he slid the blade across James's throat, severing his arteries and letting his life pour out rapidly.

The other cutters, blood collectors and flesh collectors took the blood they collected, passed around the cups, and drank every drop. They then took the cup of flesh collected from James's thigh, and passed it around so that each person had one piece. Finally, a few words were spoken by the one who had done the reading and had slit James's throat. They all took the flesh they were holding, and fed it to the one standing to their left.

My focus changed without any of my will or desire. I was forced to look upon James's face, which had all of the flesh, muscle and blood melted away and piled up on his soaked shirt. Even with the flesh of his face gone, I was still able to hear his watery voice speaking sobbingly to me. The words were not clear; they were an overlapping stampede of sounds that I couldn't understand. Somehow I could hear and feel all the pain that he felt.

It started with the tiny cuts going down my right leg. Those were not the cuts made by a surgeon, because they felt more like cuts made by an untrained sadist. I could feel the blade plunging through my pants and then easily through my pale skin. With each cut, it seemed as if my skin was allowing the blade to penetrate more easily. As the blade ripped downward, the pressure point in that part of my leg was torn out and thrown to the other side of the room. As a wounded child, the pressure point that was once a part of me seemingly stared back at me with its bloody eyes and tears.

I didn't notice that the surgeon had taken his place to my left and was cutting pieces of flesh from my leg. That person cut away the parts of my pants that were in the way, rather than cutting through them. Then, without noticing, one slice after another was made, until those middle-aged hands could unfold a diamond-shaped piece of flesh from my leg. It was as if I was watching a movie, not experiencing it myself. The person beside him worked like a nurse in an operating room. They seemed very well practiced in their movements together.

In anger, a blade was stabbed into each of my shoulders, just as they did with James. I could feel the blades sever all of my tendons and ligaments, damaging most of the major muscles in that single stab on each side. Each of my arms became useless; I couldn't have moved them even if I had wanted to. All I could do then was stand there and let those inhuman monsters tear me apart, just as they did to James, the only difference being that I was standing and he was lying down. The knives bounced off my bones when they first made contact. Those two people seemed to have taken the bouncing as an insult because they just pushed the blades into my bones, scrapping and even cracking them. Words of pain and cries for help were for some reason absent from my mouth or mind. I was living with the pain, only to endure it, as I awaited the final cut that would end my life as well.

Cut after cut just kept coming — one in this leg, one in each arm or a piece gone from the other leg — but still no one would end my life. One hollow step behind shook my soul and quickened my breath as the air in the room dropped what seemed to be 30 degrees in one breath. I could then see the breath that I had just exhaled in a thick, white cloud of mist. Even those who were butchering me started to breathe out the same thick mist. Their hands started to shake with the cold or with fright I could not tell which. All I could see and feel was how each cut had become less delicate or weaker.

Then a second step landed, and with it, light from behind me started to become obscured by a large shadow overcasting its presence past me and my tormenters. My tormenters started to whisper among themselves. I could hear that they were speaking, but it was too quiet for me to understand what they were saying. Before the one behind me could take another step, they all lowered their knives and took two steps back. That is when a third step came. With that step, I began to hear soft and dominant breathing beginning to break through. It sounded like that of a bull grunting before it ran off in a rage.

I could picture the beast standing behind me, readying itself for madness; breathing in hatred and exhaling revenge with each stomp of its hooved foot. Part of me wanted that more than all of the waiting around. There would be no more schooling or professors; only the next step of human existence. I was ready to depart.

So I thought, "Please, hurry. Bull, I do not blame you or hate you."

It could only end in one way! I didn't hear any more steps, but the beast was somehow right behind me, and its breath was burning down the back of my neck. Every hair on my neck, shoulders and back was melting. I could smell and taste the burnt hair every time it exhaled onto me. But somehow the hair on my head was left untouched. It wasn't the breath of a ravaged beast but that of someone who had already been satisfied.

I was forced to endure the methodical breathing behind and beside my right ear over and over again. The steady relentlessness of it felt almost similar to that of a clock that would just keep ticking second after second, never stopping or resting. I wanted to crawl away and scream at the top of my lungs, but my voice was empty and my body was broken. The tormenters were then faced down in a form of worship in the blood and bile that was left over from us. I hoped that whatever it was behind me would take that knife and staple those torments to the ground with it before it turned the knife on me; some sort of satisfaction before I was to die. I knew, though, that that wasn't going to happen.

Frozen between time and death, I could feel a tear moving as slow as a malaise emanating from my eye onto my eyelash. It stalled momentarily before finally exiting completely from my eye and onto my cheek. There it stayed for only a few seconds until the tear slowly evaporated into nothing, leaving only a salty stain upon my cheek; a simple reminder that it was once more a part of me.

2

Devin and Victoria

A soft and tender tickle of a feather-like touch pulled my mind back through the wormhole nightmare that I was fading into, reuniting me once again with the human race. Maybe it was part of the dream or just a glimpse into a fantasy I didn't know I had. The touch felt as if it could have been from an angel's wing. It stayed with me and kept in contact with my left cheek. The touch held a sensation that I had never known. It felt as if tiny strobing bolts of lightning were firing all over the inside of my body at an alarming and uncontrollable rate.

My heart raced as I wondered how a simple touch could hold such a powerful spell over me. I felt almost like a young schoolboy who was too afraid to look at the girl of my undying fascination, because of fear that she would know that I liked her. Somewhere along the way as I grew, I was able to put aside foolish bashfulness and gained the strength to turn and face the one who controlled the feather-like touch and the spell that was placed over me. I wished that bashfulness would have been able to take away all of the anxiety that was building up within me. I closed my eyes and took an unsteady, deep breath. I held it as if it were the last puff of a cigarette in a lifetime of smoking. The breath never seemed to end. I was holding onto every part of it just like the way a soldier would prolong his long kiss "Goodbye" just before he departed to fight a war. All the while, in his heart, he believed he would never again hold her or see her.

Even though I was pulled out of my nightmare back into the sun-kissed science room, I wasn't able to see anything yet. The room was completely black, almost as if I was living slightly in the past. I could see light off in the distance, but it was so far away that it didn't seem to matter. I wondered if it was the small part of light from my nightmare bleeding over to this world. Even my professor's words seemed hollow and empty, as if he were talking into a can that was attached to a string far away that was attached to another can in the classroom.

Something inside me told me the only way I could end this would be to turn and face the angel. The breath still lingered inside my body, but slowly, it began to pour out of my mouth as I turned and looked into her eyes. With a blink, I opened my eyes, and looked into the most beautiful eyes I had ever seen. Greek and Roman goddesses were not even an afterthought compared to her eyes. It was good that I held on to that breath for as long as I did because there was more beauty in those eyes than I could have even guessed or imagined. Even though they were as dark as an empty night, there was so much life, love and tenderness in them. They were the eyes of the most beautiful women I had ever seen. Her name was Victoria. She was the star of all of my fantasies and the answer to most of my prayers. But I was always prevented from talking to her because of my own self-pity. I never thought she would actually ever look at me, let alone tear me out of a nightmare.

Behind her, the light of the room seemed to turn on a few moments after I caught her eyes. The world somehow caught up to us in those few moments after we locked eyes. I didn't want to look away. I could have remained there staring into her midnight eyes for the better part of my life, but I knew life wouldn't let me. I was amazed that she didn't remove her hand, which moved as effortlessly as water on my cheek when I turned toward her. She was so much better than an angel, even though the way she managed to pull a seat behind me without me even knowing it was somewhat magical. She must have found the chair and sat behind me after I started sliding into my daydream about the sunlight.

From the very first moment I saw her, I knew that I loved her. Regardless of the fact that I didn't even know her. From a distance, I built a world for us in my head. She became that moment of light that stood alone drowning in my sea of darkness. I dreamt of ways of somehow parting the ever-widening distance between us, but for this reason or that, the moment vanished before it ever really appeared. I was forced to catch mere moments from the shadows where I made my home, never knowing that her soft and gentle hand would ever be placed on my unshaven cheek.

I couldn't remember her ever looking at me. Except only in passing glances, her eyes would slide past mine. They always blinked out of sight as quickly as they arrived, leaving me to wonder whether the glances were just that or if her intentions were to look at me without ever letting me know. I truly believe that it was foolish to think that way because I was only this guy hidden away from everyone else. Yet she was right there with her eyes locked onto mine with the intensity that I always found when staring down a dog but also in a very curious way.

It was the first time I had been so close to her. My breath was stolen from my chest the moment I noticed how perfectly her black eyes matched her raven hair in defined unison that most symphonies cannot achieve. Her hair was slightly brighter than her eyes and she had different highlights mixed within her hair that only accentuated the beauty of her hair. There were wrinkles on her forehead, caused by a tightened facial expression. It glistened with moisture and concern for me. She must have been able to see something was happening to my body during my nightmare.

Her eyebrows layered inward and were only partially real. Most of them were drawn on, and they seemed to flow evenly from her little, pointed nose. Her lips were slightly parted so as to let air escape easily or in surprise by whatever expression was plastered on my face. Her lips shone with a pinkish-purple color that she used that day as lipstick or lip gloss. Either way, she captured me with her lips that moment.

I craved to touch her lips, and in my mind, I slipped away into a fantasy in which I silently kissed her. Even if I would have to steal the kiss, I wished I had the passion and confidence to take it whether there in the classroom or not. I could almost taste her lipstick and feel its residue left on my lips.

My fantasy was interrupted when she spoke so softly that the ringing in my ears almost blocked it out.

"Hello! Is there anybody in there?" she said as a perfect quotation from the movie *The Wall* by Pink Floyd, which matched *The Wall* button-down shirt she was wearing.

Instantly, I blinked out of my trance. The first and only word I could say to my secret love was "Ya."

"You sure? You just look lost in the middle of a very bad dream." Her words softly lingered in the air.

I tried desperately to hold on to each word because she might never speak to me again. One by one, each word faded into history. There was nothing left to fill the void where the words were; just empty, stale air in its place. I believed if I lost the words, I might lose her, so as fast as lightning, my mind raced to reclaim those lost words. Every moment, I thought I had them, but then I instantly lost them. They always seemed to be one step out of my grasp until finally, I held them, and then they turned to dust in my hand.

"Help me" ran nakedly off my tongue like melting snow rolls off a mountain side at the first sight of spring.

At that moment, a violent rage threw itself upon me; not one of my own but one of the creatures that controlled that remembrance. He was clearly not done with me. The rage flashed like lightning and threw me, like a child would throw her doll, out of my chair. I flew to the wall just below the windows. The hit felt like it thrust my spine through my unwanted heart, then ripped it through my weakened chest until it exploded upon the wall. My head and face bounced solidly off the wall to the ground.

Flashes of what I went through during my nightmare started to awaken within me. My friend's pain and cries, which I never felt or heard, rushed over me as well. I felt the blade that ended his life but also how his blood and life force was drained into the stone sarcophagus below him. I could feel that he was trapped in that place of torment, in one form or another, forever. The power of those flashes and pains forced my body to curl up on the floor like a beaten dog. I started to shake uncontrollably. This was where my life and the dead collided.

Strobing images of the dead began to surround me, but stopped just short of engulfing me. It seemed as if I was floating in an ocean of the tormented. Their faces filled my eyes and mind, while their screams filled my ears. Everything that made me who I am was then being controlled by them; I had no control of my thoughts, my sight, my hearing, all that I felt and even what I said. As a man possessed, I couldn't stop the cries of my dead friend escaping from me into an unaware and half-asleep class. Word by word, I screamed James's pleas, begging and cursing his death in front of a very stunned crowd. Once in the air, the words captured all the ears that were in the room, even the professor was at a loss to understand what was happening before his own eyes.

Pain grew everywhere in my body. It felt as though my dream had come true, except that there were no cuts on my arms or legs. I believed that certain death was only moments away; that the real pain was waiting for me. Millisecond by millisecond, the flashes grew stronger, and my cries grew louder and louder. I was sure the whole school could hear me by then, but I didn't care. The pain was just too much for my beaten body to bear. Just when I could feel my soul being pulled forcefully out of my flesh, she pulled me back. My angel once again saved me. With each beat of my speeding heart, my soul retreated into my flesh. The pain and visions that were just thrown at me faded. Even the echoes of the screams were no longer there, and the sea of the dead somehow evaporated into nothingness. Her soft touch ended the terror that filled my heart.

Her hand felt soft upon my sweat-soaked chest. Once again, it was like that distant kiss of a lost lover that had returned. I thought how a single touch could bring me out of the hell I was falling into. Our eyes met again. I couldn't believe that my secret love had gazed upon those blue eyes for a second time. No words were spoken; only the dreadful sound of silence clanged in my ears until I started hearing a second beating. I was scared that the evil was coming back for more, but thankfully I was wrong. It was her heart racing to catch up with mine.

My desire for her was growing more and more powerful. I could hear her need for me beat through her hand, which was still placed upon my chest. Somewhere, deep within those beautiful, dark eyes, I could sense that she needed me as well. We held that stare until our eyes burned with dryness — neither one of us even wanted to blink — and with fear till our hearts slowed to beat as one.

Time stood still while our eyes remained fixed on one another. Even the ticking of the clock seemed to be stalled somewhere between reality and the world of the dead. After what seemed to be a motionless day, the clock began to catch up, ticking louder than it had ever done before. It seemed to be in some way a restart but not to my life. With only a few moments having passed, the bell rang like a banshee screaming on a wintry night.

Voices started to fill the hallways, mixed with feet walking unevenly outside the room. There was no one walking inside the room, but I could hear footsteps. I felt an overwhelming presence. I knew it was not over. It was very odd listening to everyone outside the classroom moving around as if there was nothing going on. Meanwhile, inside, the only things that were moving were my eyes and Victoria's. The room felt the same as an empty cell in the darkest prison blocks in the tomb of a forgotten city buried under the sands of the Middle East.

All of my classmates' faces were as frozen statues while they looked at Victoria and me. There was a palpable uneasiness about them. They seemed to be frozen in time and not only out of fear. Somehow, as soon as they turned to look at us, time stopped for them but not for us. The professor's mouth was wide open, as though he was mid-sentence when he stopped and looked. The ringing of the bell did not faze any of them.

I wanted to hesitate; to remain in that spot so that my angel would sit there with me in that silence. Maybe with her, that evil would somehow stay away from me. I didn't want the silence to end. It was almost unimaginable how pure and peaceful the silence seemed. Even with the evil presence that was all around me, staying here, I would just be daring it to lash out again. I couldn't tell if the peace I was feeling was from the silence, or if it was from my secret love holding me with her eyes. I did know that that peace was something I might never feel again.

"Just give in, and you can have her," a shallow voice whispered quietly in one ear, then the other.

It was like a kiss from a slithering snake; a voice that kept fading in and out of the audible range. I began to see a fog-like python wrapping around us. Victoria had become another motionless statue, just like the rest of the class. All of them were frozen in time, watching me, rather than living beside me.

"Can you smell her sweet perfume, as she is now only inches from you?" The tempting snake only paused to let me inhale her aroma, which sent shivers of passion and lust all over my body. "You can have her body lying on yours-s-s, I know you want it. I can s-s-smell the lus-s-s-t and see it burning in your eyes. Go ahead, Devin. Touch her. S-s-s-she is a-s-s-s-sleep to the reality you are in, and I'm giving you this free chance," the snake voice sang the temptation with a lisp in my ears, trying to make it sound alright.

The fog snake was constricting tighter around us, and with every squeeze, its words started to make more and more sense.

I became intoxicated by the fog and my lust, and was slowly raising my arm without even knowing I was doing it. It was as if I was swimming in a pool of lust. The voice and the fog were in complete control of me; I was like a puppet attached to strings. Slowly, the voice was pulling me down by my own lust, as my hand inched toward her breast. The warmth of her body radiated off her uncovered arm to my frozen arm. The snake voice was hoping to continue, sending me off into my lust-filled dream. I woke up somehow out of my intoxicated state, only I realized that that snake almost made me violate and destroy the only thing that I still loved in this world.

"Ha ha ha ha ha ha!" the voice sang as it continued to squeeze me. "S-s-s-sooner or later, I will have complete control of you. No amount of body heat will s-s-s-save you; it will only condemn you."

"Leave her alone! She has nothing to do with any of this," I said in a tone that showed I was willing to fight.

"Devin, that is Victoria and s-s-s-she is-s-s way more important than you," the voice said.

There was a loud tapping that somehow tore everyone out of the frozen, statue-like state they were in. They all turned toward the door on the other side of the room. Quickly, the door opened, and a few students stepped in and just stared at us as we all stared back at them. Everyone stared at the other side, waiting to see who would move first. With that abrupt interruption, I saw a quick exit to the door in the back of the room on my side. The door stood no more than 30 feet away, but I knew that I had to leave and I had to go quickly. With one swift motion, I jumped up and grabbed the hand of my Victoria and ran quickly to the door, hoping she would follow without too much of a fight. Her eyes kept looking back as we ran through the doorway.

I looked back right before I left the room and saw the intruder. It was the shadow that stood behind me in my nightmare, and it was melting away the face of one of the students that stood at the other doorway. His face turned into a melting pool of boiling cheese, dripping its way onto the floor. Even as I was running away, I could hear it hissing like acid, and the further I ran, the thicker the smell of burnt flesh that crawled into my nostrils. It became so thick that even my sight became blurry and weak. We ran into students and teachers as we were trying to get away. Some were laughing, others were confused, but most seemed to get angry and yelled at us. With every person we ran into, the shouts of anger got worse and worse.

We finally made it to the end of that hall turning to the right, where we were stopped dead in our tracks. Victoria's hand was still in my hand, but her body was pressed tightly to my back and side as we looked at the students and teachers that lined the hallway. All the faces of the students and teachers turned at once to face us the moment we turned and took that first step. Instantly, their eyes were blacked out and hollow while their mouths were open, almost like they never had any mouths at all, looking more like a mask with a hole where the mouth was. Screams of Hell came out of them. Instantly, Victoria pushed me out through the hallway. The students and teachers were screaming at us.

We pushed through the double doors at the end of the hall, and shut them behind us. But for some reason, no person or thing followed us. I knew that the shadow was somewhere, lurking behind one of the closed doors along the hallway. The hallway was even more disturbing. There seemed to be an eeriness to it that could only be found at a forgotten dock that time had not yet destroyed. This hallway was completely empty in the physical sense. Nor was there a single breath of life in it. Yet the noises of the children talking seemed to be everywhere. It sounded completely alive in every way — the voices, the wrestling sounds of clothing, their shoes on the ground, even the games that were being played, even homework being done.

Everything was extremely disorientating and confusing. It seemed as if we had stumbled into an echo of what my hell would be if the shadow captured us. The shadow figure was leading us somewhere, and everything that made me who I am told me to run regardless of where the figure wanted us to go; simply to run.

"What do we do now, Devin?" Victoria asked as she pulled and squeezed my hand to the point that it really hurt, but I would not let that be the reason I was letting go.

I listened and looked for a way out into the hallway that was alive with sound, but felt as if there was not any physical life in it.

"We need to get out of here now," I said, as I pulled her toward the closest exit.

All the cries remained in that hallway, but still nothing was physically there in the hallway. Once we left that hallway and went into the last hallway before the exit, there wasn't a single sound, but a green haze was spilling out into the hallway and started to chase after us. The haze was constructed out of all the screams and other noises we had heard only a few moments earlier. It was as if I could see those sounds in it, even though I could no longer hear it. I knew that if I let it catch up, it would be the end of both of us. Her role in this was unknown to me, but I knew that there was something about her that caused the creature to look toward her.

It seemed that that creature was always around haunting me, but never since that night when James was killed did it really reveal itself to me in any form other than a nightmare. Did that new paradox have something to do with her touch upon my shoulder or her poetic gaze in my eyes?

"Victoria!" — there was a very deep scream out of the green haze.

In shock, Victoria and I both stopped to turn and face the sound. Even with it still coming after us, we both just turned to face it.

"Daddy" escaped softly and tenderly off her tongue.

A lone tear ran down her left cheek as memories played like an old reel movie playing behind her eyes.

3

Nine months before Victoria was born

Jacob walked what seemed to be miles through an empty tunnel. The tunnel felt odd. There were no sharp groves that showed it to be manmade, but it was too perfect to be naturally made either. Either way, there were no markings to indicate how it came to be, only a never-ending passage that was poorly lit. It felt like everything was flat and stale, almost like it was a place just behind that present time and yet not quite in the past. The air tasted like a rotting corpse.

The air touched uncovered parts of his body, and it seemed as if blisters were about to erupt everywhere because of the hint of brimstone that heated the air. It made the air thicker and harder to inhale and walk through with every step. It was carrying a pack that was twice his weight, and that weight pushed down hard onto his shoulders, neck, legs and feet. One place he was surprised to feel the weight was in his stomach. He felt there was a rope tied around his waist that was trying to pull him back out of the tunnel.

He knew his feet were stepping on a strong and solid surface. It was hard to see the ground just below him, and there was no noise when he walked, regardless of how hard he placed that foot. He started to have a harder and harder time lifting his feet off the ground. At first, it felt like a thin film of mud was gluing his feet each time they touched the ground. Jacob could almost feel the suction of the mud breaking each time a foot was raised. But each time was just a little bit harder than the one before.

His feet were getting heavier every fraction of a second. Even when moving either one of his freed feet through the air, it became very labored. Due to the buildup of mud and anything else that stuck to his feet, he imagined himself looking like Frankenstein's monster by the way in which he was walking. Jacob never thought about how odd it was that he was walking in an unknown cave through the thick and sticky mud. Step after step, he trudged on.

He started to feel something within the invisible mud, and for the first time, he felt spongy ground. It felt more like walking in a yard that had been recently moistened. That brought back memories of playing football in the cool fall nights back in southern Wisconsin; on those nights when the heat of the afternoon gave wave to the cool and crisp night when he could see his breath just a bit, but he could also feel the grass made wet by the cool air. He could almost taste the moisture within the air by how thick his memories of those nights were. He could feel the chilled air tingle through his mouth and down his throat into his lungs where his body would take it in and feed upon it.

He took another step, and when his foot traveled to the ground, he could feel a sand-like material being pushed aside by his foot. The material was much thinner than just simple sand. It was more like sand locked within mud, giving the mud some sense of structure and strength but not enough to hold any weight on it. The material made him think of those movies in which dinosaurs, large mammals and other big monsters, when walking on mud, would push the soil and mud aside with the weight of their feet. Then the moment they lifted their feet off the ground, the mud would fill it in easily.

The thought made Jacob laugh quietly, even though there was no one around to hear it. There was a carefree attitude about the way he was walking. It was almost like the way you would see someone strolling through a park on a late Sunday afternoon when the sun would warm the skin, but not bake him or burn him. He walked as if one of his dreams finally was coming true; one that he long before had forgotten to dream. With each step was another step, not only physical but also mental. It was as if paradise was within reach. Most of the time, Jacob wished he could be that man walking through the park, but as he was living it one step at a time in this new world of dreams, he felt himself getting deeper and stronger with each step. The dream was engulfing him in the same way a blob would encase whatever it was feeding on. He pictured himself becoming whatever was consuming him, and he welcomed it.

With each step, he drifted further and further into the surreal existence he had found himself in. Most of him didn't want to come back from the blackness he was walking in. Even the part that wanted him to forget the dreamland and consider what he was doing right then was starting to fade into the part of his lost thoughts that was already sold. With what little strength was left in him, the unsold part of his mind was screaming "Wake up!" It kept resurfacing whenever one of his feet finally touched the ground, even though he really didn't notice when one of his feet touched the ground.

The part of his mind that was always awake tried desperately to force him to reconnect with what was really going on around him. Nothing inside him truly knew where he was anymore. Thoughts would come to him saying, "You must be dreaming", but were quickly dismissed as false and tossed out, simply because there was too much thought there for it not to be real. How could he be daydreaming? When he was stuck deep within a dream, he never had those feelings. That place was nothing but a hollow and the birthplace of all the things that were without color and contents that would made it feel real.

As he gave in to those thoughts more and more quickly, the part of him that would not let him be completely consumed by the false dream grew louder and louder until more of his mind started to feel the way in which he should perceive the cave or whatever it truly was. The air he breathed in tasted hot and wet in the same way a spa would keep its steam room, but there was no menthol in the air from the medicated steamers. The taste here was more like something that was inside a gym bag that was used over and over again without ever being washed.

The hot, wet air seemed to attack Jacob. It was as if the air was a military jet determined to leave its target without shape and without any remains. After the payload was delivered to Jacob, it exploded, ricocheting off the walls. The humid air attacked Jacob over and over again as a way of impregnating him with itself. Jacob could even taste his own breath and the stale air as it lunged back at him. Time after time, he could taste how the unmeasured air had changed the air he was taking in.

How was it that mere moments earlier, he was at peace? Lovingly, every breath he consumed, he tried his hardest to hold his breath, hoping that if he held his breath long enough, the peace and beauty would return. Bringing his dream back, even if it was only for one second, maybe the torment would end and allow him to slip away and become nothing once again. He was only able to hold his breath for ten seconds, and his head started to spin like he had just got off a wild fair ride that had lost its connection to the control box and was spinning, flipping, completely uncontrollable, making certain death almost guaranteed.

He couldn't hold it any longer. With pain and weakness, Jacob's lungs screamed as another stale breath was taken in. The air he took in was like drinking napalm that was being poured over him. His innards were set ablaze as in the case of innocent people hiding too close to a battlefield. They would try to run and hide from the liquid fire, but it was useless because the fire would rain through them in the way a flood pours over the floodplains after winter's thaw and early spring's rain.

Jacob gasped and coughed like a person wrestling with the water as they fought certain death by drowning in a place in a lake where there were no lifeguards there to help. With each cough, the volume of his voice grew hoarser and hoarser until all that could be heard was the wheezing air going in and out of the fires within him. He quickly became a crazed and desperate man. He clawed at the floor to pull himself away from whatever the thing was that was trying to kill him in ways he never knew were possible. He clawed everywhere, but all he could grab was the nothingness that he was walking in.

Images from movies passed as flashes in his mind; scenes in which a person was clawing and clinging to a muddy and very wet ground in a last desperate attempt to live for one second longer. Meanwhile, pictures of loved ones circled over and over. Then the eyes of those people turned into the empty stare that always appeared as though they were looking off to the next plain of existence. That new plain started coming rapidly into focus as each breath and each heartbeat, and life reached its end.

He saw himself fading out of that life just as they did. Images of his wife Nina lying in a casket invaded his mind. He could see her tears and he wanted to reach for them, but he found nothing but air. The emptiness of causing her pain crept over him. In the same manner, the grass slowly filled in the bare spots where he was laid to rest.

The words "Am I there, and is this all that is waiting for me?" flooded Jacob's mind.

He couldn't remember how he came to reach that place or even what event caused his death. He did know in his heart that it definitely was not the heaven he heard stories of when he attended all of those children's services in church during his carefree childhood years when all that really mattered was "When can I play with those toys?" and when playing with a boy or girl only meant that you liked the same things. In Jacob's thoughts, he hoped and prayed that if he made himself fully remember those years when he was a boy, maybe just maybe he would find himself transformed back in time to when he was a young boy. If he had the power to do that, he had died; he believed that when anyone dies, they are forced to fight their way to become a god.

Then another cough reminded him of where he was and the world that was then in front of him; reminded him there was a type of control there. No matter how much he wanted to be his own god, it would be pointless; the power that held him there was completely out of his reach. He thought about the Eastern religions in which someone would have to fight his way to godhood, but would need prayers to help him grow stronger to achieve an enlightened status. He wondered who would pray for him. No one in his family even knew if he practiced any of those religions that he was aware of. With another breath that ignited the moment his blood mixed with the oxygen, more torment and panic forced their way into his thoughts. The hot breath started to consume his fantasies of ascending to a deity, and once again, he found his arms reaching out to claw away from the breath and his desires. He would give up all his dreams, ambitions and desires if only the torture would end.

Even though he did not believe in God, he still cried out, "Jesus, please save me from this. Please! I will do anything you want."

Somewhere deep within his soul, he knew that the plea would go unheard and unanswered. Like the countless prayers he prayed every day, he cried out for help, only to get no aid.

"Ha ha ha!" started to echo and bounce off the hidden walls, just as the hot air had.

It seemed like a male voice and a female voice combined. There really was no tone or pitch to it. Yet there was structure and depth to it. His body felt the sound before his ears knew a sound was being made. It was so powerful that it shook him in a way that was much stronger than any road accident he was ever involved in. The rhythm made by the voice was so powerful that it forced his heart to beat to its rhythm. That forced him to gasp for air completely and uncontrollably.

Jacob looked like a fish out of water, gasping for air one moment, but then, in the next, trying not to breathe because of how painful that air was to consume. Jacob refused, however, to give in without putting up a fight even though he knew that something else was in control of him there and would always be. His body did not share the idea of fighting. It fought back at him with unpredictable shakes and a twist.

The voice seemed to enjoy watching him suffer. The more violence that was unleashed on him, the louder, longer and more childlike the laughter became. He felt he was a toy that was used to amuse a cat; that he was dangling on a string while waiting for some creature to devour it as the creature laughed at it.

A dark fog engulfed him. It didn't let him see the walls growing darker and thicker as the air heated up. The only light that could be seen was a glow of a fire that was burning within him. Each time he breathed out, an explosion of light erupted out of his mouth and nose. The heat of the fire started to burn, like melted metal being poured down his throat every time he inhaled. Then, pushing outward, it was like a torch when he exhaled. But still there was no relief anywhere for him.

His ears and mind started to twist and turn in the way a tornado would destroy a Midwest town. The confusion that became his thoughts were those of a man lost in the grip of an acid trip. The words that were pouring over him were the source of his madness. They were being spoken to him in different voices but all from people he had met at some earlier time in his life. Those voices changed too quickly for Jacob to comprehend fully whose voice was speaking at that moment. Then it would quickly change again. Thousands of different words were spoken all at once. Even though he could not make out any of the words, he could still tell that each and every word was thrusted toward him in anger, hatred, sadness and even desperation. He did not hear a single word or phrase of love or caring within all of those voices. The voices became so loud that they shook him, placing the pressures consistent with those of the deepest sea into his ears and mind. Rather than clawing at the ground and mud, he was trying to cover and rip his ears off all at once.

"Stop please. Enough! What do you want? Please stop!"

His words fell on deaf ears. Not only did it not stop, but the force at which the voices were coming at him increased until he started to feel his brain bouncing off the inside of his head. With each bounce, a multitude of pains throbbed through to the other side of his head. The pains were so severe that even the worst migraine he ever had would have been a large improvement. He felt his brain being turned to mush from what was being inflicted upon it.

Looking and feeling like a dying man begging on his knees, Jacob cried out, "Please, for the love of God."

"No! Not God but for the love of me!" the original but more powerful voice screamed, ending the other voices. "I want you to wake up."

Like a scared dog during the Fourth of July fireworks, Jacob jumped up from his bed. Before he could even know that he was dreaming, a large man's face made of smoke and mist stared deep into his eyes only an inch or two away from his face. The smoky face smelt like a pile of burning carcasses on the battlefields of old. There was also a fierce heat that only a blacksmith would like radiating off his face. The face was almost the size of Jacob's whole body, and it made him think of what it would have been like to stand before a giant who wanted to wage war against him. He felt as if the being to whom the face belonged was sizing him up. Cold sweat started to build within Jacob until it dripped off his naked chest. Tiny puffs of smoke from the heat of the face were caught in the falling moisture. His sweat changed from the clear color of sweat into a hazel color until it hit either his blankets or his beautiful, young bride. The colors would explode and dye whatever it hit with its own unique shade of red. The sweat that remained on Jacob still collected the colors. Those hues were more of a shadow without color or source of light. They would then burn their way into Jacob's skin, and even though it hurt and he wanted to cry out and wipe the pain off him, he could not move for fear that the face was staring emotionlessly back at him.

The pain that was created by sweat that stayed on Jacob was different from those he experienced in that dreamlike state. It felt more real than anything in his life had ever felt, good or bad. He liked it; he liked it a lot. Each burn felt as if his body was about to explode in a violent orgasm over and over again. He even held his breath with anticipating lust for the next burn. His eyes closed with the joy of expected ecstasy. He could not control himself, because the painful pleasure had captured and conquered him all in just a few drops. The embarrassment of his pleasure in the pain made him almost want to retreat back into the dream in which the fire was burning him. In his mind, he thought that he deserved the punishment he was enduring while in the vivid dream; perhaps to rid the black mark that was burned into his soul by the pleasure.

Then the face snorted at Jacob with a fire that burned the hair off his exposed chest and belly.

"Enough of your sick fantasy! We've got work to do. Now let's go," the face said as it backed away from him and out of his room, leaving only an orange glow everywhere the face went and a stream of smoke so Jacob would be able to follow.

Without even knowing how or why, Jacob started to pull back the sheets, and climbed out of the warmth and security of the bed and into the midnight air that encased it. The flooring was soft and surprisingly warm. The floor below their bedroom was always very warm, and it made his bedroom floor warmer. He grabbed a robe and some slippers from the closet to his left and started to follow the face. Jacob didn't even bother tying his robe. The back of his mind was filled with intriguing thoughts of what other sensations he would feel upon his uncovered chest. For a moment, he even considered taking his underwear off, hoping that the new sensation would be able to consume his entire body, but self-control held him back.

It was amazing how the glow that surrounded the face still gave so much residual light into the room even after it was gone completely out of sight. The light started to give way to a cold feeling which reminded Jacob of exercising outside in subzero temperatures when breathing in the air hurt with every single breath. It was almost like being punched in the chest every time he breathed, but he was so hot from exercising that sweat poured out until his clothes and body felt and looked like he had just climbed out of a swimming pool. Jacob's breath, escaping in thick, white vapor clouds, made him feel like a child standing at the bus stop on one of those cold mornings of early winter.

The smoke trail that the face left for Jacob to follow was darker and made up of a fiery smoke that seemed to fall out of the face as sweat. The warmth of the floor created a contradiction in temperature that confused his senses. On a normal day or night, such a dramatic contradiction would cause him to dive quickly back into bed and into the arms of his beautiful, naked, sleeping bride of just three months while she was still lost in her wondrous dreamland. Her dark hair encased her head, shoulders and upper arms as another blanket would before blending in perfectly with their dark red, brown and black comforter. In the gentle moonlight that filled her part of the room and her side of the bed, it was impossible to tell where her hair ended and the comforter began.

He often looked down at her in the moonlight and thought to himself how lost he would be without her. On nights when the moon was full, he would often open up the blinds just so he could look at her as he drifted off to sleep. She would always ask if he was scared or make some off the wall comment like that. Jacob always kept those secrets to himself. Maybe someday, when life passed them by, he wouldn't do that anymore and she would miss it, almost as much as he would miss looking at her with so much love.

Even on the coldest nights, when the air in their room was cold, he still found the strength to stand in the shadows while the moonlight glowed down onto her. He knew within a few moments of being in bed beside her that he would be more than warm enough to shake the chill that built up inside of him. The warmth of her body was something he never knew he needed until he felt it on their wedding night. Nina had refused to give herself fully to him until they were married. That rule of hers made him want her more than anyone he had met or seen in his life. Then, when she finally gave herself to him, he felt more in love with her than he could have ever imagined; not because they finally had sex, but because before they were married, he had felt so hopelessly in love with her. The physical act of love only deepened that. The feeling was a confusing blend of love, lust, desire, truth and peace that he wanted to have always until the end of time; the way her body pressed against his every time either one of them would breath. Even as his body would heat up to the point of sweating, he would refuse to leave her side. Turning a fan on to a medium speed was how he combated the intense heat. Every night, she would ask why he always had to have the fan on.

His answer would never change. "Because baby you are so hot, and I can't sleep without it."

Deep down, it was because of his addiction to her unknowing touch. He always wondered why he couldn't bring himself to say how much he needed her body against his. He couldn't tell her the ecstasy he felt every time her leg would brush close enough to his leg, tickling the hairs. It was the kind of touch that star-crossed lovers, hidden within the great poems and plays, could only hope for. Their mouths, hearts and souls would cry out in a way, reaching to become engulfed with the addiction. Sadly, the tragedy would soon consume their bodies, leaving them nothing more than a rotting, wrapped bag of flesh, bone, blood and dust.

His body was crying out in the hope that he would decide not to follow the face, and crawl back into bed with his beautiful bride, knowing that everything that was right and pure in his life was right there lying in bed waiting for him to lie close to her. That face had a terrible dark light about it. It was luring him into a darker content than the pull felt for herskin. There was an animalistic urge to chase after the face, and once again, feel the shameful lust that lured him out of bed. Somewhere, he heard the words ringing inside his head.

"Your lust for that face has turned you into the man you never wanted to be. Cheater!" he heard shouted down at him. It was a voice similar to an angry middle-aged teacher that would yell judgment calls at him every time he made a mistake in school.

There was a simple purity to that face, even if it was evil, and it was simple and true; not one conjured up by the world. It was not an evil that one would feel while standing next to some killer, rapist, terrorist or ruler who virtually killed off entire peoples. The evil from the face seemed to be the birthplace of some of the wickedest things to have ever happened. The face that devoured life was calling his name.

Through the lingering heat of the face, Jacob walked zombie-like out of his bedroom, not knowing if he would ever again be next to his wife. As his right foot broke the threshold of the bedroom door, reality then seemed to shift like a bad acid trip. The hallway attaching his bedroom to the stairwell, which winded down to the living room, started to sway back and forth like a child's house of fun in one of those traveling fairs during the twilight days of summer.

Pictures of his history with Nina that hung on the white wall started to shake and bounce wildly. They somehow managed not to fall, but almost as wild gunfire, the pictures slammed back onto the wall again, only to bounce off again due to the repeated affect. The shaking and twisting of the walls reminded him of an earthquake Nina and he had recently experienced while traveling the world on their honeymoon. If it wasn't for some sort of supernatural lifeline the face placed on Jacob, he wouldn't have been able to walk down the hallway to the stairs. He looked and moved more as a drunk person, who could not stand or walk, than as a man that had just woken up to such a wide range of emotions, feelings and experiences. Yet with the help of his lifeline, he was able to take another step in the direction of the face.

Leaning up against the wall, he pushed his way through the hallway one hard step at a time. Something was fighting against him. It was trying to keep him from reaching the stairs and the face. The first wave that tried to stop him was of forced memories of the love that burned for his wife. Then the quaking hallway tried to force him to turn back and check on her, but he could see that their room was untouched by the violence that was thrown upon him. Then he struggled to hear a very faint whisper. It was not from the face or anywhere else in the reality that he then knew and lived. It had a feeling of a father silently praying for his child who was standing nervously before an audience to perform. Jacob would have to shake off the power the whisper had over him before he could step forward again, even with the lifeline pulling him toward the stairs.

Every time the whispering voice came over him, he felt an overwhelming urge to fall asleep, causing the world in front of him to change into the characters of a dream. He felt he was drifting further and further toward the whisper. Some moments he felt that he beat off the attempts made by the whisper to cage him, only to find he was lost in its dream of countless pieces of time. Maybe it was just a split second or maybe it was more than an hour and the face decided to leave without ever showing him why it came to him in the first place.

With almost complete consumption of Jacob's will, the whispering voice still held back the words it was saying. That mystery made him want to know what was being said, and the idea of not knowing tore at his heart and soul. He knew it was important, and that it was at odds with the face. There was such a sense of purity and truth about the whisper that it didn't seem evil. But there was also an overwhelming feeling of judgement within the whispering voice.

Jacob had to know what was being spoken. Only his soul could hear and understand. He pushed harder than he had ever pushed for anything, and within a few feet of the stairs, like a clamp, the whispering voice latched onto his heart, holding him back. He could feel his heart trying to be ripped out from his back, then, with one big step toward the stairs, he started off after the face, while running like a madman away from the whisper.

"If you go to him, there will be no turning back." This whisper came in a quiet, crisp, strong and powerful tone that sang with a steadfast type of confidence flooding out within those hardly audible words.

Jacob could feel a power he could not describe behind the voice. The world around him also seemed to hear and feel that power. Everything quieted, listening to the words that were being spoken. Yet not even the ringing in his ears or the pounding in his chest could be heard.

The drunken walk down the hall seemed wavy. Jacob's sight had changed to that of a drunken person. Everywhere he looked, it appeared that everything was rocking like a boat during a storm. Memories seemed to settle in and even stopped the unfocused waviness that he felt and saw. All the pictures that were shaking and banging against the wall stopped moving. Then, in perfect order, each photo started to crack and shed pieces of glass onto the floor. The order in which the pieces of glass fell was perfectly timed, the oldest photo first and then all the way up to the newest. The first was a photo of Nina and him taken on their first date. The feelings that he had on the day of the photo returned to him again. He could feel the turning of his stomach when he gently pulled her close to him to take the photo in that photo booth. He could even feel his knees shaking as they did that night. In his mind, he was retracing the steps he took to when he would be able to kiss Nina's beautiful lips for the first time.

The dreams that used to keep him up at night before that first date were always of her and when he would finally be able to kiss her. Those dreams were reborn in his eyes as he watched the glass weep onto the ground. Nina's reddish-pink lipstick that she used to wear was all he thought about on those warm days of summer, which blew by like the years of a redwood tree. Even the evenings would pass into night, and the daydreams would linger on into fantasies in which Jacob always made sure to stop his thoughts from giving in to lust while hoping for love.

Then another photo started to crack and break. It was the last photo he ever took with his childhood dog. The memories that flooded his eyes were not of happy ones but ones of hate, anger, depression and regret. The arguments that he had with Nina, his parents and brothers dug deep into his soul once again. Oh, how he hated them for putting King down without ever telling him, nor giving him the chance to care for King himself! A single tear ran down his left cheek as he recalled taking a nap with his head resting on King's side when he was young.

As quickly as the pain was poured onto Jacob, it was torn from his mind, but he didn't want to lose it again like the first time he lost King. The world that went silent and peaceful from the whispering voice somehow was like a clock that was being wound up for the first time in decades. Along with the optical illusion he was in, confusion flooded his ears, mind and soul. He could not make out any of the words that were being spoken. In his ears, there were two polar opposites fighting for control over him. He was afraid that the war would destroy him if he decided to run to the face. His feet seemed to disagree with the decision to flee, and he kept tripping over himself with almost every step.

4

Devin and Victoria

Victoria fought to find the memories she had of her father's voice, but it would have been easier to remember the minor details of a dream she had a long time in the past. The few words she could pull out of her thoughts were very vivid but also very painful. She was back in her mother's womb. She could hear the depth in his voice muffled while she was being carried around in a sometimes light and sometimes dark area. But her eyes were closed by the thick fluid that she was in. How tight and safe she felt in the rare moments when she was awake! There were quick movements that would wake her up, but it was his voice that would always wake her in shock and horror. There was something unsafe about him that her mother could not yet see or feel.

The power of his voice calling out to her flooded her mind and forced a type of blindness to roll over her eyes. It was as though she was once again that little child still within her mother's womb. Blinded, Victoria was left only with her ears able to hear his voice and her heart to feel it speak. Feelings of love, fear, anger and hate mixed together with the same blend of confusion and separation as a dough, because she never knew her father at all. All she ever knew was his voice. She thought he died right there only moments after the death of her mother. All the newborn Victoria saw out of her blurry eyes was that something or someone appeared to rip itself free from some sort of prison that was her father's body.

The clear, deep voice that she heard that day in the hospital again captivated her and tugged at her chest, and was trying to rip the heart out of her. All Victoria had from her mother was that heart, a faint scar and a constant reminder of the life her mother gave up so freely for her. It was something Victoria did not want to lose. She did not want to live without it even if she could.

Despite all of her desires to flee from her father, she couldn't prevent herself from starting to walk toward it. In a hypnotic trance, she started to slide one foot a few inches forward and then the other. I tried to reach for her but her arm was out of my grasp. The noise never stopped moving forward, and foot by foot, the noise cloud started to engulf her. Even as I screamed at her, she didn't flinch. Further and further into the cloud she went until only an arm remained, and I knew that if I did not get her out then, I would never see her again.

Before I even realized what I was doing, her hand was in mine, and I pulled to free her with all the strength that was in me. But she was stuck in the noisy mass. The color of the mass started to change as soon as she touched the outermost membrane of the cloud. It was then turning into more of a whitish-green color. It blew out cold air well in front of the cloud, and very quickly I was trapped in the cocoon of cold air. I started to feel my body freezing right where I was standing, and the strength that I was using to pull Victoria out of the mass was triple the strength that I was using to fight off the freezing temperature. I imagined myself becoming a frozen statue in the same way movies portray a person freezing solid when they touch liquid nitrogen.

The cloud was working its way down her arm to where my hand was clamped tightly around her forearm an inch or so above her wrist. Even if I wanted to or had to let her arm go to escape the cloud, my hand was frozen tightly around it, just as the stone encased Excalibur. I would sooner die right there and then than flee and watch death claim another one right in front of my eyes.

Inch by inch, I, therefore, watched the cloud slowly work its way toward my arm. Even as the freezing air numbed every part of my body other than my hand and eyes, I refused to fight it. Closer and closer it crept till I could feel its breath being released upon my hand. Somehow that breath was warmer than the air that placed me into the cocoon, and it gave me a bit of my strength back. With what seemed to be more of an exhalation rather than a pull, I somehow caught her when the cloud finally repelled her.

The blob of whitish-green mass broke, and she was released. Just because the blob released her didn't mean it was done with us, and as we both fell backward away from it, the cloud grew explosively to entrap us. She was still trapped in her memories and I had to fight with her to get her moving. The deep freeze that placed me in the cocoon was shattered when we fell backward, instantaneously freeing my grip and loosening all of my limbs. I was able to feel some of the clumsiness that always accompanied frozen limbs and body parts, but the adrenaline that started to bombard my body was enough to undo any residue left over from the frozen grip that held me.

We couldn't hesitate, so I grabbed at her again, and pulled her away from the mass. Then we ran away. Her limp body and dead weight continued to fight against me, but I was determined, even if I had to carry her, to keep her with me. The hypnotic spell that she was under would not release her as easily as the cloud had. I seemed useless to free her and unequipped to break the spell that held her in that limbo.

"Victoria," I said softly due to the fact that I was still unaware if that really was her name or if I was being lied to just to ensure my failure.

For the most part, her body stayed locked in whatever world the cloud showed her, but the arm that I was holding onto seemed to soften its resistance to me.

Running as fast as my out-of-shape body could go, I ran, pulling Victoria toward the exit of that school of horrors. I knew that if we got outside, we would be safe. The door was only a hundred feet away, and the path leading to it was clear. My weakened legs began to burn as I struggled to break free with all the adrenaline coursing through my veins, just as testosterone floods a weightlifter's muscles. Her weight seemed to anchor me, but through the mix of chemicals that flooded my body, I found a way to drag her, even though she let herself be pulled along rather than running or helping me in any way. I gasped deeply and rapidly as a way of ingesting oxygen in the hope that it would give me the strength I needed to go those final hundred feet to the exit.

Step by step, we made our way closer to the exit. The cloud just continued to gain on us. I could feel its coldness breathing down my neck. If it was a dream, I would have expected the hallway to grow in length, becoming never-ending and impossible to escape. I could see the shadow of it creeping into my peripheral vision. That made me think about giving up, because there was no way to escape it. My legs were in control of themselves, and there was no stopping them.

The cold, clammy breath of the mass was not breathing over my entire body. The mass breathed its freezing breath out to form a vacuum suction that would open behind Victoria and me. The speed and power of the air being sucked into the mass almost stopped us. A few seconds later, the wind would exit, pushing us away from it. It was the only moment when we were able to open an extra five feet away from the cloud. The air was filled with cold and tasted like musty death. It made it very hard for me to breathe in the air I needed to pull her away from it.

Only 50 feet from the door to the once solid world outside that I knew, I screamed, "Come on, Victoria! We must leave here and get to my car. Come on! Run, damn it, run!"

She turned her head to me still with her lips parted with the same gap and confused look upon her face that she had when she first heard her father's voice.

My screams filled my mouth again. "Come on! If we don't get out of here quickly, we are going to die!"

From the look of sincerity upon my face or by the crackling that made me sound like a teenaged boy going through puberty, she knew that I was not joking, and from somewhere deep inside her, she felt the same. Her dead weight instantly drifted from me, and a few slips from her shoes was all it took for her to be well in front of me. Her hand still in mine was the only thing tethering her to me. It jolted me forward, almost as a dare, to keep up with her. Both of us sprinted. My steps were just a few steps behind hers, and her hand was then the one squeezing tightly to mine.

The air I was breathing in from the cloud started to make me hallucinate, and the dream in which I was in Hell's cave came back to me. All around, the walls changed from decorations and different artwork into the faces that made up the cave walls. Even the temperature that was freezing me only moments earlier turned into the hot, sweaty, moist heat that was impossible to block out or forget. The heat that radiated from the cave floor started to melt the rubber of my shoes quickly, and I could feel burns and blisters starting to form on my feet and lower legs.

Some of the faces within the wall started to scream and curse at me as I was then stumbling over my feet as I ran. Obscene words and phrases came at me from every direction. There was no avoiding the verbal onslaught that was being thrown at me. It would be easier to find a quiet corner during an indoor, heavy-metal concert. Threats and promises were being made from the deep blackness of the cave behind me. I wondered if it was the cloud talking or if it really was Hell that had come up to claim my soul.

As glass, the cave shattered without any reason. Glass shards of broken faces exploded upon me, cutting my body everywhere. Blood poured out of my mouth with every exhalation, and every time I breathed in, it seemed the glass would dig in deeper. Blood rained down, as water from a shower over my head. The heat and salt in it burned my eyes, and I could not see. I wondered if Victoria could still see me and if she was the one holding my hand. All I saw was a blood-red figure pulling me like a sack of unwanted meat.

She somehow led the way, and we hit the door with such force that the door flung open, releasing us into the world.

Instantly, when we hit the door, my hallucination was sucked out of my head and back into the cloud. The cloud, refusing to exit, stopped at the door as a siren's song, a way of luring us back in. We both had had enough of the cloud and simply turned away from it and toward the natural world that then held us in its hand.

My eyes gazed upon the world. It seemed in many ways different from the one I gazed upon only moments before while in class. The sun didn't seem to kiss the freshly-laid cover of snow. The sun was safely hidden behind a wall of cloud cover that almost shaded out the midday sky. The air that was trapped inside the cloud cover tasted stale and overused. With each breath, I could either taste someone else's breath, the exhaust from a car or truck or the slow decay that the freezing temperature would normally erase. It also appeared to me that no fresh air was being allowed to penetrate the situation. The lack of fresh air forced a strong breeze to build up. The breeze blew swiftly along the covered earth, pushing itself onto me and through my sweater to bring a strong chill on me. It forced a numbness that only the cold possesses to take over my mind. The numbness forced my mind into random empty thoughts. I was lost, and very quickly, I couldn't remember where we were off to and why we even started out that way. Shivers forced my mind into a state of panic over every thought in my mind. Victoria finally brought me out of my stupor by pulling my hand and arm very tightly.

"My truck is over here," I said to her while motioning toward the middle of the parking lot.

We both stood in amazement as we looked around the parking lot that was seldom empty. It was devoid of all vehicles, except for my truck. Even when there were no classes and all study rooms were closed, I always saw a few cars. I kept thinking that I was still in some form of hallucination in which the creature consumed Victoria as well, but the reason why it put us in there was unknown. It seemed that any second the mask before my eyes would be lifted, and we would be inside that mass that was chasing us. Slowly eating our dreams and passion, while leaving us frozen in a timeless land, I pressed on regardless, because in due time, the mystery would either reveal itself to me, or hopefully, we would escape.

"That's your truck. Nice," Victoria said as she looked curiously at my raven-black pickup.

"Yep," I said while grabbing the keys from my right pocket. Without missing a step, I hit the unlock button. Walking over to the passenger side, I opened the door, and watched as she climbed into the seat. Almost as a wild animal stalking its prey, I moved with a determination I hadn't known for quite some time to the opposite side of the truck, and climbed into the driver's seat with great ease. Even if we were still trapped in the cloud, I did not care, because we were hopefully then leaving the cold and mysterious classroom behind us forever. The leather seats squeaked as I sat, but with a quick turn of the keys and the pushing of a few buttons, our heated seats would soon be warming us. Still in my determined mindset, I shifted my truck into gear with my cold, bitter, dry and deathly hand. I could hear my heart missing a beat when I noticed that the time was 4.30 p.m. rather than 1.25 p.m., which was the time we left the classroom.

"That can't be right," I mumbled to myself.

"What can't be right? Is something wrong with the car? I hope not, because we need to leave." She stopped talking only to take in the fact that we weren't moving. "Devin, you were in such a rush to leave. So why are we just sitting here?" Victoria asked while grabbing my right arm and looking rather curiously into my eyes again.

In a state of confusion rather than understanding, I pointed to the clock on the radio to reveal what time my radio said, and without me asking her for the time, she quickly rolled up the left sleeve of her shirt that just barely covered her hardened stomach. I always forced myself to look away because I was never sure where the line between desire and obsession would be crossed. Had I crossed that line from fantasy and turned into a stalker?

I couldn't pull my eyes away this time as I traced her buttons and body curves. Her Pink Floyd shirt had ten or so buttons running up from where her waist and low-cut pants met. The buttons crawled upward, as a stalking snake, past her belly button. Then up, inch by inch, until it stopped just under her perfect breast. There the snake-like buttons sat waiting for the right moment or victim at which to strike out. I was the snake's victim and the venom that awaited me was pain and death. I willingly jumped in. Or was the snake trapping me to stop my sight and quiet my hunger for her? With a rapid, twisting attack, the snake climbed from under her breast to be exposed by another button in front and on top of her breast in a way of holding her purity back, and hiding from the world, which included me. Then, with only one more button on top of her breast, it sealed the chastity gates before opening to expose her lower neck and a pair of necklaces for the world to see.

Her mouth hung low as she gazed in disbelief at her silver watch. I needed no words from her to know what time it said, but for her own sake, she had to say it. Hearing it aloud, perhaps she thought, would break the spell, or make it not as real so that she could share her confusion with me as I did with her.

"We left the classroom at 1.25."

Her eyes darted back and forth between her watch and the clock on my dashboard. A feeling of uncertainty arose within me, but also a feeling of joy. It was the first time in years I had someone not only to talk to about this but also to share the experience with. That new feeling made me feel bad about myself, because how could I feel happy when it might mean the death and damnation of someone else? There had to be some human trait that makes us never want to go through something of difficulty by ourselves.

The heat from the seats was starting to warm us, and I could tell that it was relaxing Victoria a little. Neither one of us grabbed our coats on the way out, so the cold that we experienced inside the school and outside had taken its toll on our bodies. With my hands shaking, I reached out, and turned the heater on, and then reached down under the gauges to grab a packet of my full-flavored cigarettes. Without missing a beat, I pulled one out, and lit it up.

"Victoria, would you like one?" I said as I noticed her eyeing the packet rather hungrily.

"Yeah. You don't mind?" she said as she grabbed one, and lit it up. "Oh, by the way, call me Vic."

She took it and put it in between her lovely, colored lips, and inhaled like it was the first time she had ever smoked. Before she brought the smoke into her lungs, she parted her lips to tease the smoke with an exit, and then powerfully sucked the smoke into her. I felt as if I was watching her make love to the smoke before releasing it back to the world. After watching her make love to the cigarette, I took my first drag, and my body loved it. I knew someday I would have to quit, and oh, how I mourned the thought of that day even before it ever happened! I could feel the smoke and drug quickly being pushed through my veins and vessels. The nicotine sped my heart up slightly, but instead of my hands shaking, I could feel them being steadied by the drug flowing faster throughout my body until finally it reached my mind. Then the drug relaxed my mind enough that I could recall some of the day's actions.

The smoke exited from my mouth and then out of the car through the window. All the cars that were gone from the parking lot began to come back. Then, in the blink of an eye, all the clouds retreated to where they had been when I was dreaming out of the classroom window toward a sunny day.

"Hey, look. The time is back to 1.30 now," Vic said while reading my clock and then rechecking hers. She started to smile a little, then said, "Did you slip me a roofie when I wasn't looking?" She kind of caught me off guard before I realized she was smiling.

"Smart and pretty — now that is a wicked combo," I said with little confidence and feeling slightly awkward.

She just smiled as her cheeks turned from a faded white into a violet red that shone throughout the car.

I pulled out of the parking lot onto the street. It was remarkable how the light of the sun reflecting off the snow blinded both of us when only a few moments earlier, it had been cloudy, dark and stale. Even the wind was full of life again. There was no longer death in it. It seemed as though we had just exited from where the dead don't talk but where they fade away.

"Now, this is messed up," Vic said as she looked at the strange occurrence.

"You aren't kidding," I replied while covering my eyes from the sun.

After a few blinks, my eyes became somewhat accustomed to the sunlight. I started to notice Vic getting impatient and annoyed by the acts of the day so far. She kept flicking her ash out through a small crack in the window, while her head and eyes gazed out toward the school. The thoughts and questions that she held in her head would have filled hundreds of pages in a horror book. Trying to give her some peace, I fumbled through the stations to find classic rock music. The acoustic music of an aged rocker filled the speakers, singing about a highway and a girl he left because he was a bad boy.

"The only comfort I can offer you is this, Vic." I paused while waiting for her to look at me. Then, slowly and in a childlike manner, she looked toward me and deep into my eyes. "I can't give you the answer you are looking for or will even understand. Such moments in life when all you want is time to stop so you can catch up never happen. All that happens is that time forces us to move on whether or not we understand what is happening. If you think about it, that's good, because if we stopped every time life does this to us, we would never live," I stated while looking at her.

I think that was something I heard on TV or overheard someone say.

I pulled over and stopped the car so that I could look at her. Her face was only inches away from mine. Her dark eyes met my blue eyes. Even then, with all that had happened over the past few minutes, her beauty captivated me in a sense of awe that I truly believed only existed between the pages of some romance novel, not right here in front of me. I wondered if she knew, despite all that we had been through in those last few moments. I couldn't get past how much I wanted to kiss her, and there we were eyes to eyes, lips to lips and breath to breath. I was breathing her in as she breathed out. Her lips trembled slightly while she breathed in my tainted and toxic air. I wanted to touch her lips. I needed to feel the moisture of them, if not on my own lips, then at least, on the tips of my fingers. My heart sang with anticipation as it raced to where I could feel my cheeks filling up with blood and turning reddish. The blood raced powerfully throughout my body, mixing with the adrenaline that caused my body to tremble with fear and excitement. From the look in her eyes, I could see that she could either hear my heart pounding or see the swelling in my neck veins as my blood pulsed freely through.

To reach out and pull her to me encased my thoughts and primed my muscles, but fear of the anticipation froze all my movements. As fractions of a second passed, the fear rose almost to a paralyzing state. Aware that my chance to taste her lips was quickly fading, I had to break through, but I didn't know how to.

I started to ponder, "The longer I wait, the less of a man she will think I am. That is unless I can hold off my desire to the moment when absolution is here."

What if that was the moment? It was the same type of moment I missed repeatedly throughout my teen years with different girls, but it was always the same result. I couldn't wait any longer. I stole a deep breath of hers, then let it escape in uneven phases to fall upon her lips in the hope that my breath mixed with hers would revive my fading moment. As a way of summoning the little bit of strength and courage I needed, I kept telling myself that she wanted me to kiss her, and that she was hoping the moment did not pass her by as well. Regardless of whether she got mad or questioned my motives, I could always apologize to her later, and blame the craziness we were just in for my impulses.

Her lips acted before mine could, but in a different way from what I allowed for. She broke the awkward silence with a whispering voice often used by lovers. Her voice sounded as if an angel was singing a song reserved for those in Heaven during sunrise and sunset. "Devin, what was that; you know, back there in the classroom?" she asked with a sweetness hidden underneath a deep desire to need to know.

Settling back into the seat, I knew I missed that moment.

All I could say was a simple yet undefined answer. "I don't know. It was like I was living in a nightmare, and the nightmare was burned into my soul, not my skin or my mind," I replied with uneasiness in my voice but also a touch of anger for my lack of courage to touch and taste her lips.

I was able to see my reflection in her eyes, and I could easily tell she thought that I was lying. By the way she looked at me, I could tell she also did not believe me.

"That's too simple. C'mon. There has to be more to it than that. Like when I touched your shoulder. You were lost in a place or world within your mind that was not anywhere close to a nightmare. And when you got thrown out of your chair, you were hit so hard that your legs and arms flopped as though you were made of rubber. I've never seen or ever heard of something like that. You looked just like a doll being thrown through the air," she added as a way of digging for the truth.

"Let me think about it. I really don't want to get you involved," I replied quietly and hesitantly.

"Get involved! That thing was after me too. So, no, I need you to tell me right now, damn it!" she screamed. There was no way around it. I was going to have to tell her everything. I could only hope that she didn't think I was making any of it up and that I was completely nuts.

"I don't know. Alright. I need time to think about it."

"I'm not leaving you until you tell me everything," she

added while blowing another cloud of smoke out of her mouth and out of the car.

"Vic, that's not much of a reason for me to tell you, is it?" I said with a smile, hoping it would lighten the mood a little. "Vic, if you don't mind, could you please not ask me any more questions until I get us to my home? Then I'll tell you everything."

A small smile fell unexpectedly upon my face as the smoke from my cigarette exited my body and went out of the window. I envied the smoke because its whole purpose ended as soon as it left my body. My smile only lasted until all of the smoke was out of my car, because that was when I realized that I was going to have to tell her the truth about what had happened to my friend without leaving out any of the details. She was connected, and I knew it. How was I going to make her understand before that thing tortured her as it had already done to me?

The need to speak and break the uncomfortable silence was overwhelmingly powerful. Other than what had just happened to us, I really didn't know that much about her. In a way, it felt like a blind date that was going very badly. Even though I asked her to stop asking questions, I really hoped that she would ask another question, but why would she after the rude way I answered her?

"Vic, I'm sorry I was short with you. We're almost at my home. When we get there, I'll try to explain this to you the best I can," I stated, attempting to comfort myself, but my words did not reach her ears. She was lost in her own world.

For the next 20 minutes, we drove in almost complete silence. The radio was all that broke the invisible barrier. Her gaze was locked on the changing scenery. I wondered what she was thinking about and if it was me, rather than the events of that day. The world we drove in changed from campus stores and housing into a small subdivision. At the end of the houses was a thick and dense forest. The forest was inaccessible except by a narrow trail. My home was trapped, intertwined with the trees, bushes and shrubs that filled everywhere I looked.

"It feels like we are driving into the mouth of a dragon," Vic said when I turned into my snow-packed, gravel driveway.

Whatever thought or thoughts she was replaying in her mind became blank as soon as one tire was removed from the blacktop road and re-emerged onto the thin layer of snow covering my driveway.

"This is so cool but also very creepy," she said plainly while ducking her head down slightly in the way people do when driving through a multilevel parking garage.

Trees, dead and asleep for their winter's nap, hung over the entrance, but as we passed completely through the wall of trees, there was a very thin, slice-like break in the tree cover to allow light in. Even with an opening cut through the tops of the trees, there still was no clear way for the sun's light to get through easily. The only thing that was missing to turn the driveway into the horror story of headless horseman was a wooden bridge.

The gravel road was bumpy and poorly graded due to the changing weather at that time of the year. Branches that broke off one of the trees closer to the driveway made the ride from the county road to home somewhat like an obstacle course. The plow drivers always did their best to leave a thin layer of snow for me to drive on, and that always softened the ride, but if the driver was lazy and left too thick a layer, I would often hit a hidden branch or large rock that broke free from the gravel.

The tall and mighty trees that lined the gravel road hid the shadow and smell of death under their branches. They were so close to the road that two cars could not pass. By early midsummer, all I could hear on the road would be the gentle sounds of leaves brushing into each other. The sounds of leaves would mask the scratching calls of the branches as they hit other branches. In the winter, those scratches sang louder than semitrucks roaring down the road. Birds and other wildlife lived there, but they were quiet and easily scared. That was until the sleepy autumn's breath captured and killed all that were found. To those animals, death, which stalked them all summer, pounced as a cat that was prowling in the shadows. The forest of pain lay asleep, hidden from the cold, in a coma where it sat and waited for the season to end. Then it would slowly awaken to feel a warm kiss on its leaves.

As in a dream, my house came out of the trees and into sight. The dream was the warmth of the fireplace but it looked more like a nightmare, and a quick flash of a single raven flying off the roof made the house feel the part. The sleeping forest seemed to have taken over the dwellings of the only place where life was awake in the forest. The two-story, wooden house lay dark and quiet as though it was waiting to reveal a secret and mysterious past. Logs formed a type of protective layer. All the windows and doors were boxed out, making it appear elegant. The holes those boxes outlined looked more like eye sockets with only black holes for eyes when sunlight could not penetrate through the tree canopy.

5

Devin and Victoria

Vic just gazed out at the house as we drove up to it. Whether it was the size, solitude or make of it, something touched her soul, and whether it was a good touch or a bad touch, I could not tell. To me, the first sight of the house, as I broke free from the shield of trees and brush, always reminded me of an answer to a nightmare, one that I still haven't dreamt yet. It always felt like the end of the dream was near, and whether the actor in the dream or tale would live or die never seemed to matter. What mattered was that it was the end, and because of that, I could live alone in the middle of the demon-possessed forest.

"So, does your family own this house, or is this yours? Must be nice to be a rich kid," Vic said with a taste of resentment and distaste in her voice.

"I am not from a rich family, and my family does not live here with me. In fact, I have not seen or talked to them in years. They don't even know if I'm still alive." I paused just so I could concentrate on parking the car in the garage. "You see, Vic, after James was killed, I don't remember what happened to me for six months or so. All I can remember of that time was an everlasting nightmare until mid-December. I finally woke up and I was standing in front of this driveway. A man was standing there. He said to me, 'Here are your keys to the house and for the truck.' As soon as he handed them to me, the world behind him and around me disappeared, and I was standing alone just after sunset in front of this house, holding the keys of the house and the truck and the deeds and titles to each."

By her body language, I could tell that Vic didn't believe me. That made me a little nervous, because if she wanted to live through that night and those that followed, she had better start. On the other hand, if someone just told me what I told her, I wouldn't believe the story either.

"So, you live here all by yourself," Vic said as she stepped down out of the truck and onto the dry and lightly-polished cement floor with a hollow click of her shoes. A soft and sharp echo came, and then fell away as quickly as the logs on the wall could eat the noise up.

"Yes, I do; just me in this empty house," I answered her in a lonesome and hollow voice. "Come on. Let's get inside."

Her steps were close to silent behind me, and it was hard to tell just from the sounds of her footsteps how far behind me she was. By some sixth sense, I could feel that she was within an arm's length behind me. Her eyes walking over me, perhaps the same way they did while I was trapped in my nightmare. I opened the door for her to walk through into my house, and a strong smell of wood flung itself out onto us. I could see from her expression that she liked it very much.

A thought of summer filled my eyes and lifted my soul. That warm smell always had a way of doing that. I drifted back to a time and a place that I remembered as happy, and I was satisfied with what I saw when I looked into my own blue eyes. I didn't see the outline that shaded my eyes to reflect the nightmare that had overtaken me. The warmth that exploded from the door trickled out into the colder air and quickly disappeared through the garage until it was consumed by the cold winter air.

Nerves overwhelmed me even before half of my drained body entered through the door while reaching in to turn the lights on. In a flash, light poured into the garage, forcing our shadows to dance on different walls and floors. The warmth of the crisp carpet felt good on my feet. I could see that she also liked how the carpet felt on her bare feet. For the first time since I moved in there, I really felt like I was home.

Normally, I stayed in the basement. Its stairs were open and to the right of the door, but I stepped to the left and went upstairs to the grand room. The basement was all I needed; it was a decent apartment, except for my bedroom, which was up on the second story. The grand room had a large cathedral ceiling that sang over the living room and game room, and a kitchen was also attached to it. A hallway connected it to the rest of the house. There was a large-screen TV on a small wall, a pool table in one corner, and a few other oddities that easily made it known that a bachelor lived there by himself. There was a den off to one corner, which was where I started this journal. For some reason, I have numerous copies, because I kept on losing it and then finding it again.

"Wow! This place is nice," Vic stated, as she looked up to the cathedral ceiling that could be seen through the stairs going up. The open-rail log steps going up gave it an ageless beauty.

"I hardly ever go upstairs, but there is a large fireplace, and I'll get a fire going."

"Alright. That sounds nice," she said while admiring the paneled wood that formed an upside-down V to the ceiling.

Somewhere along the drive there, we must have fallen back into another time gap, because above the stairs, a full moon was then shining through a skylight as an ever-watching eye. The light of the moon illuminated the frost-covered skylight and the stairs as well. While we both raised ourselves up the stairs, the peace of blue moonlight started to illuminate us as well. Nights like those are usually the only times I go up the stairs other than to sleep, because I have always found the pale moonlight a very welcome friend.

Through it and six other skylights, I would spend my solitude in peace without any lights on; with only the light from those skylights and the fireplace as my lullaby. There I could always find peace in the beauty of God's creation, and for some reason, I never found any fear while meditating in the full moonlight, regardless of what nightmarish figure was awaiting me during my sleep.

The fireplace was in the center of the eastern wall of the huge living room. There were two leather couches with one matching loveseat and one very comfortable, leather chair forming a boxed-in half circle around the fireplace. There were two glass-encased coffee tables in front of each of the couches and an end table in between the loveseat and the chair. Each piece of furniture was centered by the fireplace, not the television, because the room was made for entertaining guests. Without the fireplace being lit, it was warm in the room, but when the fireplace was burning with fresh pine wood, it was almost magical. The fireplace was four and a half feet wide and three feet deep, and that was more than ample to produce a fire big enough to radiate a lot of heat. There was also a vent a few feet above the opening that would blow hot air out throughout the room and up to where two ceiling fans pushed the heat toward every corner of the room. The stone face that ran all the way to the ceiling added to the rustic appeal that the house already had.

Vic walked around the open room looking like a small child would look while standing in a new home and in an empty room that would soon be filled with furniture. In the soft and gentle moonlight, her jet-black hair appeared to be a mix of darker shades; one that changed the laws of physics by changing the color spectrum. Blues and purples that then shone from the top of her head to a little below her shoulder blades were the new colors. Sprinklings of red could be seen following over the front of her shoulders. Her face reflected the light so that I lost my breath. Her yellowish skin revealed a soft brown and a hidden white.

I craved her touch; to hold her; to kiss her. I realized that all of my fantasies about her were not even close to her actual radiance. I fell in love with her there and then. It was no longer my mental image of her or lust and a dream I was chasing. Somehow the moonlight let her reveal herself to me without even knowing it, and I knew then that life without her would be incomplete and worthless.

She turned, and without a word, her gaze locked onto mine, and she opened her soul to me, and through her gaze, for the first time, I could see she desired me as well. As if it was out of our hands, we walked toward each other without blinking. I could see her mouth trying to find the words as she stepped toward me. Her lips looked silky and wet, and were slightly parted. Almost by fate, our paths led steadily and recklessly to each other. For the first time, every move I made was perfectly made and timed. It seemed the world, as a whole, was holding its breath, waiting and hoping for us to touch.

Closer and closer we came with each step. We were getting so close I began to feel the warmth of her body entrapping me. I could taste the cinnamon of her gum each time she breathed out. Her breath and heat were nothing compared to her eyes, which kept bringing me closer and closer to her.

In a fluid motion, my chilled hand touched her warm and naked cheek. Destiny had us because she did not move or even flinch with the touch of my cold hands on her skin. Together we were flowing into one, even with me shaking in anticipation. My other hand possessed itself, and wrapped around her just above the waist, and with a tender and forceful pull, our bodies collided.

There was something new with this kiss. It felt like it was the way a first and last kiss should begin to be. My lips and hers met perfectly. In a way, they seemed as if my lips were made for her, and her lips were made for mine. I could tell she felt it, and with a soft moan from her mouth into my mine, I knew my dreams were not even close to how right they felt.

"I've wanted to do that since I first saw you walking in front of our school," I said as our lips parted and our eyes met again.

I could still taste the cinnamon from her gum. Her gaze into my eyes was a struggle for her to break, but after a few well-placed blinks, she moved her eyes and her body toward one of the wall-sized windows on the far side of the room.

"I like you too," she said in a way to ease her clumsiness but also to break the deafening silence that was echoing off the walls.

"It's alright, but it gets lonely out here," I said as I walked up to her.

I watched as her hair covered her head, shoulders and upper back like a midnight shadow blanketed over a cemetery in late October. My eyes were brought down from her hair toward a shape below her ribcage and her upper hips; they could be accused of stalking for their staring at how her jeans hugged each side of her butt. It looked like she was not wearing jeans but blue paint instead.

"I could just…" she was saying as she turned her head and caught my eyes shamefully looking at her butt. Then after a slight smile from her, my eyes met hers and she continued. "Sleeping right here would make me feel like I was under the stars. In a way, I felt like the stars were beckoning me when I saw them like this."

"I can't get past the forest," I said as my eyes locked onto the darkness that slithered unchangeable throughout the depths of the forest.

I didn't want to tell her about the nights I went up there to meditate.

With a weird, halfway look, she just said, "OK." Then, after a slight pause, she asked, "Devin, do you have something warmer I can wear?"

"Yeah. Down the hallway behind us, in the last room on the right, you'll find a large bedroom, and in the far corner, there's a closet that has some sweaters and longer shirts. I'll get a fire going to warm this place up."

She turned and walked off, passing a fireplace. I had no knowledge of what was about to happen and little did I know that with the events of that day, it could be the end of us. I didn't know why I just let her walk away, as if we saw and felt nothing that day.

6

Victoria's nightmare

Vic ran her fingertips over the stones as she passed in front of the fireplace. She had to feel it, to know that it was real and that it wasn't some dream she had landed in, because for her, none of it seemed right or real. Even what she felt for Devin couldn't be real, because here was a guy she'd never really met before, and he went crazy in class, and for some reason or other, he brought her into his delusion, and worst of all, she was then in a huge house walking beside a fireplace. It was too much.

"Definitely too much" is all she was saying to herself again and again.

The smell of freshly-burnt pine lingered, like a melancholy ghost during its funeral, all around the fireplace. The smell started to spread throughout the room. The stones themselves had those smells and aroma burned into them, but the smell the stones held was not rooted in good memories of bonfires with friends. No, they held the reality of what a shadow is. The shadows they held were no longer of this world or this dimension. It was almost like those stones were not even from this earth but from another time and constructed under different laws of physics.

Her memories devolved into an attack of depression and sadness. They were like wild waves that encased a sleeping Jesus and his disciples while they were traveling on a rough lake. She, though, was unable to control the winds and seas, so those waves pounded her, and they started forcing feelings that were long held captive and safely locked away.

Even though she did not want to relive or remember those feelings, it was too late because they were being thrown at her. Then a dense fog similar to the ones that linger on freezing coastal states, collapsed throughout her mind and soul, and somehow she was no longer next to the fireplace, and her fingers were touching nothing but the fog.

Where tears of sorrow should have filled and consumed her, feelings of true peace were found. A gray and dirty gravestone hidden under an old oak tree started to emerge out of the fog. Out of her body, she was able to walk all around it, but couldn't read what was written on the stone because of a thin and slimy cover of moss. It was almost like a camera spinning around an actor in a movie to show confusion. She couldn't stop the spinning, nor slow it down.

Closer and closer she spun around the mysterious grave. A desire to know whose tomb she was standing over became stronger than even her will to live. She had to know who it was, but something from inside of her was pulling at her to stop as if to say, "You are not ready to see or absorb it."

Her soul was screaming, "Let me die if you must, but I need to know!"

The fog began to laugh at her as it pulled her or her life force back a little, just like playing a game of tug of war with a dog.

"Do you really want to know? Ha ha! I think not! I can taste your fear of not knowing. It has awakened me, and it is so refreshing." A thick voice hovered in the fog that thundered louder than the atom bombs that were dropped on Japan. "I could feed off that fear and anger for another thousand years. Do you want to know? What will be more filling? I should give you a taste," the voice said with tremendous laughter.

As those words ended, Victoria found herself being pulled back to the stone grave marker. Closer and closer she came. The breath of her soul and its heart were on fire with anticipation. Oh, how she wanted this, and how this feeling became everything to her! Not even the embracing of a lover could feel this intense or the first time she was truly kissed.

Even as she fought those memories, they came without ceasing.

Initially, it was the young boy's face. First, the face cleared through the thought and then his body's shape began to take form. It was Tyler, the boy she wanted to be near to for more than a year. He became the only thing she could focus on. The joys of that moment in her life overcame her; she was temporarily in that moment and time. She could see herself writing his name next to hers with a heart around them. She felt the nervousness of that day; how she had waited until the time of the party, because he was going to be there as well. Maybe they were going to play spin the bottle or another kissing game, and she would finally be able to feel the lips she has been dreaming about pressed tightly upon hers; to have her body held tightly by him as she tried not to be a bad or sloppy kisser. The party came and went with one of those games being secretly played out of the sight of the birthday girl's parents. She could feel the tears starting to come as she walked away, but whether through fate or blind luck, she never had a chance to kiss him. She thought that the next day would not come, and that life would end without her ever tasting his lips.

Her footsteps echoed then louder and emptier than they did on those dark nights leading up to Halloween.

"This is how life's supposed to be," she thought, "alone." Who was she to demand such a person's affection and perhaps love?

Out of the fog, a hand came and touched her right hand. Fear and confusion overtook her as she jumped and screamed a little. She could hear the heavy breathing of someone else. Her rapid heartbeat rang inside of her. The world she was in froze. As soon as it did, her soul was pushed out of her younger body so that she could watch what was happening. That moment she was watching would play slowly forward, before rewinding to when her hand was touched. In a way, it was like coverage of a football game, and a person kept reshowing the same event repeatedly until finally it just paused so she could walk her around the memory in a way of recalling every detail in it.

She could see herself mid-scream and slightly off the ground from jumping. The hand was all she could see of the person touching her and causing her to jump. The rest of the person was hidden in the fog. At that moment, her memories of the event faded and vanished. It was almost like she was experiencing that moment for the first time. She didn't know who it was or how it came to be, and it seemed like the fog was blocking out everything but the hand and arm on purpose. The fear of losing that memory forever frightened her. It was important, and she knew it. It was the beginning of the life that had brought her there. Was it the voice that controlled the removal of the memory? Was the voice her soul torturing herself for some sin she could not place?

She wanted to scream — but couldn't — and beg to have it back. There was, though, no ground to kneel on or fall upon; there never really was. Even when she heard the echoing footsteps, she never felt the ground. The only way she knew there was ground was by being able to hear it. Her screams and pleas were nothing. No matter how hard she wanted to scream, not a single sound came out of her. She wondered if her lips were even moving, but they weren't.

Tears were able to come, and like a person still lost in mourning, she lost herself to it. All she wanted was death. Oh, how sweet it was to long for death! Joy is what she felt for those who had exited the world. What is the physical world but a sickening testing place where one was being judged for the afterlife? Could she will her own death in order to save her family members the embarrassment of having to live with a suicide in their family? None of them will ever understand or feel the joy of death.

"Please come to me. Please. I'm begging you!" screamed over and over in her thoughts, passing through her mind, as fluid as her blood rumbled out of her heart.

The tears had changed into tears of denial. Denial of her death was too much. The world and time had all gone away, trapping her within that moment while not letting her know what was there. Only nothingness...

Years faded away like butter on an oven-hot roll. Generations came and went all around her in a blur. Even the prophesied end of the world came, and then another world came as well. She only wondered for a moment if it was from the same god, or if this was just a step in which one becomes a god. She didn't care or even want to care. Her desire to die was all she knew and wanted to know until darkness finally came to the world, and life all around her exploded into a void of nothing. Even so, she and the hand upon her right shoulder within the fog never changed.

"Victoria," a shaking voice came from behind the hand. She knew the voice, but she could not remember the face

it belonged to. It was so many lifetimes and cares in the past. Then, as a shot from a sniper to a target's head, the moment came back to her. The shaky and cracking voice behind the hand came to her, and she started to remember everything. The party, the anxiety and the sadness of it all exploded as Tyler's face jumped out, just as a ship breaking through the last bit of fog.

"Let's walk home together," Tyler said with a slight bit of fear in his voice.

She could feel his eyes, staring at her tear-stained eyes, and with a blink, she was back within the body of her past self.

She heard the words "OK. Sure." fly over eagerly from her lips in response to Tyler's question.

He stepped beside her as she waited for him. She could tell he was nervous and not very experienced. It made her feel a little bit relaxed to know he felt the same.

While they walked that autumn afternoon, their hands would brush against each other's, but both of them didn't want to be the first one to grab the other's hand. They talked and laughed at the silly things the other said. Slowly, the angle of their steps brought them closer and closer until they were walking so closely their hands were on top of each other. She felt a bit of nervousness she couldn't explain, and the level of their discussion slowed almost to a stop. She wanted to touch his hand more, because every time they touched, her body would tingle with a sensation that she had never known.

With little steps, to keep their hands close, Tyler matched his arm swing with hers. He felt it too, and powerful feelings of lust, passion, desire and fear pulsed through his veins. He was so scared that she didn't want to hold his hand. His hand was there; he made that move. If she wanted it, he hoped she would take the next step, which she did unknowingly. She allowed her fingers to become intertwined with his, and her face went red with embarrassment. Almost like magic, their hands became one. That was the first time either one of them had held the hand of someone they dreamed about. With every step, the awkwardness faded and they were just two people holding hands. They even walked a few extra blocks just so that moment would not end. They walked until the day quickly came to an end.

In front of her home, the two stood with both hands in each other's. They both wanted to hug and kiss the other one, but how were they supposed to turn holding hands into that? All they were able to do was tell each other "Bye" and "I'll see you on Monday". Then, letting go, both started to walk away.

"Victoria, I forgot to give you this," Tyler said as he held out a heart-shaped necklace. "I always thought of you when I went into the store, so here. If you don't like it, you don't have to wear it," he said in a way of sounding unsure of himself.

She was speechless. He thought of me too is all she could think about. A little embarrassed and red-faced, she stepped closer to him. When she grabbed it, she noticed that it was a nice necklace; in fact, the weight of it shocked her. The necklace was shaped with a heart inside of another heart, and appeared to be silver. How could she thank him for such a gift, and what would her friends say when they saw it? She felt as if she was soaring through the air like Superwoman.

All she could manage to say was "It's beautiful. Thank you so much."

"Here. Let me help you put it on," he said as he took it and walked behind her.

She felt like a movie star as she held her hair up so that he could attach it around her neck. She could feel his fast breath on the nape of her neck. It kind of tickled and excited her far past any other moment she has lived up to that point. She turned around and found herself in his arms. She could feel his body softly pressed against hers. She once thought that she wanted to be held tightly like that. It wasn't Heaven; it was paradise. Perfectly, her hands went around his waist as he lowered his lips to her, and she raised her body to meet his. An explosion of lust and confusion filled her body. She could feel his heat, and he could taste her lip gloss. For what seemed like a lifetime, they kissed each other with passionate, open lips. Their bodies were overcome with those new sensations and a desire to crave each other's touch and taste.

Like a bolt of lightning, her memories of that were wiped. A shallow and empty feeling overtook her mind, heart and soul. She then felt lonelier than that dreadful day when she left him before a local dance, and she saw him holding one of her friends as close as he had held her, if not closer. She didn't know if that was his way to hiding and forgetting his pain. The betrayal of his love that he so willingly bestowed upon her had become his prison. He was not alone, but he felt as though he was suspended in the depths of a black, hollow void. Life could not survive there, which was where he wanted to be, because without her, what made life worth it. All that life had to offer him was a lie masquerading as joy and love; it really was nothing more than a gray, melancholy existence filled with false dreams and empty promises.

At that point, she did not know that tears were fighting to grab hold of him. As much as he hated her for the way she stole his heart, only to eat it and spew it out with all other digested food, he still loved her and craved her, but couldn't have her. So he took Victoria's friend, because he wanted to hurt her too, but then, within the makeshift ball, he regretted that decision. It was too late, and he knew it. She also didn't know that somewhere within his tarnished soul, he would hold her forever, and if the time came and fate brought them back together, he knew that he could not help but feel the loss of her all over again. His life would forever be wrapped around her, mixed with a lifetime of what-ifs.

The moment was over and she was standing alongside that gray and dreaded gravestone, alone and brokenhearted just as she was on the day of the dance. Staring at the single stone in a motionless and dreadful way, she couldn't help but wonder where all of the other graves were. She looked like she was a statue created only to stare unmoved at the gravestone, while locked in a circling web of mourning. Was she standing on somebody, and if so, did it really matter? That thought sent a chill down her spine like one of those chills that she believed to be the Holy Spirit or some other otherworldly experience.

"You have been gone for so long that I forgot that I brought you here to feed on your misery as my main substance. And to answer your question, this is not just any cemetery. No, this is my special place. I am unsure what misery I'll bring here. Well, that is other than yours, of course. Ha ha!" the deep voice said as it returned. "I know you know not who or what I am. Maybe I'm a god or a new god who came here to overthrow the old impotent one. You have read your Bible and went to church like a good little girl. Have you ever wondered about the difference between a judgmental father who destroyed the world, and the loving, forgiving Son of Man, who was crucified on Calvary all those centuries ago?" he said in a soft whisper behind her left ear.

She could even feel the warmth from his lips, and taste the staleness within his breath. She thought of him as a cat toying with his food right before chewing its head off. She wanted to scream, or say something. The silence in between his words seemed like a trap she fell into and was too much for her to escape. She couldn't take it, and she wanted that thing to feel the helplessness that she herself had felt since coming there.

"Oh, I know how you feel, and I am aware of the torment that is flooding through your veins. It makes me happy to see someone who has caused so much pain to another feel what you are feeling. It is not what you want, but it is an answer."

As his words ended, she blinked and found that she was standing in front of the gravestone. Dirt and years of rot were pulled off it. It didn't start at any side or corner, but it started six inches up from the bottom and in the center. It appeared as though letters began to be engraved right before her very eyes on the gray gravestone. At first, there was a line maybe two to three inches long. Then numbers, both to the right and left of the mark, came out, first a three, then a nine and a nine again popped out, and then a one to form "1993".

She smiled to herself when she read that, because that was the year she was born, and for some reason, she always loved that year regardless of where and why it was written. Then she felt a little more attached to that '1993' than all of the ones she had seen before. There was depth in those numbers — something very familiar — but also some distance. It might have been easily dismissed as déjà vu. She couldn't dismiss it, though.

She was in a place of nothing. She couldn't recognize her own form. All that was there was a non-descriptive whiteness that engulfed her. She could remember that she knew words like pain, love and hate. What were they, though?

"This is what sleep is in between dreams," she kept thinking, every time she faded and melted into the white nothing. "Maybe this is what created God," she wondered to herself. "Is this God's mind that I'm locked in? What am I but an afterthought that, with any luck, will fade until sleep consumes me like a fire consumes the fuel it burns?"

She knew the word 'fire' and that fuel was what it burned, but what that fire and that fuel looked like she was unsure of.

"Maybe this is what dying really is" was her last thought before darkness overtook her. The whiteness she was swimming in was turning pitch black.

A bang loud enough to break every bone in her body screamed out into the pitch-black sea she was then part of. She did have a form, but it was broken in every way, and her depth was the thickness of a sheet of paper. She could see every heartbeat pushing her chest and abdomen up and down. Then another bang thudded against her. This time, the noise went through with such a velocity that she started to burn. Her eyes were never hurt or allowed to close, so she was forced to see it all, whatever it was to be. Huge shapes started to form, as quickly as bullets firing out of an automatic machine gun; they were of all sizes and of different colors.

Throughout the process, there was a great light. It was, though, different from what she thought a light was. It was everywhere and nowhere all at once, and every time it spoke, something exploded into an existence. Then there were times when the words would shake apart something that was large so as to show all who witnessed it who it was. It seemed as if everything was part of the light; nothing was truly separated from it; even the smallest parts of darkness had to look at the light.

Victoria continued being thrown throughout the whole thing. Through those balls of fire, she would pass. The pain of burning was the least of her tortures. It was the pressure she would feel as she went through that drove her to a level of madness she never knew existed. What was that light and why was she being tortured in that way? Those questions would quickly fall from her thoughts as she froze solid, and then instantly was engulfed as she passed through it.

Time was no longer a concern. It was all happening to her at once; too quickly to realize what was happening until it all stopped. She was gone. Whatever happened was destined to happen with or without her. She began to understand that what she saw was the beginning of everything. She was becoming part of a rebirth. It was not something she was merely watching. No, she was an unwilling participant in it. As soon as that thought came to her, she was ripped away again. Those thoughts were placed in a locked room inside her mind; the same locked room where she had placed a lot of those horrible thoughts throughout her life. The smell of cinnamon and apple filled the air, while songs played very loudly from the stereo on his desk.

She was then in Jack's room. He was the first one she gave herself to. He was not much different from Tyler. The only difference to Victoria was that Jack was present, and Tyler was not. Drugs overcame Tyler as he drifted further and further down life's over-driven road. The worst part was that he really didn't care. He enjoyed the high too much. He fell in love with the high. It was a love that he thought he could control, but the lure of an endless bliss drove his need for it beyond his control. He ached for it to be pushed into his veins, and it quickly became the only constant, one that would not leave him like Vic did when she disemboweled his love.

Jack was the one in whom she hid her torn heart after she broke up with Tyler. In his arms, everything felt so natural. Every time she thought about him, her whole body would shiver and ache for him. She finally felt like it was something she could handle and easily grow into. For months, Jack and Vic had been together. It was amazing how easy it was for the two of them to love each other. They did not have many classes together, so they settled for those stolen moments in between classes, at lunch and after school. Even though she wanted him more than she ever wanted anyone before, she held him off. Very, very slowly, Jack started to break her defenses down. It was not with begging, threats or deception in any way; it was how he kissed her and held her; it was even the weight of his body stretched out on top of hers. She was feeling again the sweat of their bodies, and she remembered why she could not wait any longer.

Those sensations swept throughout her soul as countless waves of her feelings back then clawed their way back into her heart. Over and over again like a raging sea, she was overcome by a love that hurt so much. The only way to calm the rage down was through his touch. It was more powerful than any drug or high she had known. It was not her touching him that she desired. No, it was his love toward her that she once again ached for. It was so overpowering, her mind was flooded with an intoxication of love, passion, sadness and shimmers of the fear of loneliness that entangled her every time she thought about Jack.

She knew then why he looked at her like that. The poems he always wrote for her had always been a mystery to Victoria. For the first time, she felt the ache that he had for her. The heartbreak she caused when, without explanation, she left him was revealed to her. He felt as someone might when a loved one disappears and is presumed dead, but no body is ever found. There was only the blackness of mourning a love that was all he knew. No one could ever replace her in his mind. Songs he dreamt about writing, if he were a musician, burned into her mind in the same way as they tortured him. The words of those songs grew inside her like they were her words and songs.

She could feel how, with a glimpse of hope, he tried to reach her, even if only through his mind and dreams. In his mind over and over again, he would drive to her house. Every bump, turn, stop and acceleration was perfectly timed. Maybe, with the right will, she would see him again and his tears would all fade away. The emptiness within his belly was eating him from inside, as a madness flashed across into his mind.

He treated her very well, so why was she leaving and dating some of his friends? She remembered how he would call her late in the evening just to hear her voice. Jack began to beg and welcome Death to sit upon his left shoulder, waiting for the perfect time to pounce, like a cat onto a mouse. Even his nerves were without shape, but on a state of alert. It was the first time Jack had ever found love while pushing past the boundaries he had imagined. Before, it was only a word he would repeat to his parents and relatives. Never had love been anything but a dreamer's dream to him. It was completely untouchable. There was no way he could survive without that kind of love touching him again. He refused to let anything other than the love he had for Victoria fill the void he then felt in his heart.

Tears that never stopped became who he then was and would always be. For that reason, he began to live in the darker corners so that no one could see his tear-stained eyes. He was the one who loved without needing anything in return. With that love taken away, what did life still hold for him? Vic could feel and see the daydreams Jack had about a shiny, stainless-steel razor; about how beautiful a sharp blade would feel as it sliced through his wrist as if it were red hot and his arm melting butter. She could feel how he longed to taste his own blood as it gushed out of his left wrist. She even could feel how he fantasized about the punishment God would inflict on him. In his mind, it was because anything other than this lost feeling would make his punishment worth it. Oh, how he wanted to bleed and forget about life! He wanted to touch the other side. He had become enchanted by those thoughts about death. Each night, he prayed that it would be his last day, even hoping death would take pity on him and do it, rather than it happen by his own hand. It was not because he was scared. It was because he knew his parents would be driven over the edge, and he couldn't become the monster that Victoria had become to him.

On certain nights, when he could just barely stop himself from ending his life, a soft and gentle song was just barely audible. If he stopped and tried to listen, the song would disappear like it was in the wind, blowing this way and that. The song was always the same one. He heard different parts of the song, but only slightly.

There was the joy he felt with knowing that Victoria would come to see him as he lay resting, because it was essentially the tortured poem that he had always wanted to write. He thought that to die while smoking would be the truest form of a symphony, which only the likes of Beethoven could compose. His final poem along with the song he kept hearing would tell of love, loss and death. The true beauty of death overtook his every thought. He began to see it truly as the last form of peace anyone could want.

Victoria could also feel how he would lie there on the cold bathroom floor wondering how the angels or demons would come to get him. Would they descend like in the movies? Would they just appear suddenly? Would there be a fight for his everlasting soul? Would he even be himself, someone or something anymore? She understood that what he truly wished for was nothing more than an eternal, black sleep in which he would become nothing. She also understood that he wanted to savor every moment of dying.

He even prayed, "Please, God, let me live till my last drop slivers through my own inflicted cut before you permit me to die. I want to feel the pain until the very end."

It was like the notes playing on an out-of-tune piano when they would linger before the ending.

There was such a peace that was blurred by the pain, as Jack thought about death, and even more so, his own. The most overpowering feeling she felt was of his never-failing love for her. It was like the food he ate and the water he drank. But it was also the poison that was left on Romeo's lips when Juliet kissed him for the last time. To Jack, Victoria had become both the poison and Juliet. She could also feel how he wished she was there with him right then, waiting to take her trip to the next world with him in a lovers' suicide. That was so that they could be free; wrapped together in a blanket of darkness in a place where their friends would no longer be able to find them and tell them it was time to move on. They were jealous of what Victoria and Jack had; they never were able to find someone to love them as completely as Jack had loved Victoria.

The moment melded with her. No more could she feel the love she had for him, but only his desperation to hold her. She felt trapped within a cruel time loop of feeling and pain that she inflicted upon a boy she loved without question at one time in her life. Time moved slowly as she was frozen there in Jack's soul, and tears she begged for were held back; she couldn't cry because of her being locked in Jack's form and memory. Those tears never came, and the weight of his love for her, as well as death, felt like all of the oceans, lakes, rivers and waterways drowning her. The mourning Jack felt was so strong and powerful that hopelessness stopped her heart and burned into her soul. Even though she did not have a body, she somehow felt all her bones break, then rebuild over vast amounts of time, only to be broken again. With each break, she could taste her blood being forced through her mouth, nose and eyes. She wished more than ever she could go back and hold him again, and just be there for him that day, but it was not to happen. She was frozen in his obsession. With the edge of a razor resting on his skin is how she found him.

The smell of fresh tulips and flowering trees overwhelmed her sense of smell. Snapping logs over an outside fire tickled her ears and warmed the soft, crisp, night air. Victoria could taste the charcoal and lighter fluid in anticipation. The first outdoor smell of cooked hotdogs was everywhere. If Heaven was real, that was how she hoped it would be, because for her, that was all she could think of.

Eternity was always there, though, and she believed that with it, came the end of all things new, of beauty and of fulfillment. The outstretched hands of forever's gray, spider-like webs engulfed her. That sent her to a place that smelled of ground partially frozen. The grayness transformed into a gas and made up all the air around her. It looked almost like a thick fog. She began to taste it with every breath. It revealed that it was more than a just a color. The grayness brought with it a freezing mist that encased her naked body. That forever was so much stronger than the beginning, because it was Jack's forever, not hers. The capsule of pain had imprisoned his soul. It was all that was left of him. The destruction she lavished upon him turned him into that grayness of forever, and it was then there to swallow her much like how she devoured his heart.

She wondered if she would have a chance to right this lie of a life she lived in the next reality; if she would ever remember the savagery that consumed Jack because of her. What about all those others she never gave a second thought for? She wondered whether the life she had just lived was her first attempt at righting her wrongs.

Shivers ran down her entire body with the thought of her having to feel the pain firsthand. If she did go back, she would choose to be the predator no longer. She would change from being the one who preyed on broken men to fill her need; she would become the prey. Over and over again, she would be there for the sole enjoyment of anyone who sought her out to use her and abuse her.

As those thoughts filled her mind, she unknowingly started reaching out to find a cold razor. The feeling of the blade piercing through her left wrist was just out of her grasp, regardless of how hard she reached for it. It would be beyond ecstasy if she grasped the razor and plunged it through her pale skin. The thought of red life pouring out of that pale skin filled her with a joy she couldn't fully understand. Oh, how this would be more fulfilling than a drink of water for each soul burning in Hell!

She even thought maybe after she sliced a thin line down her arm, she would clean off the blade by running it across her lips. In a way kissing the blade, just like how she always dreamed her last lover would kiss her the moment before she died. She wanted to taste the finality of her own life before everything became black.

The blackness that invited her in was deeper than eternity and longer than forever, and only the reaper itself knew the way to. No boatman would be there to escort her to it. There was only a never-ending path on which she would only have the blackness as her one and true friend. Hopefully, the pain that was giving back to her would be diluted into even the faintest recollection of it. She also hoped that the blackness would destroy her shadow so she would no longer have to look upon her disgusting features mirrored back to her.

She could feel her soul reaching out to her. Her soul wanted to hold, caress, and squeeze her tighter than even her loving foster father would do to her when she was a little child running to greet him at the door. If she had a body, maybe she would be pulling her knees to her chest, hugging them.

She thought of a movie in which a person who committed suicide lived the afterlife lost in an ever-shifting sea of faces. She thought that would be justice. She welcomed that emotionless sea of faces almost as much as she welcomed the blood-stained razor.

Only pieces of her past could be reborn within her thoughts. Those memories were always and only ever ones of pain and sadness. She felt that it was a way of torturing her more because she could feel Jack's and Tyler's pain so much stronger when those thoughts were poured upon her. She kept thinking she was forgetting something very important. If she could only remember it maybe, just maybe, she would be able to leave. Leave to what, though?

She never saw another floating soul anywhere around her, but there was a voice saying over and over, "What was it? Think, Victoria. I know I know this. It has to be there somewhere."

Very rapidly, all the pain began to dissolve. The gray fog was ripped apart by an explosion of rainbow-like colors shining so brightly that she couldn't even look away to find an escape from the light. Finally, there was a break in the light. It was small, but it was big enough that if she looked there, her eyes were better able to focus. The light drifted until it was shining out from behind the object obscuring the face. Curiosity was then in control. Even without an effort, she pulled herself over toward the object. Every bit closer that she clawed toward the object, a body was formed. The body took the place of her old one. New sensations started to erupt within her.

How could she have forgotten that wonderful feeling? Thoughts of Jack's hand upon her sent shivers throughout her body; thoughts of their bodies entwined in the summer heat in a house with no air conditioning and no ceiling fan on. At least, it felt like there wasn't one. The mere thought of that heat made her body sweat and explode back to life. Taste took over, and it was Jack's lips pressed together. She tasted sweat and tears of joy.

With the speed of a cannonball, she was shot out, only to fall upon an area that had no grass, landing just two feet before the object that was blocking the light. Just as she landed there, the lights behind the object disappeared, leaving her partially blinded for a few seconds. It wasn't blackness; it was a shade of night. The calls of frogs, crickets and owls and other wild, nocturnal sounds flooded the air.

The breeze was gentle and cool. It felt like a summer night that was almost perfect; one on which she could go outside after the sun departed, and sit cuddling by a campfire while making s'mores. The taste of a lemonade-flavored beer drowned her tongue with every sip. It was the type of night when the moon failed to rise, but that was more than OK because with the moon not reflecting the kiss of the sun's blinding light, every star shone brighter and deeper into the night sky. She thought if she could go without blinking, she would be able to look further and further into those majestic views of the heavens.

"Heaven! Ha ha ha! Oh, I needed that laugh. This is definitely not Heaven!" a voice shouted at her. "With all you have seen, touched, and felt, you still think this world here, which I created for you, is Heaven?" The voice only paused to let the words sink in.

Victoria couldn't even speak if she wanted to. She had instantaneously been frozen into a motionless statue as soon as the voice spoke. Fear, anger and a sadness she could not explain swept over her. All she could think about was all the time she had spent there having to endure the pains she had inflicted upon others. Everything she knew would be gone.

"No, no, no. That isn't what this place is. It is a place where time does not have the same meaning. Here tomorrow is today, yesterday and every other single day. The time you are looking at exists only inside your mind, because you are still a living human and there is no way for me to break those bonds that you have forged with time. In my world, such things as age, degenerative disease and death are not present, but you will still feel time as it passes slowly by. You have spent around

10,000 years drifting in their pain, which is now yours," the voice said as if it was teaching a class on cruelty and she was the subject and student.

The light from the stars filled the night air, and the figure started to become visible. She could see the gravestone again, and as she did, everything came back to her, like a lighting that created a tree-like giant throughout the night sky; one that reached not only from the clouds to the ground but also to the ends of the earth in two different directions throughout the sky. It left the onlooker partially blinded; all that could be seen was a white shadowy silhouette of the lighting.

"Devin!" she screamed with so much force that the hold over her was broken.

It was so powerful a break that the body that had been torn from her 10,000 years earlier had come back, and it was hovering over her ghost like an image that she had become. The body was not complete yet. It was being made. She watched as the figure hovering over her started to form a human shape. There were electric sparks everywhere within the body. She could see through because it was transparent. Layers of her body were reformed, and they moved closer to her. She could feel the electricity of life flowing from her body. The never-ending stream of electricity ran wildly between the two parts of her as they were pulled together. The closer they got to one another the more powerful the surge became.

Her vision began to become impaired as her body bled into her soul. She felt its powerful surges trying to pulse in the same rhythm as her heart. With each pulse, her heart and soul grew closer together. She was holding her breath in the anticipation of what such a connection would be like. She tried to hold her heartbeat in the same way she did when listening to a song that was lingering on a note that was faking an ending, and then, just like when the music began again, the pulse would let her release her breath. Even before opening her eyes, she knew that her soul was resting safely within her, because the pulse and heartbeat echoed like a grandfather clock throughout her entire body.

She remembered that she could only see a few numbers on the gravestone before. As she was then able to move, she wanted to know more than only those numbers; she wanted it all. With the first movement from off her back, she felt tingling and stabbing. It reminded her of when one limb would fall asleep and then begin to wake up again. It hurt whether she moved or stayed still. Over and over, she wished she could force her body to wake it up in order to stop the pain. Despite the pain, she had to know what was written there. Slowly, she started to crawl awkwardly toward the stone-like grave marker.

The voice said with the confidence of a womanizer at last call, "You can crawl all day and night or even for 10,000 more years and you won't reach or read any of it if I choose not to let you. I am the one who chooses everything for you; whether you live, die, love, hate, breathe, or become anything. I am your god, and through your pain, I can once again become strong enough to lash out at those who tried to restrain me. I am now higher than the highest, and the Devil and his minions kneel at the sound of my breath."

The voice laughed as it seemingly started to walk away. Victoria was convinced that that thing — whatever it was — was not a god but some spirit, demon or leftover energy from when time began.

"You are not God. A true god would certainly not need anything from me."

She spoke with anger as she found the strength to stand up on her wobbly and unsteady legs, while looking for the voice so she could destroy it. Why couldn't she stop or destroy the voice? As she grew in physical strength, she could feel that the voice was backing away from her.

"You do not want to fight me, little girl, for I am beyond you and your understanding," the voice said in a way that made her think it was mocking her.

"If you are a god, why do you need my pain? A true god has more strength in his breath than anything you can come up with."

As she finished speaking, the fog fled out of the area, and a physical world began to form beneath her feet. She could feel the grass under and around her sockless feet. A shadow started to emerge 15 feet from where she was standing. It was a giant creature; of greater height and dimensions than she ever realized any creature could be. As quickly as it started to become visible, the creature that was the voice she heard backed away, and melted into the fleeing fog, as if they were one and the same.

Her attention returned to the gravestone, hoping that with the voice gone, she would be able to make out why it was so important that she had to watch all life disappear over and over just to get there. She could make out the 1982 – 20. That was it. She looked for water, because she remembered watching her Japanese friend Airi wash off her family's graves with a wooden ladle when she went with her to support her as she prayed to her ancestors. There was no water or anything she could use to wash the dirt off.

With her body completely restored, she figured it would be easy just to wipe off the stone to read it, but as she walked forward step by step, she could easily tell that the stone was blank except for those numbers that she could read. Victoria was in disbelief. She couldn't believe her eyes. Touching it would be the only way to know for sure. She expected the stone to be dry. Instead, she felt a softness like silk. The disappointment in her heart was even more than that of a grieving mother who had lost her child in the name of freedom and peace. All the time that she spent there was for nothing.

"Why?" she thought to herself.

A mixture of anger and sadness overcame her. She had to restrain herself from ripping her chest open and tearing out her heart, then throwing it deep into the dense fog that imprisoned her. In that fog, she hoped that maybe the swamp critters would devour it slowly and painfully. At least, she would then not feel anything ever again.

"This place is not for you. You must return to Devin. He needs you more than you need your heart to live," a new voice gently said to her.

She felt as though the tone and how the words were used seemed almost fatherly. There was no way that that voice and the one before were the same. After the fatherly voice ended, she could feel a pool of love surround her, and she started to melt into it. She felt herself falling onto the biggest pile of pillows that there ever had been. She had to close her eyes then because the brightness of some light encased her. She drifted into a dreamlike state.

"You must remember the pain, but even more than the pain, you have to remember the love before that pain," the new voice said as it disappeared with the light that was behind the gravestone.

Like a sucker punch, the new voice re-emerged out of nothing, only this time, there was no light. She felt alone but within an engulfing crowd, fearful and blind, but she could sense all the angry people around her. She felt hunted. All around her were people that were stained with sweat. The sweat and steam of them pressed against her. Cries and screams filled the air as one by one, a person was pulled under.

"What are they being pulled into?" she thought.

She knew that it was Hell, and all the words used to describe it weren't even close. The smell of sweat was not of a human body but of its soul. She could taste it, see it, feel it crawling onto her, and breathed it in with every breath. The taste was that of a moldy peach that was lying in a pit of waste before it was pulled out and bitten into. It would explode all over her face when she bit into it, dripping down off her chin to her chest where it would corrode her chest as the juices would land on her uncovered skin.

The smell of the souls erupted onto her in waves and fumes. Some were quick, like a rushing river, but most were slower than the rising and lowering of tide on a frozen and wintry shore. It was almost as though she could not tell when one would end and one would begin. Sometimes the sweat would be so thick that it seemed like a dense swarm of mosquitoes waiting in a cloud for their prey. When the sweat penetrated her, it was as though she was decomposing outwardly from deep within. It wasn't merely a physical feeling; it was deeper than that. Almost everything that made her who she was began to be erased. The process was leaving just enough so that she would not be able to forget who she was completely. The parts that were left to remind her were becoming harder to bear. It reminded her how breathtakingly beautiful she was; the way her eyes sang with perfect harmony that was reserved for queens and mythical gods; her voice would heal the heart of anyone that heard her speak; her skin would kiss anyone with an explosion of passion if anyone was so lucky to feel her touch.

The hot, sweaty air that she was breathing in stayed within her, and formed a cloud inside her. The cloud then impregnated every tissue, organ and bone, along with her skin, till it was done transforming her. She could feel the sweat becoming her. She felt as if she could not even walk away, because the sweat had locked her in place as it finally leaked out of her pores and onto the ground. There the sweat grew veins that fastened her feet to the melting ground. The room became nothing but empty people or souls or whatever they were.

The voice returned. "Ha ha! You thought I was an angel or a god. Angels only do God's bidding, and I am sorry, Victoria, but God has left thousands of years ago. I find it funny how people beg and pray to him. The prayers they send up find my ears. Soon enough I will use their pain to give them a small sense of hope. Then I'll wait, and sooner or later, the world will distort their sense of hope into something seemingly divine as well. What is even funnier is that you thought that that hack before me was a pagan god, demon or even me. He is nothing more than a failed experiment and one I may have to be rid of myself. All of this before you is all that there is. No matter how long you live, this is the only thing God truly has given you and every other worthless soul that was ever born.

Because of this, I will send you back to what you were 10,000 years ago. It is a way of torturing you for the rest of your days." The voice ended in a tone that was as colorless as the fog that once imprisoned her.

With a flick, everything around her vanished as if it had never ever been there. Victoria's thoughts ran unrestrained. She felt like some mental patient locked in a padded room, drugged until she was so lost that her mind did not even recognize the physical, sexual and mental abuse that was being perpetrated. Laughter faded from one ear to the other as quickly as lights would flicker on a dance floor.

There were words like "Don't worry, sweetheart. I will always be here. Ha ha ha ha! You are and have always been mine." Somewhere from deep within this deep singing voice, she could hear, "Kill him. You know you want to."

It was like a slimy parasite's voice clawing from within until it escaped into mouse-like screams.

"Devin. Ha ha! Yes. Kill him." Those little screams were too many to count, and they all seemed to be arguing with each other about the ways in which she should kill this person named Devin.

Victoria knew that the name Devin was supposed to mean a lot to her, but what she didn't know was who owned that name. The anger she felt toward those little screams was some new feeling. In her whole time in that realm, she never felt an anger that had structure like that feeling created in her. There was a depth as well to that feeling, so much so that the depths pulled at her, ripping her from the clenching hand of the possessive monster that trapped her within herself and the darkness of that realm.

7

Nine months before Victoria was born

An uncontrollable flame took control and seemed to explode behind Jacob, pushing him toward the U-shaped stairwell at the north end of the house. It always seemed colder in that part of the house. Jacob and his wife Nina seemed to feel as if there was a very sad presence that occupied it. That sadness would imprint itself upon anyone that lingered there too long. Somehow exiting this world in any form seemed to captivate the lingering person. Jacob would often find Nina standing motionless with tears about to flow down her face on nights when he came home late. All he could do was crawl up the steps and stand behind his wife. He was hoping that the sadness within the cold area did not swallow them into it.

They imagined a child who fell by accident while playing innocently too close to the stairs, or even slipped out of its parent's arms. She always had her own insights into her views about the supernatural, referring to it because of her Japanese heritage and eastern beliefs. She rationalized standing there and invoking whatever spirit, demon or deity had made its home at the top of the stairs.

Jacob thought she always just fed off him, because she never said anything until after he said something. He saw the shadows bend and shake as they approached, and heard the whispers in the middle of the day beckoning him to venture into unused alleys between buildings. His dreams always seemed to have a hint of truth to them. He wished he could hone his ability so that he could focus it to his benefit.

He knew that the cold was not of childhood sadness but of complete desperation and utter loneliness. He could hear the faint echoes of a song that took him many sleepless nights to track down. It was the song *We Belong with the Dead* by Inkubus Sukkubus. He could hear the words ring out like a poetic, suicidal dream as the pale-skinned, 38-year-old man sat upon the top stair with blood pouring out of his wrist. Above it, there were cuts and marks of self-inflicted pain that had never seemed to fade. Curiously, they only went deeper and stronger with every new cut. Holding a picture of a young girl on his lap, and no matter the pain that was sinking into him as his life poured out, he refused to look away from it. Jacob could not help but wonder how a loving God allowed so much pain to come upon him, leading him to end his life. How could God really condemn him to an eternity of pain and suffering in Hell? Was that just one of the many false Catholic dogmas that plagued his life?

Jacob could see the little bit of color slowly drain from his face. Sadly, even his tears seemed to stop. He wanted his last tear to pour out the second after his life stopped. At some point, his eyes began to lose their focus on that reality and started to focus on the spiritual world. They bounced their focus back and forth between realities until he could no longer see anything of the physical world.

For a moment, the look of perfection and bliss came upon his face. It was the moment before judgment; the moment when he was finally free of the bonds and chains he had been dragging. In that moment, he was able to look at himself sitting on the steps, drained of all life. It looked like he was a figure in a museum. Time was frozen just for that moment. At that moment, he was released, but there was more to that stage. A song he'd never heard before started to ring out. It was calling to him, and it finally took him away.

Jacob looked down to the first landing, and there lay a lady. She was dressed up in the clothes of a businesswoman trying to look sexy for her boss. Her skirt was an inch or two above her knees, but the thigh-high, fishnet stockings revealed more the desire to please than to work. Her blouse hugged her body as a second skin, which showed that she preferred not to wear a bra and that even in her late thirties, her breasts were still perky and strong, mimicking the work of a gifted plastic surgeon.

Her face was covered with white makeup like that of a geisha. It was very doll like. Her lips were as red as the apple that witches would employ to poison princesses in fairytales. Her eyes were blacked out like two lumps of coal as a way of stopping her from seeing the world. A small trail of blood trickled out of the small bullet hole in the center of her head. There was no other blood anywhere around her that showed that she had been killed somewhere else and then moved there.

By the look of pain on the man's face, Jacob never believed for one moment that he killed her and placed her there. Jacob did some looking into it at some point to see if there was any truth to any of it, and he found out that there was a family that lived there 20 years earlier and the wife slipped over some clothes while walking down the stairs carrying their newborn daughter. Her daughter slipped out of her hands and broke her neck on the stairs as she fell. It was ruled an accident, but one of the grandparents didn't believe her and blamed her for trying to get attention. They captured, tortured, and killed their only daughter and placed her at the first landing of the stairs dressed in the form of a doll they buried with their granddaughter. Jacob knew all of that a few weeks after they moved in, but he never told Nina any of it. He liked letting her believe it was her own mysteries that she needed to solve.

For the first time since they moved into the house, Jacob wasn't able to see the father, his misery, the picture or his doll-like wife. It was just the memory of those events that ran through his thoughts. He actually wondered if those steps were in fact the first steps in a long and winding descent into madness. A small smile briefly fell upon his face as he thought about this possible madness. What if he was already trapped in madness and this was all just part of his delusion? He thought of himself being that father and the family as his own that he lost. He thought that somehow the life force that was draining out of the father's wrist was stopped by someone else or by some so-called miracle that trapped him in that new, shaded reality; a reality he could not escape; a place filled with lies and false truths.

He raced through his mind as he tried to remember the faces of the father, daughter and above all, the mother, but just like when someone loses someone that was very close to him, recalling that person's face was almost impossible. He pushed his mind harder than it had ever been pushed before. He tried to find something that would tie him to them and their faces, but in all his efforts, he only found blank spots and faceless forms. All he could see in his mind were pale pumpkins for faces and only a spot of blood thrown here and there for depth and meaning.

It reassured him that he was trapped in his mind and maybe those stairs were the way out, but to accomplish that would mean that he would have to descend past the things that sent him into lunacy. But if that was true, who was that person he had been sharing a bed with? Those pictures on the wall couldn't be made up. Even though the mind is very powerful, it is not capable of so many details that are so meaningless. Jacob really had a pull at his heart to walk back just to see his beautiful wife lying fast asleep like his own personal angel sent there to guard his heart and make him want to be a better man. No matter how hard he wanted to or how hard he tried, he could not turn around nor step back to look at his sleeping angel. There was something unmovable behind him that would not let him walk back, and the ground that held his feet would somehow block his steps even if he had managed to push back the unmovable force behind him. So there was nowhere to go but forward to the uncertain stairway. The pulling and pushing he felt seemed like he was being magnetized. The face that brought him out of his nightmare and down that path seemed to have the opposite magnetic force, pulling him harder and faster by the second. The pull was more than just his body; it was as if his soul was connected to that face. One moment, it was just a step forward, and then the next, it was almost a leap forward. The leap was one of true glee and unremorseful lust but not just a physical lust. Jacob also lusted for the knowledge that the face had. Empowered then by his newfound lust for truth and answers, he placed one hand on the polished smooth railing to his right and the other on the textured, blue drywall to his left. The railing was beading with sweat while the drywall was melting. His hand sank into it as easily as falling into a mud puddle. The beading sweat felt more like sap from a maple tree deep within an undisturbed forest. The sap was so sticky that it was preventing his hand from sliding down it as easily as he had hoped. It was a hard fight to slide it down half an inch or less. As Jacob's left hand sank halfway up to his forearm, he looked at the wall and thought of it as if it were bleeding with the blood from his hand that was pushing through. It appeared as if the wall was dying a very slow and agonizing death. All the pictures of him and Nina along the stairs, filled with their hopes, dreams, vacations and heartaches were all alive once more.

The breeze from the mountains that littered Japan and over the top of the snow-covered volcano Fuji blew through and over, him. He could smell the gardens of flowers below Mount Fuji. The humid Japanese air was subdued by the cool air flowing off the mountain peaks. It was late spring, but there was still a thick covering of snow on the top of Mount Fuji, and in the breeze, some of that frosted air blew the heat away.

With another picture came the taste of saltwater that sprayed from the ocean surrounding the islands of the Pacific, showering him all over again. The humidity hit him harder than a prize fighter could ever hit, and even though he hated the humidity, it was then part of that paradise, and he was able to relive it. He could taste the foods from all the different nations being cooked as he and Nina enjoyed their adventurous life. The smells then made his stomach crave some of those foods.

8

Victoria's nightmare

A long screeching exclamation of a simple word expressing horror slingshot her eyes open.

"No!"

The mellowness of the subtle light was blinding in its own gentle voice, almost like waking up in the middle of the day to a bright and burning sun, only to find that after two blinks the world all around was a frozen land hidden within the shadow of mist. She blinked, and saw that it wasn't light that was coming into focus but the memory of a faded dream; a dream that was once was so strong that the thought of it alone could hold her whole world within its grip. But like an overworn pair of jeans, the tiny fabric that made up the glue that bound the dream together dissolved into broken hopes, anger and even frustration. Millennium after millennium had ripped that dream apart, and scattered its remains into multiple dimensions.

Fueled by her anger, the hatred that ripped her away was more powerful than an electrified magnet made to lift cars. Her magnet was one of extreme power and precision because fabric after fabric that was ripped apart was then being instantly reconnected. In the same motions as waves brought on by a tsunami, the dream imploded back together. Too much, too fast, the tsunami would not slow or end. She felt the weight of the waves, the horror and fear that so many before her felt only moments before they died because of the unending waves. She had become completely vulnerable to the waves, and she knew that the tsunami would bury her in a grave of exploding dreams.

The next wave of the dream tsunami was filled with the smell of soft, evergreen woods with a sprinkling of maple. Her dream was being catapulted at her, as though she was the sun and her dream was a comet whipping around her. Only she did not want her dream to be dissolved, or to fade, nor be stolen from her hands again. The smell was so strong that she could almost taste every floating smell. But then only a split second before she could enjoy the flavor, the smell of it left her mouth. It seemed so close as to tease, like one lover might do with another, just before they kissed.

The wave of smells wrapped around her, clinching her like a python squeezes its prey each time the prey exhales. Unlike the dying animal, she wanted to exhale her breath in order that the smell would wrap closer to her until that wave wrapped her so tightly that it became a new skin replacing her old skin. Then, like a rip cord being pulled from a parachute, the smell was ripped from her. She felt her skin being ripped from her muscle and other soft tissues. That made her feel more naked than she had ever felt before. It was the most truthful exposure she had ever been involved in.

Faster, higher and stronger, those dreams began to come at her, rolling over the years she was tortured, and her endearments were washed away. Not that those waves took the memory of what she had seen. It was more like cleaning the dust off her window. With each cleaning, she could see more. But she could not tell what was beyond the dust. The flickers of the dream began to brighten up the side of the glass she was sitting on.

Soon a thousand years of torture were laid aside for this dream. Then, one after another, the years she had been gone blinded her from where she started all those years before; parted the dust so she could return to where she was before. This feeling of knowing that she was going back to where it all began stopped her from truly looking. She was afraid that if she did go back, there would be nothing but another beginning repeated over and over again, and she would have to go through whatever it was that she had just gone through. Was it pieces of Heaven hidden within rows of Hell? Was she nothing more than a character of some insane writer?

The reality of not knowing where the dream would lead her made it the worst torture she had to live through. It was worse than any of those that the first voice tormented her with for those 10,000 years. She couldn't even remember why she was even facing the menacing dream that loomed over her like a stalking lion. When she tried to remember why and how she got there, her mind pulled her through the dust closer to the answer she wanted. Over and over again in her mind, as she was squeezed through it, the name Devin rang repeatedly in her ears. Who was he, and why did his name matter to her?

Glimpses of her dream became visible, and to understand it, her body divided itself into two separate beings; one, her physical self and the other, composed of her mind, heart and soul. The physical portion stood tall and strong like a spectator watching her mind put the dream back together. She felt like Moses standing in the parted Red Sea; standing in the center where she could see where she was going, but more so where she came from. She could feel the sea all around her as it was forced to one side or the other. The smell of dead fish and the taste of the sea were deeply within her mouth. The mist from the evacuated sea was able to escape God's clutches, rained down upon her, but it never made it to the ground as a powerful wind forced the mist up and out again. A powerful thunderstorm was at one end of the sea, while the flickering land of promise was on the other. She somehow knew that the land of promise was a lie, and that within those borders, her 10,000 years of pain were hiding.

It also felt like the land where the Sirens from the tale of Odysseus, an ever-vigilant land of destruction, was calling out to her from within the strong wind. She was not stuck in a nightmare in which if she ran to the safe exit, the destination would slip further and further away. No, it was as real as real could get, and with every step, she felt the weight of her horrors pulling at her, like little floating wave monsters, trying to pull her down so she would be trapped in those horrors.

She fought with everything she had. While she started to pull, crawl, fight, and peel her way out, the past started to flash before her eyes, just as lightning in the middle of a hot July midnight thunderstorm might flash. Flashes of her when she was young were revealed to her first, and then middle school exploded into high school with only a brief glimpse of Tyler. Jack's face was everywhere, however it wasn't just his face she was seeing. It was more like she was marinating in their ancient love. Her most vivid and amazing memories of him filled her, driving her forward and pushing her to keep going.

She paused for a moment to regain her strength, but then those 10,000 years collided with the force of a crashing meteor on the moon's surface. She could feel and remember all the pain she had caused and all of those feelings she felt while within the borders of whatever hell she was escaping. She prayed over her memories in the way that she would have when rereading a book, hoping for a different ending. She knew that if she didn't push herself past it, she would never escape.

Her body was on fire as her muscles tried to pull her to safety. It was as if all of her bones were breaking one after another. Tears and sweat mixed together in her mouth. The physical pain was so forceful that she didn't believe she could push on. Then a new face started to appear. It was not a face like any other that she had ever met or remembered meeting.

She could not make out who it was or really anything about the face. Victoria could feel how the face felt. She could see how blue the eyes were without seeing anything other than the shadowy face. She drifted toward it like a ship without power being pushed toward shore. Even though its eyes held a great amount of pain and tears full and of mourning, she knew that she couldn't break its heart and soul like she had done to those before. The name Devin rang, though, like a hundred trumpets sounding for the king or queen. The power of that name shook her, and then, like a dragon, his name swooped into her, and ripped her out of the storm.

At first, it was like waking up from a bad dream. She really had no idea where she was. Only later, she realized that she was standing beside a large fire. It was a stone fireplace. She could hear a voice talking in the other room. Faintly, she could recognize where she was, but she didn't trust her eyes and senses anymore. How many times after trusting in her feelings had she ended up in a never-ending maze of torment?

The other realms started to dim in the same way as the bright light of a camera flashes, and then, every time one blinks, it gets less and less bright. Initially, it's all that can be seen, and quickly, it fades into a shadowy figure of the light with each blink until the impact of the light becomes only a memory not a painful event. Memories of the day began to fire rapidly within her thoughts, and she relived them all at once. Those flashes were so strong that even her vision was consumed by them. Before her eyes were given the blessing of seeing the real world, those thoughts of that day became her only sight.

Everything around her looked as if she were back in the classroom. Even her senses were the same as when she was there. The coldness of the room and air was everywhere, and through her foggy breath, she could see the coldness as well. The coldness sent shivers down her back, and radiated to her arms first, then to her legs. Tiny goose bumps exploded all over her body. The hairs on her arm stood up as if to conceal a larger amount of hot air closer around her body.

The echo of a proud professor sang in her hears. Oh, how she loved the way his voice flirted with various deep tones, then kissed a tenor voice every time he taught a new formula to the class! She had no mythical desire to be with him or an obsession. It was only that he, without knowing why or how, became the father figure that she never had. She never knew her real father or mother, and throughout her life, she enlisted a few different people to be her parents. All she remembered of her parents was that her mother sacrificed herself so that she could live, and that her father left, never to return, as soon as his wife's life ended.

A voice was echoing in her ears, and the tone of that voice destroyed the dam that was built by time deep within her memories. From that voice, she could smell the fragrance of his cologne mixed with his cinnamon-flavored gum. She could feel the warmth of his hand from when she would walk beside him so that the mass of the crowd would allow their fingers to touch without him even knowing it was her. It was his eyes that stole her heart with only one glance.

"Vic, if you want, I'll go and get you a sweater, and you can have a seat here by the fire to warm up," Devin said as he stood behind her after the fire finally came to life.

Vic stumbled over her words, "Ah, s-su-sure. That would be nice."

When he walked past her into a dark hallway, her mind finally recognized where she was, who she was with and why she was there. The first thought that came to her was whether it had actually happened or if it was merely a moment of thought that appeared to last forever. Had she really experienced it, and then had she somehow been returned from the evil she could not name? It was an evil that was strong enough to freeze her heart while also trying to turn her soul into coal in order to force darkness to overtake her.

9

Devin

Parts of me wanted to turn on the hallway light before I stepped into the darkness. But with Vic standing by the fireplace watching, I thought turning the lights on would only prove that I was a wimp, or let her know that I did not feel safe with her. Then she would want to leave. Better to plunge into the darkness. I always felt as if there was something living in the shadows of my home, and because of that, I hated going into dark rooms. I even placed nightlights in every room so that darkness would not totally overtake the room. There had been times when I thought the lights were either broken or needed a new light bulb, but when I got within a foot or two of the nightlight, I would find that the light was on the whole time.

It seemed like my senses were picking up something hiding just out of sight, and it sent shivers of goose bumps up and down my spine in an uncontrolled vibration. I always thought that the shivers on my spine were God's way of saying that he was right there with me, but when I tested this theory of mine, I discovered that it was my own mind that created those sensations. Knowing that I was alone and that God was not with me, I felt naked and exposed as I entered into the shadows. I wanted to run, like a child who was scared, to my room, which was all the way at the other end of the hallway, but it took everything I had to resist the urge, and to walk slowly to it instead.

I kept mumbling, "There is nothing there", but the mumbling in itself brought on a new type of fear. If I was wrong, and something was indeed in there, I had just given that thing all the power I had, and let it know that I was scared of it. I also wondered if it could hear my ever-rising heartbeat, mixed with my breathing, shaking like that last leaf left on a tree as winter approaches.

My bare feet were massaged by the carpeted hallway; not too thick, with just enough cushioning that made me feel like I was walking on the clouds, leaving all of my cares and anxiety in this hell-ridden world out of touch. With enough thought, I could almost taste the cold damp air from the cloud. I didn't even care if the lack of oxygen or the laws of physics would kill me. All I wanted was to be there. After a few feet, the imaginary cloud started to cause friction. First, my left foot sank into the floor. I paused only for a second, but it was long enough for my mind to synch with reality, because of my mental drifting by walking in the clouds. Within that moment, I realized that I was deep within the shadows of the hallway, and darkness was everywhere. Some of the areas of the darkness held different shades of shadows. At the end of the hallway, there was nothing I could see, which was not quite right, because I knew there was a nightlight there, and that it was working, because I saw it before I stepped into the blackness. I could almost imagine sets of red and white eyes looking at me, but as I strained to readjust my sight, there was nothing there again. It happened repeatedly to me, but not only from the dark, impenetrable area. It was everywhere but nowhere at the same time.

Three feet ahead of me on the right, there was a glow living within a part of the shadow. At first, I could see waves of shadows rippling out past the door that was well into the hallway. Taking another step with my right foot, I could no longer feel the carpet. Instead, it felt like I was walking in the woods but not on a path. I could feel something breaking under my feet, but I didn't know what it was. I tried to rationalize my thoughts by telling myself that I dropped something there, and I was then standing on it. But I knew that must have been a lie because if I dropped something I would have picked it up. Then I thought maybe someone broke in and then the burglar dropped something. For some reason, the thought of someone breaking into my house and that they might still be in it was better than thinking about an evil being in the shadows waiting for me to get close enough to strike.

Just before my right foot finally came to rest on whatever I was standing on, I felt it break through what seemed like a web of twigs to rest upon a hard, slippery, rock-like ground. The shadow waves in front of me started to whisper in colors of red, gray and blue. A blanket of heat swelled out into the world within the hallway. Instantly, a feverish sweat poured out of me. I could see paint by the door starting to bubble and blister. The rock I was standing on started to boil, then melt.

I instinctively covered my face as I fought the ground to free my left foot. It felt like I was standing in deep mud that locked my foot when I tried to pull it up. I was pulling not only my foot but also all the mud that encased it. Finally, my foot was freed, and I could take another step. I don't know why I couldn't just turn away and head back into the living room and grab Vic to leave. I felt as though if we did leave, both of us would be in even more danger. Even if this meant death was certain, I would be more than OK with it. What was one more day living when I was going to be dead forever anyway?

All my weight was on my right foot. I felt the weight of my body crush through the softened rock on which I was standing. I was instantly buried up to my ankles, and reached out to the wall to stabilize myself, but the heat boiling out of the wall burned my hand and arm. All the paint bubbling up showered my hand, arm and right side with the heat it was storing up in blisters like bubbles. I tried to scream, but my voice was taken before I was able to scream.

Panic struck me as I realized that that was indeed how I would die. It had to be one of the worst ways to go. I thought of the witches that were burned at the stake and how the fire was set up so that the fire would burn them to death before the smoke would kill them. I thought of my body being barbecued like a burnt piece of chicken. Then time stopped for me.

I wasn't frozen, but time was. It stopped right after some of the paint bubbles exploded. I could see the spray from the bubbles everywhere in the air. It was amazing how all of the different shapes — every speck of melted paint — looked. Some formed a perfect sphere, while some looked like a bullet. Some looked like a bowl with the front going slower than the back, some looked almost like plates, and some were even colliding with others. There was every shape that a person who devoted their lives to geometry could think of frozen right before me.

I was able to see all of that because as time stopped, the red glow from the door was very intense. Not only did I have to shield my face from the heat, but the light was blindingly intense and was constant. My eyes never adjusted to the light. My face started to accept the heat, however.

Before looking at the ground, while half blind, I placed my foot down. It felt like I was standing suspended by a large group of interwoven, thin branches. The branches would bend and bounce, but not break. I couldn't even hear cracking, popping or snapping, so I assumed that I was safe. I placed more and more weight onto this type of springboard until I evenly distributed my weight. Slowly, I started to put more and more weight onto it while I tried to pull my right leg free. I looked down and behind me as I attempted to pull my foot out, I couldn't see anything below my knee because it was completely immersed in a blackness that for me was indescribable. I felt my right leg beginning to free itself as I put more of my weight on to my left. At that moment, I realized the reason I was not hearing the cracking, popping and snapping was because I was in a vacuum, like I maybe was somehow transported into a different dimension. Panic stricken, I glanced back toward the living room hoping that Vic was still there.

I didn't know how I could live if what had happened to my friend happened to Vic. I could feel her screams tearing me apart. I could also feel the ripping of her skin as though it were mine. I could taste my blood exactly when she would be regurgitating her own. I could smell my bowels as they were ripped open and systematically taken out of my abdomen. The smell of my digestive fluids mixed with the bodily waste from the bowels was worse than the smell of death itself. My body started to turn cold as my blood rushed to the floor, taking the little life I had with me as it spilled.

All around me laughter started to echo. The laughter came in different octaves and speeds. Initially, the laughter, like that heard in a house of fun, seemed to reverberate from the ceiling to the floor and back to the upper corner where two walls met. Then it somehow drove the laughter into my chest. I could feel the laughter ripping my eardrums apart. The wetness of blood steamed out of my ears. I tried to cover them to block the sound, but like everything physical around me, it was frozen in time. My soul was screaming, but still nothing happened. All that could leave my mouth was my dry and scratchy breath. Then it was like the laughter hit me with the force of a sledgehammer being dropped off a skyscraper onto my chest. The laughter became so low that the tones were no longer inaudible. Only through the vibrations could I tell that there was a sound at all. Then the high-pitched laughter came back. Like a seesaw, the two pitches took it in turns with the different pains that were being inflicted upon me. One moment, I could feel all of my bones breaking, then, in the blink of an eye, I was reconstituted, only for the process to be repeated. Between those two indescribable attacks, I began to hear the song of the essence of a dream softly singing. The song filled the holes between the two punishing tones. The beauty of the soft song spoke to my heart and soul. My soul longed for that song. I found myself begging in silence for the laughter to change pitch so that I could hear one more note, even if it meant that I would have to endure the pain. The song finally started to become the primary audible sound. I believed that it was the song of death. The laughter must have been the process of dying. The painful laughs started to join in. Their pitches started to move like a snapping rubber band flying through the air. The vibrations of the laughing were not in tune with the other sounds, and they started to shake the walls to the point when they started to bend and crack. Showers of the powdering drywall began covering my head, shoulders and back while the vibrations shattered the frozen world around me.

Then the floor started to buckle like a restless ocean. For some reason, I still was trapped in it, no matter how fluid it appeared. I constantly tried yanking my foot away from the floor, but I couldn't break it free. I hoped that with every rise and fall of the floor, I would be able to use that motion to free my foot, allowing me to leave the hallway in order to face whatever was next. The dust from the breaking and cracking drywall was then so thick that I couldn't breathe without coughing. The dust was becoming extremely suffocating. Then a new fear arose; the fear of being buried alive by the dust. Chunks of drywall and wood no bigger than golf balls began to explode over my head, shoulders and back. Other pieces that were slightly larger bounced off my arms. My right leg that still was not free was being buried under debris.

I was hoping, even begging, that the fire that once surrounded me would melt the floor or would somehow atomize the floor. That would allow me to fall unharmed to the floor below. I knew that that scenario would put my body in a more hazardous position. What could I do, though? If my leg was not permitted to leave, I would die from asphyxiation. The stories about people who drown and are brought back to life rang hopefully in my ears. Would this death be like the pleasant dreams that I heard filled those drowning people as the water overcame them?

I just knew there would be nothing pleasant in a death like that. It would only be the powerful, tightening grip of death squeezing my life slowly away, almost like the grip of an anaconda as it constricts its victim. I wondered if this was death; if the reaper was the one behind the laughter and the song. Could it be that this was God enjoying the torture and destruction of his own creation?

I whispered over and over in my head, "What good is it for me to show my rage against God now that I am within seconds of meeting him?"

I'd dreamt of the anger I felt for him, and dreamt of the time when I could tell him. My anger was the only thing I had that gave me the strength to keep on living after witnessing what God allowed to happen to my friend James. I truly prayed and hoped for the second death, if it truly was a second death.

"Do you really think it is that cut and dry? C'mon, Devin. You're not that stupid," a deep voice spoke quietly out of the glowing, red door.

There was no panic, anger, scolding or condescension in those words. It rang more like that of a corporate boss instructing a subordinate as to why something is done a specific way. Certainly, it did make me feel like a child being talked to by an older person as to why dirty jokes are not appropriate during a family Christmas party.

The voice explained, "God, as you call him, really is so far beyond you and me. However crazy it may seem to you, it is not what you think it to be. You have taken a step into a realm that does not support life as you know it to be. But this is not the first time you've touched this world, is it?" The voice stopped to see how I would react.

"You mean…" I was cut off before I could even finish the thought let alone my words.

"Yes. Although time doesn't matter here, it would be many years for you. For me, I just left that scene where this creature you now face was created. That was during the time of ancient man. I was there to take James before that atrocity claimed him. I am Death, so I do not take kindly to something taking that which is mine." A slight bit of disgust was in this masculine voice that was overlaid by another softer tone that hinted at being more feminine. "You and Victoria will endure much before the night is done. Hell, Heaven and the creature will all stand before you two. You can choose death in any of these places, and I will come. But if I come and you fail due to fear, you will spend eternity in a pit of anacondas and hell hounds. They will kill you over and over until God finally becomes bored with all of us and moves on to his next creation. At that moment, we will wish for those man-eating snakes and hounds born in the fires of Hell." He stopped long enough for his words to sink in. "I will come to you again without my sickle and as a friend, so do not fear our next meeting. That is when you will be given a weapon that can kill the creature, unless you fail and give in before the appointed time."

As his final words ended, everything around me evaporated; the burns, the cuts and the dust in my lungs were all gone. The speed at which it was gone was quicker than even the fading moments of a dream early in the morning. The red glow from the door on the right in front of me was then only a low, humming nightlight. Weirder still was that the darkness was no longer there, and I didn't even have the feeling that the darkness usually caused in me anymore. It was so far gone that I couldn't even remember how it felt. How it imprisoned me, erasing all light surrounding me.

I even felt that the air that I breathed before all of that started was finally evacuating my lungs. What was that dust I breathed in while facing death's sneer? Was it all part of the illusion? Was I really breathing it in? I must have come back to the moment before that happened. Something I couldn't understand was how my breath left me, but the beating of my heart was louder and stronger than I had ever felt in my life. Even when I was in school running track, playing football, wrestling or in a lover's embrace, the pounding of my heart never reached such a rate.

I forgot that I was not the only one in the house. The echo of Death saying "A lot will be brought before you and Victoria tonight" stuck with me. The words telling me not to fail because of fear rang louder. What if she let fear take her? How was I going to tell her that without her thinking I was completely nuts? I knew if I was not told, I would have given in and let fear take me, because I had been ready to give up since my friend was taken by that creature. I somehow found a strength I didn't know existed, and I turned to face her. She was standing close to the fire in a trance-like state that open fires do to us all. What was the lure that I always found in them? Was it because of the way the flames moved in their fluid pattern? Was it how the flames wrapped themselves around a log differently every time? Or was it the flickers of the flames? There is always a quiet peace from within while watching something burn. Is it because deep down, we know that that is all that awaits us when we die; the never-ending flame of the unforgiven?

My eyes seemed to become like those of an eagle soaring high above in search of prey, but Vic was the object of my love, not my prey. She couldn't see me because I was hidden in the darkened hallway. It wasn't the same type of darkness that consumed me in the hallway before. It was just the natural shadow that typically encased the hallway. I couldn't take my eyes off her. It was like I had fallen in love with her as she just stood there unaware. I took her whole beauty in. I marveled at the way her thick, jet-black hair hung loosely over her shoulders and was parted so most of it rested softly down the middle of her back. I loved the way the light from the fire shone off her hair. At times, her hair looked a deeper black than the darkest shadow I dared walk through. Her slightest move would reveal purples and dark blues that lay dormant until the right light shone on it tugged me as I watched. Her hair seemed alive on its own. Her skin was slightly golden, almost yellow, in tone. Her Japanese features dictated only part of her face and body. The darkness of her eyes made them appear bigger, the whites of the eyes giving shape. Her high cheekbones provided a unique depth that allowed her smile to be bigger than any I had seen. Her nose held a perfect balance between depth, height and width. The skin above her upper lip was smaller than that of anyone I had ever met. But in the limited space, her upper lip had just enough room for the perfect natural curve, like the ones models would spend money to achieve. She always seemed to accentuate that feature. I never saw her without a dark line that traced the outside of her red lipstick. The events from that day took their toll on her lipstick. Her lips were still red but to a lesser degree. In some way, it made me love her more.

From the safety of the hallway, I could see the different colors of the fire reflecting off her face. I wanted to rush over and tell her what Death told me, but I was lost in her beauty. From the first day I saw her, I wanted to rush over and talk to her, but I knew in my gut that if I brought her into my world, she would end up dead, just like my friend James. I was so used to my dreams about her that I didn't know how I was going to step from fantasy into reality. I often dreamt of holding her from behind, wrapping my arms around her. Our hands would be interlocked. As we stared into a fire on a cold, winter night, I would hold her close enough that I could feel her breath. I would welcome the tickle of her silky hair. I would squeeze tight enough to let her know she was mine but soft enough to know I was hers and hers alone.

Even though I had been totally released from the trap death had me in, it refused to let me fully return at long last to the land of the living. It appeared, however, to be a way of torturing me by letting me look at and dream about my unspoken love, but then refusing to let my eyes blink to keep my focus on Vic. Death was showing me the strength I needed, and let me stew in those thoughts.

Moments passed by and she quickly faded into a blur. A burning pain grew in each eye, but not seeing her clearly became more powerful than any desire my body ached for. I felt a hunger that no food could satisfy. Only she could; it had always been only her. Forcing my eyes to find some form of clarity became a driving rage within me. I knew I would happily die repeatedly just to be able to see her clearly one more time. I wondered over the years since James was stolen from the world why someone would sell his own soul for a moment of glory. At that moment, I discovered why a person would and what my price was.

An alarm of laughter filled my head.

"Is that it?" sang out, devilishly hidden within the laughing itself, in a deep, dark voice of a confident man.

Finally, I was allowed to blink, and a new film of tears covered each eye, bringing Vic's figure into perfect focus. I wondered only for a second whether any of it was real.

The dream started to take hold of me again, and as much as I fought to stop it, I also welcomed it because with that dream, I could touch her once again. But I refused to give into that dream for another moment. She was then right there. I couldn't let myself retreat to my dreams because then I would surely lose her forever. Even with the craziness of that day, I knew that it was my moment. In some weird and twisted way, it was the answer to my prayers. Thinking that it was how God answered my prayers made me laugh because of the timing. I broke out of my trap, and started to walk toward her. I felt like I wasn't even walking. It was like I was watching my body walk, as if I was in a first-person video game. It had to be a video game, because I couldn't control what was happening. Step by step, I emerged out of the dark hallway. She did not yet see me. Would she smile, laugh, or say something, or would she be upset because I didn't go and get a sweater or blanket for her? Another step, but still nothing from her. I still had little or no control over it. I had the confidence of an alpha-male lion ready to pounce on its prey. The only sense of her being my prey was that I longed to feel her close to me. But the drive pushing me was so animalistic and more powerful than anything I had ever known or felt.

I was three or four feet out of the shadowy hallway, yet still within the darker side of the room, moving directly toward her. The fire created a permanent shadow to the side of the fireplace. I still had no control over my own body. I wondered who or what was really in control. I also asked myself what the goal for the one who was operating me was. Was I to become like a Hollywood version of a caveman, who grabs hold of a woman, grunts, and then forces her to go where he wants her to go? Was I really the one pulling the strings? A nervous sickness tugged at me. That feeling was the only way

I knew that it was still my body. I felt that if I was nervous like that, I still had to be in control, at least partially. That realization made me feel both more relaxed and worried. Out of the shadows, my body leaped, as though I came out from nothing. She looked at me and I could see the reflection of the fire in her dark eyes and the flames dancing differently in each eye. The reflection was so accurate that for a moment I almost expected to feel the heat that only a fire has pulsate out of her as well.

I could feel heat as I stepped an inch within her personal space, and to my amazement, she also stepped toward me. I then knew the heat I felt was somehow from deep within her. Both of our hearts started to pound faster. I could see the colors of her cheeks, face and neck start to darken into a reddish tint, either from the physical fire or the fire within her. Even though I could not see my own face, I could tell by the overwhelming, hot flashes that I too was changing into a redder shade. I wondered if it was how one person unintelligibly tells another he is lost in lust for the other. She moved toward me as a way of telling me all I had to do was reach out and grab her. Nerves seemed to freeze my movements and hers temporarily. I was paralyzed by fear but not of rejection. It was more of a fear that she would accept my advances. I knew that I was completely in love for her, but would this turn out to be another letdown? Would she become the next great letdown of my short, ever-drifting life?

Once again, my body moved, without my consent. I could only watch as my right arm clumsily reached out around her waist to pull her toward me. The movement of her body to mine was dreamlike. We somehow moved perfectly; almost like dancers. Her arms reached around me without accidentally bumping mine. It seemed like we had been holding each other for a lifetime. Her eyes were then only inches away from mine, and were focused upon my lips. The heat, weight and pressure of her body made me want to hold her tighter and longer. I wanted our bodies to be made out of wet clay so that the potter would make us one. Our hearts would beat only after the other's did, appearing to echo the other. I could smell and even taste the cinnamon on her breath as if it was the first time. Her breath was anything but steady, and sent waves of cinnamon blowing over my face, almost exactly the way wind moves relentlessly across a frozen lake.

Then, for a moment, as time became unimportant, her dark eyes blinked, and looked into mine. It was within that lost time that all of the dreams I had of her became real. My lips finally found hers. Neither one wanted it to end. Seconds faded into minutes, and they would have dissolved into hours if we had let them. I didn't care what happened in that classroom, in my hallway or even all those years before. All I cared about was Victoria.

10

Devin and Victoria

I no longer felt as though I was a spectator of a first-person video game. I finally felt that I was in control of my own actions. I could feel a heat that Hell could only dream of every time our lips touched. The fire that was burning deep within me seemed to be oozing out from my skin. As I touched her cheek with my shaking hands, chills poured out of her soft skin onto my rough, unsure hands. Her hair felt like how a cool mist would in the heat of a desert in late afternoon. I found myself in a state of lust, and by some divine inspiration, a poem mustered softly out of my lips to her ears.

> I've waited a lifetime to live.
> While crying onto an empty and hollow night sky,
> with only a thought of you to quiet my loneliness.
> My heart and soul
> would be swallowed up by your sight,
> only because I knew that seeing you
> would leave me
> the moment when I watched you walk by.
> I would close my eyes
> to burn your smile, eyes and lips
> into my mind.
> Every day was different,
> yet somehow every day was the same.
> The sight of you became my breath,
> became my food,
> while your perfume of lilies
> overcame everything

that was blocking my sense of smell.
On days of perfection,
your arm, hand or shoulder
would gently brush my body
and it would stop me where I stood,
forming me into a statue
that had to watch you keep walking by.
Like a puppy,
whose master is walking out of the door,
I would stand
and let my whining heart scream from deep within.
I would crave them all night
so that I could once again
find you before my eyes drifted out
and dreams filled my eyes.
Over and over,
I found myself dreaming of you,
until the sleepless night
would once again claim me,
and all my consciousness
would grow dull and stale.
I once more would be allowed to walk
in my dreams among a sleepless night.

As I ended my poem of her, an uneasiness overcame me. My lips retreated slightly as I questioned why I just spoke those words, and in all sincerity, those words were gone and partially forgotten as soon as they exited my lips.

Looking at her, trying to catch her beautiful eyes. I could see and feel her breath quickening to a speed that was reserved for sprinters on a track running for an Olympic gold. She moved her head to mine again, and I caught her tongue smoothly licking her upper lip, and then, as if it was rehearsed, both of her hands flung themselves onto the sides of my face, and before I could even think or react, her lips were on mine again. The feeling of her hands was like I was being touched and caressed with a love I knew nothing of.

As she pulled her lips less than an inch away from mine to whisper, she said with a smile, "I've always dreamed of what your lips would feel like, Devin."

Her arm wrapped around my lower back, and with mine, I held her tightly to me. I could almost reach the elbows of my other arm as I squeezed her. There were so many thoughts going through my mind that I started to forget about everything completely, except for Victoria there in my arms.

After what seemed like forever, Vic looked up at me with her shining, dark eyes and asked, "Devin, what's going on here? Something very nonhuman is going on all around us." She paused to await my words.

Withdrawing from her slightly, I unwrapped my arms from around her, allowing me to grab her hands. She seemed to fight my movements at first, but with my lead, she released her grip of my body, and held my hands firmly. It seemed like it was her way of saying, "If I can't hold you, I will lock my hands to yours so that I never lose you." I led her to a couch to sit down. The weight of what I was about to say forced a tension headache to explode in my head. I was somehow able to pull my hands free from the soft kung-fu grip she had my hands in, so I could rub my eyes. I'd always wondered what good rubbing them really did, because it never seemed to relieve any pain. Her arms refused to part from touching part of me, and found their way to caress my back, as I was bending down to rub my eyes. I sank back into the thick cushioning of the couch.

The way in which I looked at her must have appeared to reflect someone who had been lying and was then finally coming clean. Anxiety clearly spilled out from my face. I could tell Vic understood the magnitude of what I was going to say and how much the event had changed not only me but the way that I, at that time, looked at the world. Her left hand massaged the base of my neck while her right hand lay motionless a few inches above my knee. The way she looked at me with a curiosity and pain made me feel like she was truly concerned about me. It felt good to know that she cared.

I expected the walls and world around me would be pulled apart to reveal just a new type of nightmare to stop me. Part of me wanted to retreat away from her so that I didn't need to speak about what happened. I thought many times that if I could just forget, maybe it would all disappear. Only in my dreams, locked away behind barriers, would the truth I hid be found. I had also found myself longing for the moment of time when all I knew was utter loneliness. Oh, how sweet the loneliness can be!

A poem spilled out softly.
In that place where blackness
is dissolved into the nothing that created it,
I find my thoughts walking.
In these empty spaces,
a shadowy dream is where I can now live and breathe,
reluctant to love,
knowing that the pain of loss would always be present.
Even though in here I may be bound and wounded,
at least, there is freedom from the pain of loss there.
Here I may still inhale the breath of life,
but I ache for the hidden shadows where I can hide.
I cling to my heart,
and pray that death would consume
and break it into dust.
But will my soul once more have forgotten?
Or will I suffer until the blackness of that place
dissolves my soul back into nothing?
For what is a soul but a faded memory
of a life it once was lived?
I clung to a gray substance
that was the reality between my life and the blackness,
in the same way as a child, afraid to swim,
clings to the side of the pool.

There was no life here,
only my desperate thoughts.
I made the absence of life
my food, my air and my death.
Will it take me
before I find love and piece it together?
Or will it first throw love in front of me,
only to find the right time to break it,
ripping it from my bloody and scarred fingers?
I have become the lover
to the shadowy, black nothingness,
and I crave it
like how Romeo craved Juliet's kiss
the moment before the poison
emptied its fatal nectar onto him.
But it was the kiss of death
that answered their lover's wish.
I dream of that kiss;
of that sweet death
that would release me.

"What are you talking about?" Victoria asked.

"What? What? Oh, I was just babbling about how to say this." I hoped she believed me without hearing it all. "Well, I don't know if you are going to believe me, but I am not going to lie about anything, so here goes."

"Don't worry. Given what I've just seen over the past few hours, I'm very open-minded," Vic said, trying to reassure me. "Very open-minded," she added easily and convincingly.

I had no knowledge of what she had been through, but I knew that with everything that was being thrown at me, she must have seen something that I was not aware of since we left that college classroom.

Enchanted by the fire, I began, "I know that there really is good and evil in this world. I don't mean evil like that of some person, groups or government. No, I mean real evil; the kind of evil that dreams up what those people, groups and governments do, and it's not about life. It's not about killings, torture, rape or destruction. No, it's about complete destruction of everything we hold dear to us. It's about taking our souls and then using them as tools to inflict that which the owner wants."

I paused to let it sink in while her hands slowly fell from off my neck and leg.

"I guess, like any story, I have to go back to the beginning. I grew up in southern Wisconsin. It was nice. I really liked the fall weather. There was something about the crisp air that somehow always mixed itself with all of the colors from the dying leaves and grasses. I loved the way the leaves would crunch under my feet as I walked on a sidewalk or when I would plow through a pile of them with my bike. The feeling, as well as everything slowly dying all around, just made life seem that much more meaningful. The whistling of the wind through an emptying forest always brought a sense of evil and decay back to where beauty once thrived. It always seemed to push my summer desires to the side and force me to embark on a new task, such as finding a new love interest or friend.

It always felt more electric during the fall. On top of all that there was the illusion of fear that grows each day as Halloween approaches. In all fairness, it might not be an illusion at all, for there really is a darkness to that time of year. Whether or not that is what draws me to it, I can't say, but in the deepest parts of my soul, I loved the feeling of it.

That time of year was quickly approaching again, and all of my old feelings started to begin to tingle with excitement. Maybe I longed to see what the darkness was, or maybe it was more about the peace I felt with it all. James, my best friend, and I decided that we were going to pack up our guitars and head out to the West Coast. We weren't really sure if Seattle or Los Angeles was where we wanted to go. All we knew was that regardless of where we did end up, we would find a way to become famous, and our songs would be heard everywhere.

We had been playing and writing music for years. I was the one with the formal training whereas James was the kind of player that didn't adhere to music theory; he just played. He liked to listen to music that was new, and find ways to write in that style. I combined the storytelling of country music with a 1980s style of guitar work, and then added a 1990s style of poetry in order to deepen the feeling and make it sound authentic. All in all, we were a good combination.

James was only an inch or so taller than me, but he was built like a bodybuilder. His other passion was sports, and he was very good at whatever sport he played. He turned down numerous scholarships in order to pursue a dream involving music. I would be lying if I said I was not jealous of what he was offered, and maybe that is why I always pushed for us to leave the area together to be rock stars. He was so good at sports. I think he knew that if within a year we weren't going anywhere, he would go to one of those schools that offered him a scholarship.

I've never liked Fords but a gray-haired, smooth salesman in his fifties somehow convinced me that a little-used pickup was perfect for me. I regretted it from the day I bought it because it just never seemed to fit me. It ran fine, but it only had a four-cylinder engine and the cab was very small. It did not feel like a man's truck. It was more like it belonged to someone who was playing at being a man. We put a very ugly, cheap camper over the back to keep everything dry during our travels. The truck was a greenish-blue color while the camper was an ugly, off-white color with red racing strips down the middle of each side. I could only imagine what we looked like driving down the road. To top it off, the truck was a manual, and had no power windows or air conditioning. Having that camper on made it even hotter. The lack of cruise control made the purchase very stupid. Who's going to buy a vehicle that does not have cruise right before leaving to go almost the whole way across the country. It wasn't one of my better ideas. James did not like stick shift. It was very funny to watch him try over and over, only to fail so horribly. I thought that by the time we reached our destination, all of the gears in the transmission would be shot. I would tease him every time the truck bounced while he shifted. It didn't matter how much time he spent driving it. Either he was just doing it to piss me off, or he just wasn't getting it. No matter, it was fun and entertaining to watch.

We were well past the 15-hour mark of our drive, somewhere in North Dakota. The land all around us was as flat as a placid lake. The wind started to die down as the day began to cross over into twilight. Small amounts of sunlight were still holding onto the day in an attempt to squeeze out the last breath before night completely took over, as though trying to give us all just enough light to endure the shadowy night of death that was standing at our door. I looked toward the sun, and even as it was burning through my eyes, I could not look away. I held onto it, and somewhere, without knowing how or why, I started writing a poem of love and desire for the sun. James knew that when I started down this path, it was best to sit in silence until the moment passed me by. These are the words as I remember them.

> My breath is quickened
> as you stand frozen before us.
> Like a giant, you look toward me
> but never see me,
> for I am nothing but a bug to your immense wonder.

> I crave to stop time
> in a way of holding onto you
> for just a little bit longer.
> To my uncovered chest,
> I would lock and hold you
> to allow your warmth to fill me,
> and then out of me it would explode.
> I reach, but I only find air
> and nothing to hold to myself.
> My body aches for you
> and my soul is now lost as I look into this setting
> sun.
> For you are, and will always be, my warmth.
> Or is there somewhere?

Or is there someone
who could hold you closer and tighter
than my pale and weak arms?
I lie here naked and exposed
before the light of the day dies
to beg for your touch.
For if God would not let me have you,
maybe this ancient sun god of the Egyptians
will bring you to me.
I can't mourn any longer.
The feeling of unending mourning has become my
life, and why I live and how I must now die.
I reach again,
just hoping that you would see me,
but there was nothing.
My love and desire burns,
never ending, for you, as I promised.
Yours has been burned out.
Or is it that it was never lit?
I hate myself for giving
my heart, body, soul
and whatever innocence I have left to you,
because like a vampire,
you sat and waited to feed off me,
taking all that I have,
and leaving me with nothing
but the taste of a hangover in my mouth.
I hurt, but I still love you.
Or is this just something I've made myself believe?
No! Your promises I still hide in my heart
that someday, as you have said,
we would become one again.
Sun, please don't fade.
Just let me hold you a little longer.
Because she may be looking onto you,
as I dream, and plea unto you,
as a beggar who has craved her,

but now broken by the coldness within her heart,
I need your heat.
Please! Keep us both held to you.
Take my breath and give it to her,
and hold me
as my life fades out.

I finished just as the sun settled past the horizon. There was a beautiful blend of violets, orange and soft yellow, while shots of green sped through. Dark blues gave way to the softer versions within seconds of each other and then bounced back to the deep, dark blues when colors bled out and away from the departing sun. There was an amazing illusion in how the clouds that were surrounded by the blackening sky still sang with life in a parade of pinks. It always reminded me of the mountains of Albuquerque, New Mexico. Every day, they would sing with their luminescent glow to the hard life of the desert below. When I drove through New Mexico and saw it, I believed it was the sun's way of apologizing for the long day of heat that it poured out across the desert. I wondered if, within that apology, the sun tried to dampen the dryness with promises of rain, only to find out that the promise was a lie when the sun brought forth a new dawn.

There was something growing in the darker parts of the clouds. It seemed as if, one by one, the thriving life of pink was being put out with the same anger as I'd just used to put out an over-smoked cigarette butt. The darker clouds, which seemed to intertwine with the rest of the softer clouds, began to eat them up until they encased each cloud that was devoured in the same way as the smoke completely consumed my hand when I exhaled. There was something about how brutal change could really be. What made it more than just a cloud eater? Was it something I felt? But by the reaction on James's face and his physical expressions and movements, it was evident that that change was gripping him even harder than it did me.

It was hard to explain how all life just seemed to drain out of him. His face bled off the colors, like they were being washed off him. Everything about him seemed cold. I don't even think that people on their deathbed would have the same lifeless image tattooed on their face as James did. The force of whatever came over him was so sure of itself, and the outcome of that was going to be not only unchangeable but undeniable. His eyes seemed to sink, and mirrored those of a rock star, who shot his life away through needles in the arms, poisoning the veins. Darker and darker his eyes grew as the shadows around them seemed to come alive. It seemed those shadows were trying to pull his skin into his eye sockets, mimicking two small black holes that drained life in opposite spiraling patterns into the vacancies where his eyeballs once had been. Shadows flashed out from his eyes, but then pulled back with such violence that tiny waves could be seen on his cheeks.

An acoustic guitar slowly began to play throughout the cab. It was a very well-known song that was dedicated to all color fading into the absence of color. The music seemed louder and crisper than anytime I had heard the song. It tugged at me, making me embrace some form of solitude that I had never considered before. With the sound, the setting sun and James's appearance, I felt as though I was being pulled into those tiny black holes, my body into the one on his right side and my soul into the other. I wondered if all my thoughts and consciousness would go with my soul or my body.

In an attempt to save at least one of them, I turned my gaze away from James and toward the darkening sky. It was only seconds since I looked away from the clouds and to James, but in those precious moments that passed without my look, the world turned into the same blackness that was sucking life out of James. It felt and looked as if it was 2 or 3 in the morning. There was no light anywhere in the sky. There was a hint for a second on the horizon, but that hint was stopped almost as quickly as the notes in the song faded or changed.

The song drew closer to its first chorus. I could feel the electricity in the air building along with the song. Everything seemed charged and ready to explode. All the hair on my body began to lift from the static that was then deeply imprinted in the air. As each note grew louder, my hairs grew a little bit more.

The little bit of light that was allowed to shine out from the truck's headlights showed a world that appeared to be hiding. The cattle in a field were all running as fast as they could away from us. The wild animals, hiding in silence along the roadside, started to take off when we got alongside them. The birds that came out of nowhere started to dive-bomb houses along the road and even at the road in front of us. There were so many birds flying into things that they seemed like large pieces of hail. I looked on with horror while James's driving never changed. He remained on course, as if all of that was solely in my head. I also wondered if it was the result of over-drugging my own mind when I was younger. James's hands that once shadowed that of a bodybuilder seemed at that point as old and frail as someone who was in his nineties. The skin of his hand looked like it had been vacuumed closed, like when people store clothes for the season.

Every imperfection of the bones in his hands sang through the skin. His whitish skin seemed to be like that of a porcelain doll. There were some places that you could see how the red from his veins was trapped, being pinched, because of how tightly he was squeezing the steering wheel. The contrast between how the white of his bones shining through mixed with the dark red of his veins, highlighted in lines on his hands, was as mesmerizing as a bonfire on a cool and crisp fall night. With my eyes returning from the sky and locked solely on James's hands, I was unaware that we were slowing down. James was getting off the interstate. He never said anything. All he did was drive. I couldn't even tell if we got off smoothly or erratically.

I cannot say what happened first. James lunged one hand off the steering wheel and onto the shifter just as a bolt of lightning exploded maybe 50 feet in front of us. It hit the road like a mini nuke, and sent pieces flying in all directions. When pieces hit my truck, I retreated instinctively into a fetal position or at least, the closest I could get to that while stuck in that horribly small cab. As I covered my head and neck, I could feel the glass beginning to be blown apart. I could also hear the pieces of stone ripping through the plastic center of the window. The hairs all over my body started to stand in anticipation of the softening impact.

Split seconds passed without even the chance of a breath or it being released. There was no time to think, but for some reason, my thoughts never stopped. I felt like the world I was living in was paused, and my consciousness was removed and placed aside to watch. My sight seemed to be withheld from me so that all my other senses were heightened. I was on fire with a new awareness, or at least, I thought I was. Not only could I feel the shock wave as it embraced me, but it was like I could see by feeling each one of the hairs on my arm wave and fold to embrace the shock wave. That sense of touch was so much more defined than any visual glimpse of any sunset, breath of love or sorrow of death. It was more defined than the sight of a passing funeral procession and truer than that first kiss that gave birth to love.

I thought perhaps that it was the beginning of my death and I was already on my way out. Maybe the lightning striking the ground also struck me, stopping my heart and blinding me. The heightened sense of feeling could be my body's way of fighting for life with what little power and energy that was left to restart my heart, but my blood just sat there getting thicker and thicker with each missed heartbeat. There is a type of beauty in death. I longed for it to be mine. It seemed like perfection.

Fantasies of my death filled my mind and took over my every desire, twisting and turning them into a mortifying longing for my end. Like a fly trapped in a spider's web, I just got more and more tangled. I wanted it to be true, even more than a vampire could wish to watch the rising sun with its own eyes. I didn't care about what I was going to lose or who I would never meet. All of that was nothing. Even if the place I went was dark and filled with hate-filled rage, it still had to be better than all of those unknowns that lingered in life. I could feel my soul whisper from within, pleading that Death would not pass me by.

I could feel Death burning the hairs on my neck with a cool that burned. I could smell each hair melt away. It was a fire that did not burn or consume my flesh or soul. I felt like a shy lover standing in front of the one I adored with my naked back opened before her, and even though she only stood a breath away, it seemed as if we were an ocean apart. I pictured death behind me, slowly sliding closer, half man and half beast. By my heightened feeling, I could see his hooves stomp the ground. I could taste the death of all those he took from the stench blowing out from his taurine face. I wondered how much different his next breath would taste to his next victim after he ate me. Would my stains of life be anything more than a stench to the next victim?

Time still did not seem to have returned, yet for some reason, I was allowed to hear the rocks bounce off the truck or through it. The vision of a space shuttle being pelted by thousands of meteorites tearing holes all over the hull flooded my mind's eye. Maybe my ears were gone just like my sight, but I could hear words that sounded as if they were hidden underneath a murky river water. I hoped those were words from my loved ones that I was about to be joining. Would it be God I'd go to join? Were those the words of the curse that would send me to Hell? My mind raced as I thought about the different stories of the hereafter. Would I be dining with my ancestors in the halls that were described in ancient pagan religions, or would I be burning for the sins I committed against God, who had hidden himself from me? At the same time, I began to feel like a samurai, a chieftain or a shadow warrior for the ancient pharaohs, and sensed the overpowering rage of conquering that the Viking warriors had. Was the conquest part of becoming a god? Was I food for one who has already climbed the stairs to godhood? I didn't care if this was any of those. The fantasy I had drifted into was my only reason for being there. I was sick of the staleness of life. Life seemed too boring to be real. It seemed like the only ones that ever truly live are those that are characters in works of fiction. Movies always fail to depict an exciting life properly.·

I began to think of the people who really led exciting lives; lives that seemed to start new almost daily; lives in which love and passion fueled their fire to burn like those of first loves, and above that in which one's heart and soul wouldn't mourn every breath taken. I believed life was nothing but a poor, tedious book that never seemed to end. What would it be like when God decides he has had enough? At some point, he would move on from us, because he is our beginning and our end. But thinking that we are also his beginning and end would be to limit the limitless.

I wanted to sink into nothingness. I wanted the death that was falling upon me to close on me like a Venus flytrap. In fact, I knew deep within that if I wanted to live and step out of the shadow, I could take that step. All I had to do was open my half-closed eyes and take a breath. Yet I refused even to consider that, and closed my eyes tighter.

I could feel coldness descend upon me like the color of night on a gray, wintry day in the depths of a leafless forest in Wisconsin. I could not see my breath, but I could feel it freezing as it started to gather in my lungs before exiting. My throat burned with frostbite as my frozen vapor crept up and out of my mouth. The slow and fading speed at which it crawled left me gasping for air that I no longer needed. I could feel my tongue begin to contract as the cold, burning, tingling and numbing feeling took over. My tongue started to crack and break as I moved it back and forth. With everything that was numb, there were still a few taste buds left, and I could taste my own freezing blood as pieces of my tongue broke off and fell lifeless within my mouth. I felt a sense of relief, knowing that I would die, by a thing that took my blood from my tongue. It was almost as though death was kissing me and sucking my life out at the same time. It had a very vampiric romance to it. Maybe, in death, life finally would become more exciting and real.

Pain plowed through my body as the cold started to drive through my teeth, flicking each nerve. It felt like my dentist forgot to allow the novocaine to sit long enough before drilling into my nerves. I felt somehow that I deserved the pain, so I did not let it stop my descent into the abyss of death. Then, without warning, my frosty breath hit my lips, and as soon as it started to pass over my lips, I felt them chap, crack, break, bleed, and freeze shut before the first wave of breath passed over them. It was like the final phase of the vampire's kiss in which our lips finalized the kiss.

It was as though the frost was as close to an instant death as I could get. I could not tell if I was already dead, in the act of dying or in a new form of that twisted book. Was I still, in fact, alive? Was it just that I had been knocked out by the blast? I had been knocked out before, but I was never so aware of my time while out. I knew, therefore, what I had just experienced was different. If it really was death, I wanted it to last. All my pain turned into pleasure, and I craved more of the blood that I had lost through my tongue and lips. I began to wonder and hope that my eyes would crack, and tears of blood would roll out of them, half frozen but still with enough liquid that gravity would push them down toward my mouth.

Oh, how cruel this life really was to those who learned how to feel and bleed! I wanted it to touch my lips one last time. Even if they were numb, I would be able to feel the weight and pressure placed upon my chapped and cracked lips. I still refused to let death release its grip on me. Maybe it was my soul or ghost that was climbing out, and my body was unable to set me free.

James's voice called out to me, "You going to get up so we can get something to eat, or sleep all night and bitch about having to eat gas-station food again?"

11

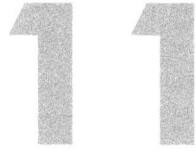

Nine months before Victoria was born

The stairway called to Jacob, like the quiet dream of a middle-aged man right before the crisis takes hold of his heart and drives him to change his life. The stairs seemed to pull at his feet, like he was being worshipped by those stairs. He could almost feel all the strands of the carpet reaching out as if they had arms and hands. For a moment, he felt the godlike feeling that rock stars or actors might feel as they are clawed at by their worshippers. Jacob could imagine the intoxicating lure of that power.

The lure became everything to him. Even the memories that were crying from the wall were just photos of memories and nothing more. The smells from when those memories came alive seemed to leave a residue on his lips and tongue as a tease by failing to crawl up to his nose so he could once again breath it in. The humidity that he dreaded all of those nights as he prayed against the approaching dawn became the melting world around him, but his skin was left naked and uncovered by the heat.

As the melting wall oozed onto his hand, he felt nothing but the pressure and strength of the carpet reaching up and grabbing hold of him. Even the wall that trapped his arm had then been transformed into another worshipper in his mind. The only time the wall or carpet released its grip on him was when it was time to push him further down the melting stairway. Jacob felt like he was sliding down a hill that had a new and fresh coat of powdery snow and he was the first one to ski on it. There were no steps for him; only a slow, well-thought-out descent into the total madness that waited for him at the bottom. If it was not madness, the descent could only be brought on by a few possibilities. But in any case, there was no going back.

First, madness would mean that everything he had ever known would be nothing more than a dream or delusion he was sucked into. Second, it would also mean that the beauty sleeping beside him would not be in his bedroom. Jacob wondered if she actually existed, or was merely a part of his living dream. But how could this madness explain the way her hair tickled his nose while he slept, or how her lips pressed against his were softer than the innocence in the eyes of an infant as it slept?

Jacob's mind quickly shifted from thoughts of madness and what he might have lost as soon as his feet landed on the flat platform. They turned 180 degrees before allowing him to descend again. It was the first time he could remember, since starting down those stairs, feeling something solid under him. Jacob once again started to think about the thing that originally drew him out into the eerie, dreamlike state, only to open his eyes upon that massive face staring back at him. Even the vision upon which he had been fixated faded away. Everything seemed to be back to normal. The tickle that he felt before starting down the stairs was still moving up and down his spine, never stopping. All over his body goose bumps gave him the feeling that someone or something was with him. That made him feel like he was not alone, but drifting in the dark Mediterranean Sea, much as Odysseus did after he lost his whole crew and was at the mercy of Poseidon. It was not, though, the loneliness of being in the vacuum of space, but resembled the loneliness felt when standing motionless in full view of moonlight.

His anxiety and fear melted away as though he was too hot for those traits to cling to him any longer. In between heartbeats and breaths, he was no longer waiting to hear the deep sound of that beast he pictured panting behind him as a way of pushing him further down into whatever state of madness or hell awaited him. The heat he felt pushing him along and down the stairs was not there anymore either.

Searching for an answer to make sense of what he'd just experienced, Jacob stood there, looking back at the stairs he had just slid down. He couldn't move forward or backward. Jacob became a living statue. All he could do then was remain motionless on the platform of the stairway. The pause let him delve more deeply into the thoughts about where he was heading, and built to a breaking point. But he was unable to explode, due to the stone, concrete or marble statue he turned into. Maybe this was Heaven, Hell, insanity, the bathroom or merely another unexplainable nothingness that didn't quieten his curiosity. Those thoughts only made him want to know.

He remembered his high school and the years just after when he enjoyed any and all sorts of drugs and other escape mechanisms and psychedelics. LSD and mushrooms were some of his personal favorites. For $5, he could trip on LSD. The world around him would no longer be anything, other than five-to-ten-minute segments of time, and would then become lost in the next rabbit hole of his thoughts. One time, he combined LSD, marijuana and nitrous oxide. As soon as the nitrous oxide was inhaled, the world became twisted and reversed. Everything solid turned into a gas, and everything that was a gas was a solid. Liquids became viscous like paint or gel. People seemed vacant, not there; almost like their skin melted away into steady streams of goo slowly dripping onto the floor. Buildings, once made of brick, mortar, steel and wood, seemed as if they were made of paper, and all he had to do was lean against them, and he would fall right through. Voices screamed from within those buildings when he walked by. He couldn't make out any of the voices. His mind put false words and sounds in the holes, trying to make out the conversation. But those sounds were nothing but a very loud, unrecognizable vibration. Jacob's brain treated what had just happened to him the same as a psychedelic trip or perhaps even a flashback.

The bottom half of the stairs was open on one side, so he could partly make out the dark room below him, but the glow of orange and red radiated about 20 feet from the stairs, and was shining into a mirror that was nearby. It was such a dominant reflection that he could not be certain if the light was merely reflecting, and not shining, out of the mirror. There was an eerie darkness within the mirror, even though the light that shone onto or out of it was bright enough to illuminate most of the room below him. The blackness was not merely the lack of light. He could almost make out some type of movement within the shadow on the other side of the mirrored glass.

The thought of what he was walking into gripped him harder than before. Even though he was no longer scared, he knew that something was not right and that that might not actually be his stairs. But if it wasn't his stairs, where was he? Was the dream he had before the face dragged him out really his death? Had he actually died in his dream, or was he facing the death that came to take him to the afterlife? Because of his lack of faith in God, Jacob wondered if this could in fact be a never-ending spiraling stairway to Hell that would get hotter and hotter as he descended. Perhaps, as soon as his foot hit the ground, he would be brought back up to the top of the stairs to start over, like Sisyphus with his rock going up a hill. That pattern would repeat itself over and over until that phase of Hell's torment ended, and he would be removed to face his next torment.

"Whatever this was and wherever it leads me, is it really my choice? I am the one and only person or thing in charge of what happens to me," Jacob said to instill confidence in him, while also trying to convince himself that there was nothing there within the supernatural world.

12

Devin's story

The truck was bouncing all over because James was driving a bit on the wild side as he was pulling into the parking lot. It was a truck stop with a restaurant. In fact, the sign high in the air read "The Restaurant". I guessed that the owners didn't care all that much about things like names, concrete parking lots, health inspectors and hairnets, but other than that, the food smelled enticing while we were pulling into the parking lot. There were a lot of semitrucks parked on the sides and back of the lot, and that's typically a good sign of quality and cheap food.

The night sky was dark, but the storm we were in was gone. There was not a tingle of electricity or a wet surface. There was not even a single cloud in the sky; only the full moon floating half asleep and naked in the midnight sky. Even with the full moon, it was harder to see into the depths of the night than upon any other night. When the moonlight was completely absent and distant, even the faintest dream of walking in the moonlight would be considered a taboo. The moon seemed somehow to be the opposite of what the moon stood for. Instead of reflecting the light of the sun, the moon collected whatever light was shone onto it. It was like a parasite that latches onto a host and slowly drains it of everything. That is what that imposter of a moon was doing, and the face that stands strong and proud, with the many craters, had fixed its hateful gaze upon me.

I could feel the hateful gaze consisting of betrayal, brutality, death and consumption as I tried to refocus my eyes on the row of semitrucks and empty trailers that lined the edges of the parking lot. They looked more like modern tombs than moving offices. The windows of the trucks were either blacked out or a shade was drawn. That made the tomb image all the more realistic. The small number of lights in the parking lot were upon the fronts of the trucks. The spaces behind and between were a wasteland of shadows that seemed to change like ones within an old colonial house.

The uneven surface caused by potholes rocked the small truck back and forth. The occasional stone that shot out from the weight of my truck pushing down on it sent a shiver of fear down my spine as it popped loudly. I got the same feeling I would get when hearing silverware scratch a plate or when someone creased paper. It was as if I could feel that part of my soul was being ripped harder every time by the moon. I was in the grip of two evils — my fear of what was awaiting me in those modern tombs and the soul-sucking moon.

A flash of whitish yellow broke my concentration, allowing me to find my center for a moment. The sign above the door read "Mag's Diner", and it flickered on and off. It seemed that James had had the idea to park the truck right where the sign was flickering. As if there was only one path, he sped wildly toward the parking spot. There were only a few other cars scattered throughout the parking lot, but no other car seemed to be heading toward us or the diner, so I wasn't sure why he was in a rush.

I know we were talking, but even then, I had no idea of what he was saying or what I was saying, for that matter. I could see his mouth moving and even grinning as we approached. The flickering light lit up his blue eyes with an almost gothic mist that clashed with the soft, white glow from the light on his skin. Even with us being half a parking lot away from the diner, the light pierced through the parking-lot lights to show its power over us and of what lay ahead. The light refused to shine on me, leaving my face hidden once more in the dark of the cab. Like a stalker, I was left gazing out the front window, in which I saw a darkened reflection of myself.

I could see my mouth moving, answering the conversation with James, but our conversation resembled a movie scene from the early 20th century when movies were silent and words were written in after the scene, but no words ever came. The moon's pull seemed to have taken me completely out of my thoughts, leaving me a mere spectator of whatever I was witnessing, rather than a participant.

Worlds divided James and me. My world was being driven into another one in which shadows and storms began to rain. James's world, however, still had light and predictable events. I could see the lightning starting to begin once more in my world. First, it was merely flickers of electricity between the parked trailers, but then it grew into light that engulfed the parking lot. I wondered if I would wake up this time; if I would find that I was in fact the prized experiment of some crazy scientist trying to live out a childhood dream of bringing a monster to life after death.

The explosions grew louder. That time, it was as if they were inside my own head. With every flash, I was increasingly blinded, but I could still see a grin on my face growing bigger and wilder, and making me less like myself. Then, with the rumble of thunder, I felt a hand grasp me, pulling me just enough out of my body to let me know I was not in control of it.

My skin became completely numb and without feeling. I was like a zombie; I was able to keep breathing, to talk, and even to move. The movements of my body were no longer my own. I was a receptor that could only refract the desire that was in control of me. I thought that my death dream was taking me — that it really did take me — and the storm that erupted because of the lightning in front of the truck was also an illusion that could not capture me. The wake from the storm was returning to take hold of me, never to release me again.

The strange sense of peace I felt while I thought death had its grips on me re-emerged for a split second. It was long enough for another phase of thunder and lightning to build up to a final crescendo that shot down with the pure force of domination. Destruction was the only possible goal as the bolts touched the ground. That bolt, no doubt, was meant for me to see. James never seemed to notice the flash or earthquake under him as thunder resounded off everything. It must have been the moon that was reaching for my soul. It lashed out with anger, and exploded onto the earth. Everywhere within sight constituted the explosion radius, but the center of it was Mag's Diner. Everything else was rolling balls of flame caused by the fallout.

The flames started from the diner as the windows and doors blew out. There was nothing to those flames other than color and depth. The heat that produced them was slower, so the force pushed them out. The flames did not swallow whatever was in its path, but seemed to go through whatever it was. They looked like they were ghostly and didn't affect anything. I watched as they passed through the trucks and up the high, dirt embankment that rose up to the interstate behind some of the trucks. A wall of sound also pulsated out from the diner with the power that was reserved for weapons of mass destruction. Everything but the truck James and I were in was pushed aside from the diner. The sound wave was similar to that of a tsunami. As soon as it seemed to give way or end, there was another wave that pushed forward, causing even more destruction.

Whatever had hold of me seemed to burn with the fallout, and I was released back into my body. Instantly, the fireball and fallout were gone, but I was still lost to James and the land of the living. I was back to staring out the shadows between the trucks. I could almost picture dragons hiding in the shadows of the trucks as they waited for the perfect time, when no one was looking, to break free and burn the world. I wondered if they were also part of the fallout.

13

Nine months before Victoria was born

"Ha ha ha ha ha ha! Is the basement floor cold on your feet?" the face said in a mocking tone as it pulled Jacob through the house and into the basement before he could even think about what was happening to him or consider where he was. Everything was a blur to him because of the speed at which he was rushed through it. For a moment, he wondered if it was his own doing and if he was walking or crawling through the house, the way he did a few minutes before. The memories were so strong and overwhelming that his mind blocked them out as soon as they came back to him. He could not believe that there was an evil force in front of him that wanted to consume him. It must have been his own freewill that dragged him down there.

Different colors began to lash out in a parade of colors changing rapidly to reflect that of a strobe light. Dark and stubborn lights attached themselves to physical objects. The lighter colors could only be seen through his psychic ability. Quite rapidly, the two different realities began to blend together. Areas in which shadows still clung to the corners were impregnated with the lighter colors. The depth of those shadows looked similar to how artists use shading to establish depth in a painting. The lighter colors kept flowing into the shadows until all that remained was a gray blur. Every now and then, the passing of a bright light of perfect white kissed his sight. For a moment, the color was so bright that everything around him seemed to fade out, and it seemed like all the other colors were not really there in the first place. But like many times before, that moment was being drowned as the darkness overpowered it with the tenacity of a swarm of locusts. He felt as if he was a junkie desperate for a fix, but his drug of choice was not something he could easily find. It was buried under that gray darkness. The light was completion. It was happiness and the feeling of being unconditionally and completely loved. He knew that there was nothing that he would not do it in order to find it again. He didn't even care what the outcome would be.

"Please don't let it end," Jacob kept saying with tears pouring out of his eyes. He wasn't sure if the tears were from the loss of the light, or if it was from being pulled throughout the house at such a high speed, or both. "I will do anything. Please don't," he pleaded one more time, but the deep colors of blood red, dusty blue, Seattle gray, Los Angeles haze and rainy-night black, along with the darkness that lies within all shadows, screamed out.

But he didn't know it existed all around him. It happened with such a force that he was sure his house was going to fall on him. The basement walls and floor started to crack and blow out. Cucumber-shaped holes formed in three of the four corners. They were three feet wide by six feet long on the floor, and the same on the walls that connected to them. It seemed like there were veins that connected the holes to one another. Those veins looked six inches wide and did not follow any form or pattern. The veins appeared to embrace the theories of chaos. Each one had a different color that glowed from the crack-like veins. One was blackened red, one was dirty blue, one was gray, and one was a color that Jacob had never seen before. It seemed like it was pure yellow while at the same time somehow black as night. The colors of the holes seemed to coincide with the vein that drained into or away from it.

Screams came out of some type of beings, and pulsated out with whatever color from the hole they started. Every time the colors grew darker, the screams seemed to grow louder and became more desperate as well. Some screams sounded bipolar. Those sounds coming from one source sounded similar to *a cappella* choral singing. Each note was accompanied, but others formed some kind of musical chord. Buried under the sound of torment and suffering, those chords formed a melodic ballad of sorts. It would have been quite breathtaking and peaceful if it wasn't so eerie and dark. The pain that was twisted between the mortal sounds and non-mortal sounds held anger and hatred toward each other but also for something else. There were no pleas to be heard. The only words that were understandable were those that were curses toward God. The darker the shades of color grew, the louder those curses became.

In the corner that was left untouched, a black hole started to melt away the upper corner. No scream came with it, just the decaying sound of the drywall, insulation, wood and brick melting away. The hole was much more appealing to him than the other ones. The hole was black, but it wasn't black like a dark room, a shadow or even outside. It pulled at the light that was in the room, and it seemed to feed off the light. It grew darker the more it fed upon the light. Unlike the other holes, in which heat, fire and lava could be seen shooting out almost rhythmically, that hole had a cool steam that seemed like it could burn away flesh from the cold grip of frostbite. The hole started to open as it ate up more of the surrounding light, even the light that was coming out of the torture pits of the damned. All the holes seemed to grow darker as the new hole sucked the colors into itself. The vibrant dark colors that painted the basement in that anti-rainbow were then only tiny specs of what they were supposed to be. Even the screams that were entrenched with color, were fading into the voices and sounds that were still too far off to make out, but were fading the same way an echo does.

With every pulse that the black hole made while eating more light, faint whispers started to bleed out of it. At first, they were too quiet to make out what was said or even the language that was being spoken. Every so often, a laugh could be heard; not a loud or long laugh; barely even audible enough to know for sure that it was a laugh. As soon as Jacob thought he could direct his ears to the laugh, it was gone. All it did was make him want to listen more intently. He inched himself closer as he listened without knowing that he was doing so. It was almost as if he was hypnotized by the anticipation of the next noise. But still there were only the tiny whispers that were just out of reach.

The hole extended four and a half feet down from the ceiling, and it was there the growth seemed to stop. The dimming of the lights of the room that was made by the Hell holes no longer looked effective. It was like they were no longer giving up any more light to anyone or anything. Jacob then edged himself a foot away from the black hole in the corner of the basement. He could even feel the cold that surrounded the outside of the hole, but he could also feel a heat emanating from the center of it. It made him feel like he was standing inside a stove set at its highest temperature.

As a way of pushing himself away and out of the heat, he raised his hands to the outer side of the hole, but he had to move them away just before either hand touched the edges of it because frostbite had already begun to take hold. He couldn't understand how or why there was such a difference between the center of the black hole and the freezing edge. If it wasn't for the pain of his hands, he would have dismissed the difference as nothing more than an illusion made by extreme heat. The frostbite was different from any type of cold he had ever felt. It held all the solitude of the tundra and the bareness that only something that cold could drink from the world, but somehow there was still a beauty in the power it had. Maybe, somewhere deep inside, he knew that the cold was not a mere coldness that life could touch or even hold. There was a joy in that to him.

A whisper was heard, telling him that it was time to let go.

14

Continuing to tell Victoria my story

The bumping, swaying, rocking and creaking of the truck could not break my concentration out on the parking lot where the light seemed to have been swallowed up by the blast that had just engulfed everything. I had my head resting on the window, because the cool of the window felt very good. Even with all the rocking and jarring, my mind was focused on the lights. The cool of the window pressed solidly against my temple felt as close to paradise as I will ever get.

How could those lights be so dark while lit at that time of the night? On the darkest nights, in the deepest trenches in the oceans, on the lowest bowels of Hell, the tiniest flicker of light could be seen from everywhere and from all angles. The tiniest bit of light could even be seen if something was blocking the line of sight by how the light radiated all around the object into the darkness. But those lights were shining as bright as they were designed, and yet it was still so dark that I couldn't even see the ground below the truck.

I felt my heart race with fear as a thought flooded my mind that that was death once again teasing me before it took me. It was in the same manner as a young puppy plays with the first animal it kills, only to mourn the death moments later when it realizes playtime is over. I wasn't sure if I had enough heart to take another letdown. Would another letdown leave me half mad or wild?

Fear or heat from the day forced a single bead of sweat to break free from the hair next to my right temple. It ran down my unshaven cheek. It weaved in and out of a thin beard to my chin. It was not enough to cool me down, or do much more than change my train of thought. What was it that was waiting in death's arms? Every time the droplet was forced to redirect its path, it tickled just a little, and that almost brought a smile to my face. I lost track for a moment as the droplet plunged into my thick goatee. It was the only area of my face on which I was successful, at that time, in growing thick facial hair. I sat there with the same anticipation I'd had while waiting for a Christmas morning. I waited impatiently for what would happen to that tiny bead of sweat. I had to restrain myself from reaching up and wiping it away. It seemed as though the droplet made it through my goatee more easily than it had through the little bit of stubble I had on my cheek. Just like an unwavering soldier, the droplet ran with its own battle cry down my naked neck toward my thin and undefined chest. Unlike the cold feeling that I felt when the droplet rolled down the side of my face, I couldn't sense it. It seemed as if the droplet was unreal; a figment of my mind.

A thick fog began to grow up over the gravel as time began to go backward. It seemed as if we were losing ground rather than getting closer to the diner. Somehow, even with us not moving forward, we still managed to be bumping up and down in the truck. The time changed in a blink of the eye. It was midnight, and we were still in the same spot. It felt as if we were like a spirit that was caught in a never-ending loop. James thought nothing of it. He didn't even seem to notice. I was not in control of my own body. The fog got thicker and thicker until it was hard to see much more than ten feet in front of us. My eyes started to play games. I started to see people all around us. They seemed to be walking without any purpose. I could feel their loneliness; it was something like a sickness that could be caught and passed on to someone else over and over again until everyone fell victim to it. This loneliness had no cure, but it enforced newer and deeper depths of the sickness as it spread. No words were spoken. There was only the steady sound of regret, and there was also an emptiness. Something was bringing them there, but for what? How could James not see them or feel it?

Scraping sounds burned my ears, as one of those people bumped into the truck, because they could not see it. The fog grew even thicker until it was so thick it became the air I was breathing. The fog was laced with fire, and the fire traveled with the mist as though it was being breathed from it. It did not taste like fog. The taste of it was more like smoke. More and more people bumped into the truck as they marched harmlessly by. Every so often, I got a glimpse of a hand or arm being burned as those bodies walked by. They didn't even seem to notice that they were on fire or that their flesh and shirts were melting into a pile of goo. The smell of burning flesh emanated through the fan of the truck. The heat from outside started to rise rapidly, and with it, a thick and impenetrable web of humidity came from everywhere. Heat waves started wandering into the mist. The fume waves were hard to focus on because the fog offered nothing to look at in order to find my depth perception. The heat all around us changed into the type of heat that long days spent in a sauna couldn't contend with. Inside the truck, the temperature stayed the same, as when the fog started. With the intensity of a solar flare, the heat licked the outside of the truck, and with each lick, the heat tore a tiny piece of the truck away. It seemed as though the heat was determined to break through whatever was shielding us from it.

With one of the first licks of heat, each rubber tire exploded, and began to melt into puddles of nothingness, one after the other. Still, I felt no heat or fire from the melting rubber. Then the paint on the hood began to bubble. It started to pop, just like tiny fireworks exploding all over the hood. Some even blew liquefied paint onto the window. I could smell a mix of burning rubber and burning paint with every breath. All I could do was remain there, and wait for the heat to do the same thing to my blood.

I imagined what it would feel like to have my blood pop free from my veins and skin. Would it burn or would the heat be so intense that every nerve in my body would also be ripped apart when my blood was forced out in such an aggressive way? Would the heat bring back the cold touch of death, or was the heat all that was left for me?

The sound of loud, hooved feet approaching from my rear brought the thoughts of my impending torment to an end. Then I feared the touch and kiss of death. It was getting too real. I knew where I was. I could feel it in my bones, but I could not say the name of the land of the dammed because that would make it too real. Closer and closer, the hooves came as the heat finally invaded the interior of the truck, and it started to melt. First, the vents and the walls around the vents started to melt and drip onto the floor. I could hear a hissing sound as each melted ball fell to the floor. The heat was quickly transferred to the dashboard, which started to drip onto us. For some reason, it seemed that those balls of heat didn't affect me. My clothes just hissed, like the floor did, when they landed on them. The steering wheel began to melt, and was reshaped around James's hands. James just continued to talk as if nothing was happening even as the melting steering wheel set fire to his hands. He still smiled at me, saying something about how good the food smells from the diner. I could see his skin turn to liquid as I awaited the coming of the hooves, which were accompanied by more scratching sounds, being made on the side of the truck. Those things or people that were walking in the fog began to pile into the back of truck. It seemed like they were rushing to get me. But I could not take my eyes off my friend, who was melting in front of me. His veins boiled each time he tilted his head back laughing. His blood poured out. Part of the steering wheel landed on his waist, and instantly, his clothes were engulfed in flames.

Some of James's clothes burned to ash, while other parts just melted into the puddles. The fire was moving up his torso. Flashes crackled every time it burned through his shirt and touched his skin. His blood was so hot that it became an enriched type of fuel for the fire. When the smallest amount of blood touched any part of the fire, the fire grew in intensity, so much so that the cloth ceiling liner started to drop bits onto James. They looked like tiny little bombs being dropped on a carpet-bombing run. Over and over, they kept dropping.

The flames worked their way up until his entire torso became a roaring inferno. All of his clothing was gone. Each layer of skin was slowly removed. It looked like the fire was skinning James one layer at a time. First, his outer layer was removed in part with his clothes, but the rest that remained seemed to slide down his body, revealing the next layer. At first, that layer was a gentle shade of pink, but then it blackened as circles started to move outward until one hole merged with another. That layer seemed to be erased instead of sliding down.

Out of the holes came a layer of muscles. I could make out every line and the differences between muscle and tendon. The tendons in his arm broke and shot off from his muscles like broken rubber bands. Then, one by one, his muscles started to fall off and into the puddle of flesh, blood, bones and the melted parts of the truck. The larger muscles landed with loud splashes.

The heat of the flames was too much for his chest to hold. As soon as James's last muscle, from his neck, landed in the puddle, a loud explosion occurred. His organs had been turned into smooth, polished stones, and rolled out of his chest onto the floor. Those stones landed on the accelerator, and the engine began to scream as it wound up. The flames moved up completely covering his head. I could no longer see any part of his head, and the fire seemed to burn without consuming any more of him. I heard hissing and popping but nothing was allowed to leave the flames.

The humanlike creatures clawed and scratched at everything while they piled over each other trying to get to me. Over and over again, they rocked the truck back and forth until the rear window blew out from either the movements or the heat. I looked back toward the shattered window, and noticed there was no one reaching for me. There was only a group of humans with unshaped, clay-like faces. Each one sat neatly beside each other like they were waiting for something from me or from someone else. One after another, they formed an opening in the clay where a mouth would have been. Screams poured out of their mouth-like holes as soon as they were formed. The screams resembled that of monster-movie dinosaurs calling out to each other. Louder and louder, the screams filled the air until that was all I could hear. My ears felt as if they were inside a drum set while the drummer was enraged by cocaine and determination, and hit the set harder and louder with every strike. Somewhere from within those screams the solid and distant sound of hooves came slowly and steadily.

I thought those hooves stopped, gave up, or went after something else, but I was wrong. The hooved monster had sent its lackeys to find me, and then to signal to it when they had found me. Closer and closer it came. Initially, it sounded like a small horse, but very quickly I realized that I was wrong, and by the depth each hoof made when it landed on the ground, I could tell that that thing coming at me was extremely large. Soon its sound began to be more like a car that needed a new tailpipe, then it mutated into an American motorcycle that prides itself on being loud. Within moments, the noise picked up and began to sound more like that of a locomotive plowing uncontrollably down the line.

James continued to laugh at a feverish pace, even though he was little more than a skeleton with a pair of bulging eyeballs. Rocking back and forth, he reminded me of the sadistic crypt keeper from *Tales of the Crypt*. The scuffs of the hooves dug with bass tones within my ears as they tried to stop the behemoth. Chains from the hooved monster lashed out in violence, as they too were stopped along with the thing's momentum. The chains wanted to let their master know that they did not approve, but there was no stopping the torment that awaited me.

The monster's lackeys moved like bugs avoiding a swatting hand as it made its way to the rear of the truck. With a powerful, raging hand, the monster plunged its claws deep into the rear quarter panel, and slowly moved forward. It walked with such skill and patience, making sure to draw every ounce of fear and anxiety out of me before finally facing me. I felt like I was watching a horror movie and waiting in the dark at the point when the music just stops, and the character is just about to open the door even though the character knows that that is where the Devil himself is waiting to take hold of him. Then a breath is taken, and everyone thinks it's all over, only to have the monster jump out from the corner of the room.

I didn't fear the claws that were ripping the truck apart because I did not yet feel anything from that place. It was the monster's eyes that I feared. What would those eyes that might have looked upon God look like? With one more step, I could smell the ripping of the metal as it was torn apart.

"It's the eyes."

I heard chanting from the mouths of those humanlike beings that were piled in the back of the truck. It was coming from the holes that were made in their clay faces. I didn't have to guess what it meant, because I knew somehow that I would be looking into his eyes. With just one look, almost like Medusa, my face would turn into clay.

It clawed over the tire, and with every step, it seemed that it was getting harder for the beast to get to me. The truck was rocking with more force than I had ever felt. It was like I was about to be thrown completely out of it. I could hear his hooves stop by the rear of my door, and as I peeked out at the mirror to see if I could see anything, all I saw was the fog and smoke growing thicker by the second. The monster's breath penetrated through the busted rear window and even through the window of the closed door next to me, and it smelled of stale death.

"It is not clay. They are denied any expression," it said in a voice that touched the depths of fear that I didn't know existed.

147

For some reason, I reached up and locked my door.

"Ha ha!" he laughed as three razor-sharp claws shot through the middle of my door far enough to cut all the way through me, but I still felt nothing.

With a tug, the door was ripped off, and I was staring face to face at a weathered-looking, 70-year-old man standing outside my door. The eyes of the beast I feared to look at were nowhere to be found. The heat, fog and clay-faced humans were all gone. I was back in the parking lot. I screamed, jumped, and plunged back into my seat just as James was about to get out of the truck.

"Ah!" the old man laughed as he walked away from the truck and headed toward the diner.

Some of his friends were with him, and they were laughing too. Some of them even resembled those human lackeys that were without faces in whatever hell I had just left.

"Devin, whatever you are on, you need to share it," James said as he pushed me off him and back into my seat. "I'm hungry. You look like it would do you some good to eat too," James said.

He shut the door and walked in.

Feeling finally returned to my body and it seemed like color came back to my face, but I couldn't shake the fear that there really was something way off with that place. Time changed again; it was then almost 3 in the morning. Semitrucks lined the lot everywhere, but so did other cars. The diner was encased in a thick fog that had the same taste as I experienced only moments before. Everything seemed and felt very ritualistic, from the appearance of the people that were there to what they were wearing. I would have thought that the bulk of people there at that time of day would have been people trying to sober up before heading home or people that were working in the establishments that aided in the consumption of alcohol throughout the night; not the almost Halloween-like atmosphere that we walked into.

There were eyes all over. All around the parking lot, there seemed to be a stalker-like fixation with us. But James somehow seemed completely oblivious to it. He seemed to be drawn to the people like the sailors of old and the call of the Sirens. I alone seemed to be aware of it; Odysseus similarly was alone in hearing the song of the Sirens.

Dread filled me as I reached for the truck's door handle. I hoped there was a way to postpone the walk or even the first step. With some force that was not mine, the door to the truck flew open easily. I was standing before I could feel the gravel beneath my shoes. I wasn't numb anymore, but my movements happened so quickly and without thought. The ability to feel was overwhelmed by the simple act that it happened in the first place.

I felt naked; exposed to the world all around me, as I stood there outside in physical form in front of all the hiding shadows, flickering lights and the hungry moon. There was nothing to crawl behind or blend into, as I stood in an open parking lot waiting for the next thing to happen. The few lights that lit up the foggy parking lot somehow cut a hole to expose the uncertainty that radiated from inside me. There were eyes everywhere, and the light seemed to reveal the breath of thousands of the dead and dying hiding in the shadows and watching us. They seemed to be breathing in rhythm all around me, and even though every bone and muscle in my body said, "Run!", I knew there was nowhere I could run to.

With fear and anticipation, I took my first step. The way the gravel gave way to my weak and trembling foot was shameful, but it gave me strength to take the next step. The gravel was well compacted, and there were few large stones. That made my walk to the sidewalk a fairly uneventful one. There were tingles all over my skin, made up of chills running up and down my back, because I felt like I was being pulled back to the row of trucks. It was like I was a puppet and only then finding out about it. I was without knowledge of who my master or masters were. Was it the clay-like faces, or was my master the one with the hooves for feet? I knew it could not be the moon, because since the fog slithered in, the moon had retreated from sight. There wasn't even a shadowy outline.

Without sound and with very little grip, it was my right foot lifting me from the world of gravel and nightmares back into the world of men and buildings. James was already at the door waiting for me to enter with him. With one long stride, I plunged into the new reality. He opened the door as soon as my foot was less than its full length off the ground. At first, there was a strong suction of air that helped keep the door closed, but as soon as James broke the seal, the door flew open angrily like a vengeful warlord coming home to find his wife in bed with his lifelong friend. The vacuum that had held the door shut began to push air out toward us, blowing our hair wildly and our clothes tightly against our youthful bodies. The air pushed the smells that were lingering toward us like a swarm of mosquitos on a hot July night. Stale and fresh cigarette smells clashed with each other as fresh coffee teased the pot that had been burning and dry for most of the day. Perfume from the wait staff flirted with the smell of old, sweaty men that had been driving all day, but the most overpowering scent was the lingering smell of the charbroiled burgers.

The sound of some wannabe cowboy singing with a forced Southern accent just so he could sell himself as a cowboy played quietly out of the speakers as we crossed the threshold. Violently, the door shut behind us. No one seemed to care, or take any notice. There was a heavy-set waitress in a yellow-and-white, striped dress that ran down a few inches below her knees. The sleeves were about four inches long but were tight at the end and puffy at the shoulder. There were three buttons down from her neck to her chest, and she could choose either to show cleavage or dress on the conservative side. She wore a name tag (Ruth) just above her right breast. Ruth chose to have the top two buttons undone for comfort. She had large breasts, and wearing her dress any other way would have been difficult and uncomfortable.

She was hunched over the counter facing the door as we walked in. She wore very bright blue mascara wildly around her eyes and black-as-death eyeliner to help the blue stand out. Her cheeks reminded me of the dolls little girls would play with. Her lips were red, and it seemed like she was continually putting on more red lipstick throughout the day and night to keep them that color. Ruth's hair was thin and big in the same style the girls had in 1980s rock videos, but the colors were yellow and blue. Her age did not seem to match any of that. She looked tired and worn out. She looked like something I had seen in the eyes of a grandmother, especially the way her skin was in waves of wrinkled-up skin. I figured she was well into her sixties.

I motioned for us to sit at a table close to the door, but James wanted to smoke and he always liked to sit at a booth so he could lean with his back against the wall and put his feet up on his side of the booth. I always wished I could be that confident in my own actions. I was afraid that I would get yelled at or kicked out, but he didn't care. He would always say with a smile, "What's the worst they're going to do — kick us out and give us a free meal?" I didn't look at anything other than the table we were heading to until after we sat down. Once we got there, I took the seat with my back to the outer wall of the building so I could see everything. It was so dark where we were, yet all of the lights were on. I could barely focus enough to see the menu after we sat down.

The diner appeared to be similar to the typical American diner. It was mostly made up of tables for four that were easily pushed together. There were booths and bar-like sitting for singles who didn't want to be looked at or to answer questions as to why they were eating alone. On the walls, there were overview pictures of what might have been that area or of well-known places in the surrounding area. The pictures looked like they had not been cleaned or dusted in some time. The ceiling was similar to those of a school or government building; a metal skeleton with rectangular tiles placed to traverse the gap between the rectangular lights. The color of the tiles looked to have been an off-white color, but from years of cooking food, smoking and neglect, the tiles were more of a greenish-orange color. The floor was made up of 12x12 square tiles that seemed to repeat the order every other line. A mix between gray, white and some sandy colors made up the floor tiles. The tiles held the most fear in them, for there was no hiding with them, and there was no way to know where something or someone was, only that someone was coming.

"Click! Click! Click!" I heard that sound coming from somewhere. I didn't know where exactly it started only that it was pointed toward us. "Click! Click! Click!" It echoed across the room as it plowed through any roadblock that might be in place to stop it. The steadiness of it reminded me of the old trains that the blues players in the South would time their songs to; an immovable, steady rhythm that would hold a beat as long as someone was willing to listen and feel it. "Click! Click! Click!"

Even though I could see the entire diner, I was blinded from almost everything that was in it. It was like I was watching a movie on an old, rerecorded videotape. Bits and pieces of the previous recordings bled through the one I was then watching. I might have been blind to what was really going on, but my other senses were working just fine. I could feel the coolness of the table, the weak and overused seat of the booth and the smoothness of the menu, which at times was difficult to hold. Whispers started to flood my eardrums and I could make out different things from people other than James. Some guy with a thick Georgian accent was talking about a storm that was heading our way the next day and that he was going to head out on a different route to go north to avoid a possible tornado. A guy with a thick New Jersey accent was telling another guy to stop talking about his Jets or they could go outside and settle it like men. Then there was a woman who was sick of men saying they were better drivers than women. She bet them all, saying, "If I can take a fully-loaded truck through the Rockies faster and safer than any of you, you owe me half your rate for two runs." I could hear all of those different conversations and feel the physical aspects of the diner. Was it really happening or were my eyes and ears lying to me?

"Click! Click! Click!" I could almost make out a shape of something moving toward us, but it looked like there was a fuzzy haze to it. The walls seemed to be dripping in the same way as a mirror drips water after a hot and steamy shower. "Click! Click! Click!" The shape swayed back and forth with each step. I began to make out a mushroom-like head bouncing up and down with each of the clicking steps. One moment, it seemed as if I was about to make out who it was, but the next, the person was swallowed in the fuzzy haze which only I could see. The haze was a sickness that was crawling its way to me. It looked similar to a group of zombies trying desperately to get over the last wall to get to the only remaining human brains, fighting each other with such force that most were no longer even recognizable as humans.

"Click! Click! Click!" I could not focus anywhere past our table. I looked at James, and could tell none of that even mattered to him. He was looking and pointing at the menu, saying something about having a bacon-and-egg cheeseburger medium with a large fry and a strawberry shake. "Click! Click! Click!" It was getting closer to us, and I could almost feel the heat from another body pushing closer to us. Even the limited light that permitted my sight was growing darker as a great shadow that has stepped in front of a bonfire on a crisp night in late October.

I felt the darkness close around me, as though it was a new set of clothes that I was told I was wearing. There was a cold, numbing feeling to it that not even my touch with death could relate to. The numbness forced its thoughts onto me, and I almost didn't care if that haze was in fact zombies that were really there to eat us. I would not have stopped them. Even the clicking of the feet no longer mattered to me. I found that I was not listening to it, nor even looking for the mushroom-like head to appear out of the haze.

Without warning or reason, my world was lit up again, and the shadow behind the haze was gone. Left and right, my eyes looked for a reason or destination. Was it in my head or like everything else that day, just another thing to add to a long list of things that went wrong on that night? The haze rebounded and grew thicker than before, as if it was trying to keep me from seeing into it. It was almost like there was a consciousness to the haze and all of the other oddities that were working together to keep me in the dark as to what was really developing. I felt like a defeated rat.

My head lowered, and it almost hit the table, but then that ever-present noise awoke me again. "Click! Click! Click!"

As I looked up and to my right, there was no mushroom head, only the haze. Then, as my head was about to lower, a flash of red no less than two feet from my face revealed a pair of eyes and the shadow that had been hiding in the haze a few seconds earlier.

"What brings you boys out here at such a late hour?" Ruth giggled as she put down two half-sized cups of water for us.

James quickly grabbed the cup and drank. She seemed to have just exploded out of the haze and seemed mostly normal, but the pair of red eyes were still there looking right at me. The eyes were right where her neck was. I wanted nothing more than to look away, but I was too scared to.

"We're just driving through," James said with a smile. "Well, my name is Ruth. What can I get you guys?"

"I'll take the bacon cheeseburger, medium fries and a strawberry shake. How about it, Devin? Remember you are doing the next shift of driving."

The eyes finally went away so I could look Ruth in the face. Something was turning inside my stomach, making me feel nausea instead of hunger, but I knew if I didn't eat, I'd fall asleep while driving, and not eating would make James very worried. So I ordered the same thing, only with a sugar-filled soda instead of a shake. Ruth took our order, and quickly hopped away to hand in our order. The haze seemed like it was being vacuumed into her back as she walked away.

"I don't know about you, but I am going to rest my eyes a bit as we wait for our food," James told me as he leaned his back against the wall and closed his eyes.

I always was jealous of how quickly he was able to fall asleep. I never could; it always seemed like my mind would never stop at night. I got up and decided to go to the bathroom, and I was amazed at how much it felt like I was walking out of my body. My feet did not make a single sound as they hit the ground, and I was wearing motorcycle riding boots that had a hard sole to them. The two chains attaching my wallet and pants somehow did not rattle or clang together as they always did. Even my breathing somehow seemed to have been stopped. The feeling was very similar to the feeling I would get right before fainting.

I heard and felt vibrating noise circling all around me. It resembled one of those moments when the world stopped. As dark and steady as a raven, the noise kept coming round and round. I could feel the spin within my eyes, and I could almost see the walls, corners, tables, chairs and people blending into one. The vibration began to sound and feel like the close but faintly-off tuning of a distorted electric guitar after a long, bluesy, string-bending solo. The vibration waves hit me in the chest with such a force it was unnatural. That caused me to stumble a little bit, but no one even noticed that my angle had changed, or they chose not to notice. The circling part of the vibration kept creeping closer to me. I knew that the vibration that hit me in the chest was there only to stall me until the one circling me could grab hold of it.

The taste of metal started to build in the back of my mouth. Initially, I was able to hold back the saliva in my mouth, but I was afraid that I was not going to be able to hold out from vomiting for very long. I could almost feel a single droplet beginning to split my lips and break free. The spiraling vibration was so close to me that I could feel the whirlwind of its cyclone twisting with a single purpose toward my right temple. While the force of the untoned vibration was pounding me in the chest through to my backbone, somehow the single droplet was able to break free and fall to the ground without the power or waves of the vibrations affecting its path.

Tunnel vision started to grip me as I got closer to the door of the bathroom. All I could do was hope that I could make it to the bathroom. Then I would be able to sit down and not make a scene, but if I passed out before then, it would make a big scene. At first, my tunnel vision was not so bad — only the outermost parts of my vision were of a grayish tint — but after a few waves of the vibrations hit me, the gray ends of my tunnel vision faded into black, and with every vibration after that, my field of vision shrank just a little. It followed the same pattern each time. The first was a gray shade. It was followed by blackness. Then my vision shrank by the same amount. As my field of vision got smaller, the decaying sight seemed to speed up.

With the little sight I had left, I could see that I had made it to the bathroom door. In my mind, I thanked God as I raised my heavy, half-dead hands to the door in more of a dreamlike motion than one of real physicality. They didn't even look like my arms. My hands, arms and fingers looked like a character in a first-person video game. I half expected to fall through the door, but with a gentle push, the door opened.

15

Nine months before Victoria was born

Jacob found peace in knowing that it might be his death. He closed his eyes, and heard a piece of music being played on a piano that was somewhat out of tune. It played a song of poetry that seemed like it was written solely for his ears to hear. Deep and slow, the notes passed as time began to become something that no longer mattered to him. His failings and successes became nothing; none of that mattered anymore as he felt the touch of that calling. A single tear formed in his left eye as his eyes blinked hopefully for the last time, and he could then hear and feel his eyelashes crack and break as they opened and stayed open. The tear sounded like an uneven ball of ice bouncing across a frosted field in the middle of nowhere.

Death was freezing him before he was even able to touch the edge of the hole. It seemed to bring an intense love affair to the dying process. The slow, lingering process was for death's pleasure, and it was what fueled death's fantasies. The person dying was its lover, and once that door has been opened and death has made his claim, there could be no stopping it.

Even as Jacob's tear ran down his cheek, the clock in the basement was then a motionless statue. The steady ticking that never seemed to stop was no longer echoing along the dark corners of his basement. He thought to himself that he would never again have to worry about or see that or any other clock again.

The cold started to sink into his skin and into his veins. At first, his pitiful flesh wanted to run and fight for life, but he knew better. The pull was too strong; like a starved vampire, who needed the blood of a human, it was too strong. His blood was slowing, and his death was quickening. He didn't think he could wait much longer for the kiss of death to touch his frozen lips, but he knew that the pleasure of his birth into the afterlife would be more fulfilling than anything he had ever experienced in life. The music in his head was shaking his soul and begging for his hand.

Jacob wished he had the power to reach out his hand into the void and pull out some heat to force his heart to explode and trap him in that state. But he knew that none of that really mattered at that point, because this was his death. In some way, he felt as though he was then making love to it, and in that moment, all bounds that time held over him were gone. If it ended up not being the touch of death making its way to give the kiss of death to him, and he would blink and be back on that stairs, Jacob knew he would be lost. He could feel how desperately he would mourn the music of the dead. It pained him to know that there was no way he could live another day without hearing that beautiful song again. The touch of his wife would not come close, and his dreams would only leave him empty, dry and without any true answer for what he wanted or craved. He would then feel like a man who wanted to kill but could not because of the laws he was forced to live by. It would be better for him if death took him then, freeing him from that torment.

Even as his blood thickened and began to stop, the cold was able to pass through him like an exploding volcano. The skin on his fingers kissed the cold even before they knew what it was. They reached and were met with the cold embrace that only true lovers knew. His fingers held onto the cold, knowing that even if they broke and bled, they wouldn't stop reaching, because the desire to be held in the embrace of the cold edge was more sincere than any he had ever known. Why must life be lived if death is the only way to free the spirit to live, and to know and feel real love? Jacob felt a deep sadness for those still alive who couldn't feel it, nor hear the song.

The music sang again with a gentle, bass line that hugged Jacob with a strength that the giant anacondas of South America could not even compare to. The music sang for him, and it was written upon his soul. He believed that the sound was there to ease his soul while being born into death's abode. No more living in the shadows or hiding behind fake smiles of pain so that questions about how he felt were no longer asked. Whether with his eyes or body language or words, the questions became a way of life that was not his. They were really only lies.

"Sing, you beautiful song," he kept saying to himself, because with the passing of every note, he hoped it would be harder for him to come back.

There was a small change in the song as the music switched from a piano to the sound of bells chiming one at a time. It was almost like the sound of marching soldiers that echoed as they walked up to a resting, flag-draped coffin.

His body was not yet completely gone, but it had already fallen too far over the cliff into death's gentle arms to bring it back. But the bells' song clung to his life with each different tone and note made by holding every note as long as possible. In this new dimension, there were different rules dictating how long a single note could be held in the ringing of a bell. Right at the moment when a note was about to fade into nothing, a different note was born with the same magic that is reserved for the creation of life, and then that new note built an entire lifetime of its own until the moment of fading away began. That note would cease, but the cycle would renew itself over and over with every new note played.

Behind the bells, the rising and falling of a chord progression sang out. The pure beauty that held him then also continued calling to him, trying to rip his soul free. All the while, his flesh was mourning the life he had chosen to leave. The song became a drug more powerful then heroin, cigarettes, alcohol, gambling or any of the other addictions that the flesh locked onto.

The cold that grabbed him held him with a love and need he never knew existed. It was in itself more powerful than all of the pain he had ever felt. With only one touch of the cold, all the other pains were gone. He wanted the cold to be everywhere, inside and outside of him, but he also didn't want to miss one moment of the precious time as it was slowly taking him. He somehow knew that it would only last until his transformation was complete and he was delivered to his eternity.

His fingers began to curve slightly as the cold sank deeper through his skin and muscle, beginning to freeze him solid like the giant glaciers of the Arctic and Antarctic. Every nerve ending flickered when the cold finally reached his bones. With each flicker, shivers shot through Jacob's body, hammering him like a fist of iron; it was slamming through his chest into his heart.

Intrigued by the hole and with no immediate threat from the hole, he decided to listen once again for the laughing. The void, though, was just that — empty. As his gaze looked into the hole, everything else seemed to become numb and distant. He could still hear the music, but it sounded hollow. It was too far away to make out the birth and death of each note. They all seemed to blend together. Even the iron fist that was trying to break through his chest seemed to be nothing more than a dead thump.

His gaze passed the icy cold exterior of the hole. His hands were still a few millimeters away from the edge. The heat of the hole didn't affect his gaze, and in many ways, the heat seemed to pull his gaze in further. His eyes began to play games with what he might be able to see. At one moment, he thought he saw a man moving through it as if he were swimming. But there were no specific features to describe the silhouette. There was only the form of a man that was recognizable. Then the person morphed into a distorted, liquefied figure. A moment later, the figure that was once the silhouette of a man was nothing more than a memory of what might have been.

Those games his eyes were playing were nothing new. He had had the same experiences when he was looking out the bedroom window late at night. He never took his eyes off the window, because he felt someone or something was standing only a foot away from the window staring at him. That person or thing was standing just out of the light in the shadows. It stood as still as a stone sculpture.

Some days, he could make out a single eye or a pair of green eyes blinking into view, but then as quickly as they came, they were gone. Frozen, he would just stand there watching and waiting until that moment when they would break through the glass. He sat there until someone else got home. He wouldn't even move to go to the bathroom. A few times he could no longer hold it. He would walk to the bathroom quickly while talking to himself so as to show whatever was haunting him that he was not afraid. He always expected to find whatever it was standing in the room when he returned.

Deeper and deeper, Jacob stared into the void with the same intensity, fear and curiosity he had on all of those other occasions. The desire to scream and taunt whatever it was that was hiding began to build. He was sick of waiting. He only wanted to see what was haunting him. A scream gushed out from the unshaped depths of the void. It burned him, leaving him deaf, for what may have been only parts of a second, but his sense of time was gone, and there was no real way of knowing how much time had passed.

Did anyone know that he was gone? Those he passed by on the street smiled gladly or angrily at those he waved at, those he flipped off with road rage and all of the ones he got the courage to ask on a date, only to be rejected — were they all gone? Was he still in that second when death began to reach out to him?

Even as the fire and heat from the scream continued to eat away and burn into his still freezing flesh, he thought about his angel sleeping two floors above him. He wondered if the music, peace, love and desire to be needed with such passion would take her and consume her as it did him. He knew that it was far greater than any one person. He also knew that it was death. He wanted her to have it and to be consumed by the same passion that was taking him.

The scream continued to ring out, but as it became less important to him, the sound melted nakedly into a vibration. Only when his thoughts turned back toward the scream could the loud, glass-shattering scream once again climb like an army of tiny mountain climbers into his ears, driving hundreds of spikes into his head. It was all in the hope of crushing it so that rivers of blood could run like the waters of the Great Flood of Noah out of his ears. Then, as quickly as they were there, the tiny climbers retreated with the same speed as if they were in the path of an avalanche that was approaching.

Soon he forgot about the hole all together, and just like the scream, the hole disappeared. He knew it was there, but Death's desires for him were all that mattered at that moment. He knew the scythe that was clapped tightly in those bony fingers would come. The unknowing of how or when faded as well.

16

Continuing to tell Victoria my story

The aroma of urinal cakes, urine, cleaning chemicals and air fresheners flooded my nose, overwhelming my taste buds. The smell was so strong it forced the blackness out of my eyes and into the vibrating waves that gave the blackness its birth. The pungent taste caused the moisture in my mouth to explode into vomit, but I was somehow able to sit right inside the door with my back against the wall and calm down.

The cool, damp floor and wall helped reset my body temperature as I tried to regain my composure. The floor was made up of evenly-spaced, grayish-light-blue tiles, four-inch squares separated evenly on all sides. The separation looked almost too perfect to have been done by a human and too perfect to be wasted on the floor of a dirty, damp diner bathroom. The light colors within the tiles reflected the fluorescent light. The flickering of it made the little bit of light feel more of a tease than a gift.

My hands quickly found and traced the mortar that made up the separation between the tiles. It was cold and damp, and at some spots, droplets of water had gathered on it. Maybe the water came from a day of condensation or from people washing their hands and the water dropping to the floor or maybe from the sweat from my arm. Somehow, within my finger movements, I could feel the coarseness of the mortar. Some of the dirt, oil and possibly even the mortar itself broke off, and tried to cling to me, just as a young child would cling to its father when standing before something that would cause harm.

I thought the bathroom was just a single toilet and sink, but I was very surprised that there were two full-sized urinals, a stall and a decent sink with a paper-towel dispenser and a soap dispenser on the wall. The urinals and the stall were on my right side, and the sink was on my left. The sink only took up a small portion of the wall, and then another wall came out to meet the countertop by the sink. The limited lighting that was in the room was blocked by the small wall that came out only as far as the countertop and left the far corner in the shadow. It was almost completely black in that cubby hole. There was no way for me to see into the shadows cast by the flickering light above unless I decided to venture into it.

Still feeling the dampness and cold floor, and with the safety of the wall behind me, I tried to regain the courage to stand up.

"OK. Here I go," I told myself, as I tried to push back and up, but with no success. "One, two, three," I grunted, while finally getting up off my butt and onto my hands and knees.

I tried to get up too fast, and those vibrations started to come back at me again. It was then, though, more like they were knocking on the door to the bathroom, trying to get in. I then had more control. After a few deep and slow breaths, the vibrations that were knocking had gone. Even the dizziness that brought me to be seated on a dirty bathroom floor was swept away.

My face was then a few feet closer to the shadow the wall created, and yet even in those smaller quarters and with my angle and line of sight changing, for some unknown reason, the shadow to the cubby hole never changed. If anything, the shadow was then greater than it was before. For the faintest moment, the tiniest bit of light, somehow surviving within the blanket of shadows, revealed something to me. I thought I saw something that was in there, only momentarily though, but then quicker than the click that turns the light on, the thing that emerged from the shadows vanished. It was visible long enough for me to see it out of the corner of my eye. The disappearing act left me wondering if it was really there to begin with or if it was merely my imagination playing games with me. All the while, there was enough fear within my subconscious to prevent me from exploring the depths of the blackness in that far corner again. I wanted nothing more than to turn my back on it and walk out of the bathroom. With the fear inside me, I wanted to leave the bathroom in such a rush that could result in me peeing all over myself. The fear didn't care if I urinated all over myself, making a huge scene. It was that fear that made it so that I couldn't stop looking away from the black hole that was dug in that portion of the diner. Maybe, it was some magical portal that led to another world and to the other side of the universe. Was it the door to Hell leading to the Devil and his minions?

The flash that revealed it to me was gone. Could it be that there was just a person hiding in the blacked-out portion of the hole, sitting in the dark, waiting until someone walked up to him? In the manner of a crazed man, he would lash out, striking terror and inflicting injuries or even death on that unaware person.

Somewhere, hidden below my own ever-increasing heartbeat, I could almost make out some sort of voice. But every time I held my breath to listen more intensely to the sound, all I could hear was the all-too-familiar ringing in my ears. In protest, I clumsily pushed myself up. I was amazed at how loud it was, yet I could still hear, just underneath my own sounds, the sound of another, but there was no direction or any real defining words or sounds. It was just like trying to listen to a single voice that was mixed with a roaring crowd. I knew it was there, and I also knew it was coming from that black hole, but there was no way I was going to walk into that shadow to see what was there.

I turned my back to the shadow, hoping that its grip over me would dissolve into the blackness rather than pursuing me any longer. The eyes of the shadow found its way into my soul as tingles and goose bumps which shivered throughout my entire spine in an uncontrollable wave of anger, rage and fear. With each step toward the urinal, I could feel the eyes of whatever was in there peering through me and into my soul. The quicker I could be finished, wash my hands, and leave the bathroom, the better.

Knowing that someone or something was watching and waiting for me made the process a little more difficult. But I was able to finish, turn around and start to walk to the sink. I didn't even wait to buckle and zip my pants before I turned around. Initially, I did not want to make eye contact with the shadowy corner of the room. I wanted whatever was in there or whatever the shadow was to know that it was not that important to me, and that with everything it did, I was unaffected. But the child in me could not resist a quick glance toward that darkness. The shadow seemed to grow; grow the way an unchecked weed does in a garden, but this was only moments, not weeks or months. I could feel myself being pulled into it like some sort of prey for the predatory shadow. Step after step, my direction was being turned away from the sink and reality to whatever the darkness was. Even as my feet started to make the first transition from tile to the decaying shadows, my footsteps went from a solid foundation to the charred ground that was in the shadow.

The crazed laugh of a shriveled, skinny, old man echoed loudly to my left. He looked to be more dead than alive, as the skin that hung from his body seemed to be pulling itself off at an alarming rate. The hair he had left was thin, broken and unkempt. Parts of his flesh seemed to be rotten, having already begun to decay. When he laughed, the smell of death escaped from him, and the foul stench of it forced me out of the shadowy corner. As soon as my feet stepped off the burnt floor, the old man just smiled and disappeared. The shadow was then swallowed up into the corner of the bathroom.

Without thought or knowing how, I managed to wash my hands and dried them. I made it back without any thought of what had just happened. The shock of it seemed to have numbed my thoughts, and it allowed me to be as empty as that shadow was.

Pleasing aromas of burgers, French fries and the different condiments helped to reshape the numbness that locked my mind from what had just occurred. In spite of what happened in the bathroom, my thoughts returned to the food that was there when I got back. James was by then forcing food into his mouth. His way of eating closely resembled that of a starved group of great white sharks. His lust for food looked uncontrolled. On the other hand, my way was more reserved. My goal was to get through it, rather than enjoy it. Food always seemed to be something I was forced to have, and my enjoyment of it was little to none. I took my time in dividing up my plate so that I could place enough ketchup in a puddle to cover my fries without having to reach for the ketchup again. The only thing I disliked more than eating was having to do something related to eating more than once. I made sure that my burger was a safe distance away from the puddle of ketchup for my fries. I always added more salt to the ketchup. After I was done with the construction of that puddle, I would pull the top of my burger off, and drown it with ketchup, because I knew they would not have put enough on it in the kitchen.

James was already halfway through his burger before I even replaced the top, and he just smiled a closed-mouth grin. His fries were just covered in ketchup. There was no puddle to dip them in, and if he added any salt, it was to the fries as a whole, not to the ketchup. As I watched him eat so carelessly, I was taken aback by how differently two friends could eat almost the same food. Between bites of his burger, he would shove multiple fries in at an alarming rate. It almost seemed as though he was either in an eating competition or he was trying to have a heart attack right there. By the time James was done with his burger, I had only taken two bites out of mine, and they were the two hardest bites I have ever taken on a burger. The meat was dry and hard. It almost seemed like someone was trying to make jerky out of it, rather than a burger. All of the ketchup I poured over it did nothing but make the bun slip over the lettuce. It almost caused the meat to fall out. Every piece of meat that I tried to eat seemed to crack my teeth. I constantly pulled out large bits of it after every few chews. After those two bites of my burger, I decided that was enough, and to stick with my fries. The fries tasted like the fish fry that that place must have had two days earlier, and even the ketchup couldn't block out the taste of old fish. I started to feel like I was going to throw up, but then I remembered that I had ordered a chocolate shake. I was nervous about how that was going to taste. James finished his, and seemed to have liked it, but he seemed to have liked everything so far.

Sometime while I was eyeing what I should try or not try, James told me he was getting up to go to the bathroom. Before I knew it, he was out of sight. I felt the air I was breathing turn to ice, but the air that touched my skin was boiling. Every exhalation turned to vapor. I just wondered what temperature the air that escaped from my lungs was after it mixed with the air around me.

The fog that once encased the diner returned, trapping me at the booth, but this time, it was alive. The fog had hundreds of little arms and hands reaching out to me, trying to dig their way into me. That anchored me to the seat. I felt them pulling at my clothes, ripping and tearing little pieces away. It felt as though I was a little child trying to run away, but like that child locked in its room, there was no corner I could hide in from an enemy within the fog. Voices from within the fog were all around. Some of them seemed to be held in it. It seemed as if the loudest voices were determined to force me to stay. Those voices seemed to be getting stronger, and they began to wrap themselves around me. In some way, they seemed to co-ordinate their actions with those of the fog. A single voice stood out from all of the others. With that voice, a reddish glow emanated from the other side of a wall. The glow pulsated through the wall, as though the color was the bit of a jackhammer and the being behind it was the air powering it. I sat watching the battle of wills between that of rock, wood, steel and mortar and the will of the would-be king or ruler of the pit of Hell, but it was not actually Hell lashing out upon the real world. It had no actual dominion over it; at least, not yet.

The fog that encased me and the diner brought a mystic or an occult-like feel to what was happening. The fog held my sight, and in some way, it held my ability to hear lower than what I would normally be able to hear. The closest feeling to that that I'd ever felt was when I was hit too hard on the head, and I could not hear, see, talk, or even think straight. Everything was distorted and vague. If I had to run, I knew there was no way I could even walk straight without falling over. I felt completely helpless. I started to slip and fall into the corner of my seat, pulling my legs and feet up to my chest.

Once more, I felt like I had failed my friend, who would have done anything for me, yet when he needed me, I was immobilized by the fear of the thing that was causing those things to happen. I only hoped that those events were not actually real and that I would wake up to realize that that was only a possibility of what might occur or that it was something that I could prevent.

I knew that there was something different there, though. Maybe it was because of the paralyzing effect or the blinding and deafening effect that was taking its toll on me. Before, I seemed to be only an observer of most of the events that night, rather than an active participant to the horrors that were happening to us, even though some of the events were very real. My hearing was muffled so that everything spoken sounded as if it was under water, but I was standing above the water. The sounds of movements were easily discerned, but all other noises seemed to morph into one.

I wanted to be elsewhere in some beautiful scene of an artist's imagination, but instead, I was here balled up in the corner of my seat, hoping against hope that the fog would simply bring the cold grip of death finally to me. I wanted out of the on-again, off-again mental trip that I had been riding for more hours in a single night than there seemed to be in a month.

"Please just take me!" Those were the only words that I could conceive.

Hope finally found a way to fade away, dissolving into that type of decay that is left for the lonely road of suicide. I wondered if, right there, I could grip the cold bitterness that death had blessed me with; if I could leap with both feet, and leave within death's loving arms, while my life drained into a puddle of warm blood on that diner table. Hidden within the fog, hundreds of tiny hands would then pull at my lifeless body in the hope of pulling my soul back to it.

Could I take that step that couldn't be undone, or could I let this notion rooted deeply in the Catholic Church stop me while death was singing its poetic song of angels to me? I could feel the tip of a blade placed on my wrist. Initially, I pictured the razor-sharp tip passing through my skin with ease. A drop or two of blood was shed with that first poke. I closed my eyes, and the metal from the blade somehow passed its taste into my mouth, and I could taste the metal tinged with my blood. I was in no rush, so I slowly pushed down on the blade. At first, it hurt, but then the pain was washed away by excitement. All of my pain and memories seemed to slip further away each time I pushed the blade further into my wrist. My blood flooded out of me, taking my pain with it, and flowed onto the table. I wanted to feel death's cold grip again. I wanted the taste of frostbite to be blended with the metallic taste from the knife.

My moment of sheer suicidal depression and fantasy was halted by fear. It was fear of life, not death. Somewhere, deep within the fog, I was able to see clearly. There were shapes of people starting to step forward and stopping. Some of them were the size of children, and some were tall, but even though they were only dark shapes, I saw their real size. The fog's refusal to hide the sizes and shapes of the people from me showed that there was a consciousness to the fog. One by one, the eyes of each of the figures started to shine with the glow, like those of a dog at night when moonlight shines on them. The sound of breaking twigs and thick branches echoed as ominously as the shapes of the bodies that had begun to change. The change seemed to push their bodies away from being human. Those changes were done in order to frighten me, changing them into some grotesque warped version of a human. The taller ones seemed to grow taller but also thinner. They stretched upward until they reached the point at which their massive bodies were too flimsy for their outstretched muscles, and began to bend forward toward me. Their overstretched arms twisted and turned into a second set of legs. They looked as close to a spider that something with only four legs could get. Their heads flattened out along the top to complete the spider look. The child-sized figures were stretched out into a diamond shape. Their arms were made longer, and their heads were stretched to almost three times their length. Their arms were stretched further than those of the taller ones, however the full length of those arms was unmeasurable, as was the strength of their arms. I was sure that each being was a creature from whatever level of Hell I was then in. Even with their bodies being stretched, I was aware that they were stronger than any creature I had ever seen.

The tiny hands that were made up from the fog started to push me toward those creatures. A new level of fear was implanted in my heart. The fear paralyzed me. I was unable to move or stop the pushing of those sinister hands, but I was unable to look away from those creatures down the hall. Their hands pushed me out of my seat to my feet. There was simply no stopping the parade. I was pushed and pulled across the tile floor. The pace was slow enough that I was able to feel the tiny spaces between each tile when my shoes crossed over from one to another. I wanted to reach out and grab something — the wall, a table, the booth — just to stop my sliding, but I couldn't move. It seemed as if I was the dinner for those monstrous shapes.

Closer and closer I got. I was almost halfway to them, but other than their shape, sizes and glowing eyes, I couldn't make out any other features. Somehow, even with them some 30 feet in front of me, I could feel the warmth of their breath tickling my naked neck. I could also taste the stench of their rotten teeth, as though they were whispering in my ear. The breath of those creatures seemed to wrap around the back of my neck before I inhaled their rotten breath. I pictured their hearts beating upon my back. Their arms were a vice crushing me tighter and tighter.

Spiders came everywhere in my mind. I felt them crawling up my clothes, moving between the little bit of hair that still managed to grow on my body. I could feel their feet scraping my skin as they slid one foot across my skin in an attempt to rip it just a bit with razor-like claws in place of their feet. The spider breath seemed to burn my skin with the venom that was in the sacs behind their long and hollow fangs. It was as if they were softening my skin with the fire from their burning breath so that when it was time to consume my pale skin, they could take their time to enjoy it. Through flashes, I witnessed their poison coursing through me. Each of those tiny, black spiders walked in a circle over and over, continually breathing fire-like balls. When the circles were finally weakened, due to heat and fire melting my skin, those spiders took their place digging into my flesh, much like a tick does in order to consume blood.

My flesh welcomed them, as though it was a hot roll on the dinner table and their razor-like feet were the butter knives. They anchored their legs into me after they found the precise spot that would inflict the most pain, and slowly and delicately, with each razor, they pierced my skin. I was amazed at how little the skin bent before it submitted to the spiders, thus allowing them to torment me. The venom of those shadowy spiders seemed to be attempting to change me into one of them. I looked down, wondering what it was that was being placed inside me.

The big, spider-like creature down the hall gave a high-pitched, clicking laugh to let me know that it was just playing games with my mind, and that nothing was really being poured into me. How could I trust that thing? It seemed to be crawling all over me, even though it was 20 or more feet away. Distance didn't matter. Nevertheless, I was in its clutches. I couldn't help wondering if those hands made of fog were actually part of the spider creature, and that its hands had already begun to find ways of gnawing me as they moved up and down my body. In many ways, it disgusted me, yet I found a dark and twisted allure to those hands moving over my body.

Perhaps it was mere fantasy that always made me too afraid to act on my own. Could it be the gothic, romantic horror that always seemed to beckon me since I was young? Normally, I was always able to find a way of living that lifestyle, which was a dark life that lingered with black clothes and dark music while painting my skin white and dyeing my hair jet black, and lived in a lifestyle that appeared to mirror the music of poetic pain topped by a distant, melodic, rock guitar playing in the background.

My eyes bore into the spider-like creature as its arms lunged toward me. Through my mind, it held me before I was even close enough to touch it. I could hear its whispers, and feel the drool from its mouth, as I become its helpless prey. I couldn't help wondering if this was what happened to my friend. Or was he behind the wall where the jackhammer was hitting? I was pushed with more intensity than I remember ever being pushed. I felt unsure if I was a food source, a prize to be won or a lover to be cherished, but none seemed overly appealing to me. I tried to find my footing, but there was nothing; no friction, no corners, no hinge or even a loose tile that could prevent me from reaching those creatures. I wondered if my feet were by then even touching the floor, or if I was being held above the floor, ensuring that I would become the thing's toy. As I was getting closer, more features of those creatures started to come forth. They all looked to be naked and of a darker gray. The color was that of a dead body after an unspecified length of time.

I could feel my heartbeat racing, as I fought with my captors to free myself, but what good was it when the hands made of fog were bringing me those monsters. They appeared to have one of two desires for me. They were either going to eat me or have a love affair with me. I was helpless, completely vulnerable, until I remembered one thing. I don't remember who told me this, but if this was a demon, there were certain rules they had to follow and one of those rules was that God is supreme, and they all must obey.

As a last resort, I screamed out with everything I had, "In the name of Jesus Christ, I command you to leave!"

What held onto me screamed and the fog faded into an imploding fire that started to vacuum up the creatures in the shadows. My feet were somehow standing firmly on the diner floor right where two walls met and formed an L shape. The glow of red grew stronger and more violent. It didn't seem that whatever owned that power was slowed by my statement. I thought maybe it didn't hear me, but then I thought that wasn't it at all. No, it was because whatever was happening in there was because either God allowed it to happen or it was outside of his domain.

17

Nine months before Victoria was born

Like vultures circling above their prey, Jacob could feel the heat of the freshly-used blade circling him. He could not seem to zero in on where the blade was. It was hidden in a shadow in between life and death. The only residue that proved the blade was there was the smell of blood from its last victim. He could taste the sweat, tears, flesh, blood, emptied bowels and whatever else was remaining on the blade. He wondered if it was from multiple victims or if it was the lingering blood from one victim that met its end just before him.

The song changed into a slow song of mourning. In his mind, he could see a day that had no light. The sun was hiding behind a wall of tears, falling like blood onto an ancient battlefield.

The generals cried, "Let no one survive this cursed day."

Drowning the grass and all other vegetation in the sacrifice of human blood, they lusted after the blood, just like they were junkies. Vampires watched in horror from the safety of the forest as the blood they craved mixed with the field to create red mud.

His vision changed to one in which a sea of black umbrellas blanketed a well-manicured lawn, but the sun still refused to shine through the wall of gray that had taken hold of the day. Looking down on the land, he witnessed a few trees sprinkled throughout the land, but there was also a fence, made of trees and metal, that encased the entire land. Large stones of different shapes and sizes littered the ground in a very orderly fashion. Cars lined the small, grid-like streets that broke up the land, and all of the people that were in those cars were already where they were supposed to. Around a collapsible and movable tent-like cover, the sea of umbrellas stood almost as still as the stone that littered the land.

He felt the bass of the voice speaking, but the words were not clear. The only sound he could hear was that of the rain singing the song of broken promises and heartache. The song brought the pain, which was being laid down within the sea of umbrellas, onto him. Like tiny little needles, each droplet that fell bored deeper and deeper into his heart.

Screams from within his own soul fought against the others, like rabid animals trying to break free, but the pain that came with the rain caved in and stopped the arguing voices. All he could do was watch the sea of umbrellas. With each droplet, a new note was heard. With each new note, he felt like he was being hit through the chest by a sledgehammer blow. He hoped and prayed that the next one would be the final one, and that there would be nothing more.

His tears and eyes were then freeze-dried. The tears that he hoped would bleed the rest of his life out were nothing. Even as the blackness of depression exploded upon him from another series of raindrop notes, he sought in his freeze-dried eyes one more tear, but his eyes vanished. He could also feel new notes pushing into his soul. He wanted to reach out and touch the life of another, but there was no one for him to touch. All of the people underneath the umbrellas were out of his reach.

The cold was finally permitted to reach into his heart, but hidden within the raindrop notes, the cold finally got there. Instantly, he became frozen in time. A dark maze of colors blew around everyone and everything in the cemetery below him. He hoped the dark maze was not there to collect his soul. He hoped he was wrong and there was no afterlife, because he was afraid of where his soul was going. All he wanted at that moment was for his light just to go out as easily as flipping a switch. He wanted there just to be nothing; not even the realization that he was wrong.

Cold mixed with fire shot through his back, ripping through his spine and rib cage, until it finally grasped his heart to end his drifting through the cemetery. Whatever that new cold was, it had a newer, darker life of its own. It had its own heart with its own heartbeat that was able to force him to do whatever it pleased. The grip of fire and cold was so painful, yet it wasn't the cold he wished for.

The fire was burning the song that was written for him away. Where did those precious notes that sang to him with an unspoken promise of a love that would consume and become all that he could fathom go? The fire part of the cold seemed to have melted the music away as it ripped through his back, and was holding his heart. There was no song that came with it, no gentle tear or frozen kiss; only a race to claim Jacob's soul. Death then made its claim on him.

"Luther, his body is yours, but Jacob's soul is not."

A steady voice echoed throughout Jacob's new world, as the new cold was pushed out from his body. As soon as that cold went out, death engulfed Jacob's body, and brought him to where he was to spend eternity.

18

Devin's story

"Devin," someone said in a low growl from behind the wall where the kitchen was. "Have you made up your mind and decided on whether or not you are going to come in? You sent away my welcome party, and now I have been told you are not to be harmed. So if you truly have any faith in that which you just said, come on in." The voice growled slowly and confidently as the red glow grew stronger.

The desire to know what happened to James pushed me forward. I walked like a man on a mission up to the old, Western-style saloon doors that separated the kitchen and the rest of the diner, and opened them. The room was lit up by too many candles to count. It seemed that the candles had been burning for several weeks straight, given the long stalactites of hardened wax that hung off whatever the candles were placed on. The edges of tables and counters were littered down the sides by those stalactites. Some of those were greater than four feet in length and close to an inch in thickness. There were candles of various colors, but most of the candles were either black or crimson. Some of the stalactites were a mix of colors. Black wax ran over the top of a thick, well-defined, red stalactite. The black wax didn't take anything away from the red. Instead, it just accented all of the different patterns that the red had already formed. The black wax added depth and shape in the same way shading in a painting does. Where red wax ran into black stalactites, there was an accenting in some places in the same way that red highlights seemed to jump out from someone who has jet-black hair. On the black stalactites where the red wax didn't look like accents, they appeared to be crying blood. The red wax running over the top seemed as though it disappeared until the precise spot further down at which it seemed to come out of black eyes forming nonstop tears.

The flickering lights mixed with the elongated wax lines added to the feeling of some castle hidden in one of the forgotten areas of Europe. Bricks against the wall somehow seemed to grow in stature but also to melt into the bricks that masons years earlier might have used to create those massive castles that are still standing. There was a row of candles that were placed on the edge of a table. I could not see the table, because wrapped around the table were people dressed in what I thought were druid-like cloaks that covered them from head to toe. The light and those figures' shadows only added to the feeling of a castle, because everywhere I looked on the walls, it appeared as if there were knights standing in suits of armor ready to strike anyone who dared to interrupt what was happening.

Perhaps they were only suits of armor. Perhaps also they were the ones who then lived as shadow beings, like wraiths, able to wear armor, and so they stood there ready and willing to step out of their world into the land of the living to strike. With every flicker of the candles, most of the shadows in that transplanted castle galloped and danced as if they were being trained by some of the best choreographers in Hollywood. In contrast, the knights stood fast, each in their assigned place.

The door I flung open was small, but to the flames of the candles, the door seemed to send waves across the transformed kitchen, the way a tsunami does after an earthquake. The flames closest to the door almost seemed to have been knocked over into their puddles of red, black or white wax, yet the knights remained steadfast. They only seemed to move their heads in order to look at the disturbance. The candles that were a little further away were only affected by the breeze from the door after it seemed to bounce off a few other objects before finally reverberating off the secondary flames. The breeze sent them into quite a frenzy. The flames were kissed by the puddles of wax that had been building under the wick. With the subtle hissing of a hidden snake, parts of the flame faded away into a void where even the spirit, angels, demons and shadow figures no longer could go.

The candles' dancing flames were mesmerizing but in an uneven pattern. Their dance seemed to awaken dreams of lust and chaos while dulling the senses with their intoxicating dance. I could feel the hypnotic stare of those burning eyes looking through me, attempting to probe me for any weakness, or feeding off my subconscious without my knowledge.

In many ways, I felt as if I was sitting peacefully at a bonfire with my guitar strumming some chords while someone else sang; with the warmth of the fire kissing my face but leaving my back exposed to the cool and crisp autumn night. The whole kitchen started to darken. Only those hypnotizing flames could be seen. I looked up and the ceiling was no longer there, pulled away right before my eyes looked onto it. Once it was gone, I could barely remember there ever being a ceiling at all. Laughter and old memories flooded my eyes.

In some twisted memory of a memory, I heard a piano softly playing a song. There were no words, and my campfire was also gone. But unlike the ceiling, I could remember the fire. I still reached for it, but I couldn't get it because my arms were pinned to my sides. I could feel parts of the memory fading into those hypnotic flames. As much as I wanted to move and regain memories of the fire, I could not. I couldn't quite remember who was there with me or what music I was playing or when it occurred. I only knew it was a moment that I wished I had back.

Then something new was starting to build up around me, but I couldn't tell where in my memory the dancing flames were looking. I had the feeling that what was being brought before me was a curse, even though it was wrapped in a time of great love. The moment was being buried under so much pain, anger and depression that I did not want to observe it. The thought of touching a love that was perfect was worth reliving, even if it meant that I would have to feel the pain that came with it. But I had to try, even if it meant losing myself to that evil.

All around me faded away. The single light that shone revealed to me a room filled with people dressed for a ball. The light was soft yellow mixed with dark purple. The purple portion of the light let everyone have their own privacy. The yellow light was fixed upon two people dancing as they held each other as tightly as they could. Even though the room was filled with all those people, the only audible sound was of the soft piano being quietly played. All the conversations, singing and dancing seemed muted. Somehow, though, I knew that room and when that all occurred. Holding her was all that I could think of, even though I knew what the outcome was going to be.

My eyes burned as I raced from one face to another, never letting them blink because I was afraid that if I blinked, it would all be taken. I just had to find the one who stole my heart before I met Vic, and look into her youthful eyes once again. Then a hand touched mine, and I knew that it was hers. Everything I wanted was there in my right hand. So I thought that if God took me then, my life would be complete. With a single step, we started walking out toward the center of the room. Everyone else vanished as we were lifted out of the ball and set down in a distant courtyard. A middle-aged man played the song that only moments earlier was all I could hear.

We began dancing, and with each turn, I held her tightly to my chest, and I could feel her heartbeat. But I could not hold her tight enough. It was as though we were melded or formed from the same piece of clay, only when it was placed in the oven, the clay broke, so God held us together. It was always enough simply to hold her, but our lips always seemed to find each other. Every time my lips came close to hers, I trembled in fear and desire. She was the first person to teach me how to love and how to feel loved. Somewhere, within that dance, I found perfection. I had dreamt about us dancing quietly alone to our own music in a courtyard covered with snow, and so there we were.

I knew that somehow that moment would pass, and I would be left alone standing in the diner's kitchen. But I refused to let that moment go. I wanted the pain of that memory. My eyes started to fill with tears as I listened to that song. Then the beauty of it started to weigh heavily on me. I could hear the plea of a brokenhearted lover begging. I almost let it pass. If right then I became a ghost, the song would be my unfinished business, because it was a poem that spoke without a single word being uttered. For a moment, it was as if the only thing that mattered was each other. It felt like we were hovering. I could feel the wind around us speeding up the higher we went. Her shoulder-length hair was intertwining with my hair.

As we rose, the song still did not fade. It grew louder. The song encapsulated us, holding us softly enough so as not to interfere with our dance. But it was hard enough to let us know that we were safe. Finally, we had a moment of peace. I had to stop myself from thinking, because over and over in my mind, I kept wondering if that moment was solely mine. Could she also be living it again? Was she really there with me again? Would she still choose to end it and walk away? I hoped that our years apart would make her realize that she was wrong. It was like a mental loop. Those thoughts kept trying to invade my conscience. I wanted to put my mind at ease and ask her if she was reliving this with me.

But all that I could whisper was "Is it really you?"

She didn't say anything. She slid one of her lace-covered hands free, and led my face so that I was looking into her eyes. I could see that she was reliving it too. The song never ended, as we stared motionless at each other. Our grasp of each other only increased. But we were then not really dancing any longer. I sensed that she was wrestling with the what-if, but I didn't care about that. All that I have wanted was her with me. So I was going to hold onto it as long as I was allowed to.

The song that encapsulated us was somehow able to fade the world around us out. I could feel that the grip it had on us was starting to loosen. I knew that that moment would soon be gone. Part of me wanted to kiss her one last time, but that part was quietened by another part of me that merely wanted to hold her and remain lost in her eyes just one more time.

With a click, we were back on the ground. The garden around us started to come back into view. Snow began falling, and everything seemed to shine just a little brighter. Out of the corner of my eye, I could see the bushes as if it were daytime. Every branch, twig and leaf that sprang outward from all of the interwoven trunks was made visible. There were even some early robins that had already made the bush home. All of the different shapes of the snowflake were easily discerned as they rested on her hair. The mix of her natural hair colors made the snowflakes glitter like diamonds. How could there be such clarity while darkness of night overshadowed this world? Every snowflake that landed on her face seemed to sit unaffected by her body heat for a second or two. Then, very slowly, it turned to water until there was only a tiny droplet of water suspended on her face like tears.

The song drifted out just a little bit more, and with it, her grip on me was weakening. Even though she was still as close to me as always, I knew we were again slipping away from each other. In her eyes, tears held her "Goodbye". Regardless of how badly I wanted to look away, I couldn't. The song started to become harder to hear, and I started to feel nervous like I used to whenever I held her hand. If the song and that moment were the last I had with her, I wanted to be tortured some more. The song continued to fade away, but as it did, the memory brought her face right before me. I almost forgot the emerald shine in her grayish-blue eyes. I almost forgot how helpless and vulnerable I was the first time I fell in love.

I closed my eyes after that, refusing to see anything else, and rubbed the tears away, never letting them fall on their own. After what seemed like a long ten seconds, I finally opened my eyes, and saw that I was back in the kitchen. It still looked like a gothic castle. The hypnotizing lights were faded out. All of the knights seemed to have turned their heads to face me. I didn't recognize any movement of the knights. They always moved when I blinked or when I was blinded by the memories. But they came with a price, and I did not know the weight of that price nor when I would have to bear it.

The people who cast the shadows that made up the knights seemed to be more fluid than their knightly shadows were. The movements of their shadows high upon the wall moved like stone figures, slow and laborious. They seemed as cold as the castle-like shadow that haunted the kitchen. Everything seemed to have grown cold and as stale as the walls of the castle. That moment was almost like some old, forgotten musician who was forced to play his own music in the city park — but only middle-aged people understood it — and those rhymes that didn't speak to anyone else. All of the beauty and life were sucked out of that place. Everyone in the kitchen seemed to be a blend of leftovers all mushed together.

My steps were the only part of the kitchen that appeared to have vitality. One after another, I easily made my way toward the table. As I walked, little changed by way of the candles and their reflection, but every step or so, a candle far off tried once again to entrap me in a looping memory. The nervousness that was building up in my stomach was sickening. It was telling me to take one of those memories and live there for as long as I could. "Wouldn't it be better there than what I was about to find on the table before me?" I felt I waited long enough, and that James deserved better than me running to hide in one of those memories.

I got to the point at which I was only a foot behind the person at the end of the table. Oddly, I could not see the faces of those standing around the table. What was in the center of the table? I kept wondering to myself, even though I was certain that it was James lying on the table with a dark, stained cloth covering his body.

There was still a thick smoke rolling over and engulfing him. It blocked me from being able to see clearly. I saw some movement at the head of the table, but to what extent I couldn't be sure. Chanting in a language I didn't know started to occur, coming from the people that were standing around the table.

The entire room echoed with their sickeningly-repetitive words. I could tell that there were three different octaves, and each of those octaves affected the room differently. The higher ones seemed to send flames into a frolicking dance at first, and then, after a few moments, the flames settled down until those tones sent all of the flames spinning in a counterclockwise, circular motion.

The medium tones attacked the metal shelving and the cooking utensils hanging all over the room. The utensils started falling to the floor, and all of the plates on the shelves started to topple and break. At first, the sudden breaking of the plates startled me, but the medium tone also partially set the knights free to hold me. With a bruising blow to each of my shoulders, I felt the weight of their shadowy world. Both of my shoulders were hit by the different weapons knights used. My left shoulder was hit with the flat side of a sword. My right shoulder took more of an uneven hit. One single point from the handle part of a mace hit me with enough force it should have shattered my shoulder. Oddly, my shoulder didn't break, yet I still felt the same level of pain that I would have felt if it had broken.

The deepest tones cracked the stone, releasing the remaining knights. Tiny pieces of rock exploded out of the wall, mixing with sand and other fine particles, creating sharp dust that sandblasted anything that was within the first few feet of the blast. Those particles seemed to have a shock-wave effect, causing those that were first contacted by the blast to explode, causing multiple mini explosions out in many directions. When brick exploded, the noise raced blindly out to a metal object, bouncing the tones as if they were arguing with each other.

I was somehow shielded from the explosion, however the deafening sound of it made it easy to make out the differences in each phase of the explosion. The room was very dusty, except for a two-foot radius that shielded me, and it did not matter what I did or where I went. If I took a step, the dust moved to include my leg and foot. The same was true for every other part of my body. Even on the floor, the dust from the explosion was nowhere to be seen as long as it was within the two-foot radius around me. It was like the explosion never happened within that radius.

The only part that attacked me already happened there in that kitchen when the two weapons nearly shattered my shoulders. But nothing changed. They seemed as if they were anchors holding me, forcing me to witness all of that. Their weight began to feel like the edge of the sword rather than the flat side, and I thought that at any moment, my arms would be ripped off just by the weight of the sword and mace.

I was being led by the sword someplace, but I couldn't tell where, because the room was still completely encased in that chalky dust. The only part of the room I could clearly see was in my little circle, but that was just enough to make me feel like I was trapped in a whitish coffin. Each breath got hotter. I could feel my body temperature rising, yet I wasn't sweating, so my body couldn't cool down. I craved that first bead of sweat, but just like so many things that night, my thoughts were ended, not by me, but by something enforcing its will on me.

The sword and mace moved me in front of the person standing at the foot of the table. It was Ruth, our waitress. She seemed to be frozen or turned into stone like the other shadows that were on the wall. Perhaps, when the knights were released, her life was given to her shadowy knight. The table looked like a sacrificial altar as if it had been taken from a land far away and from a time before most countries even existed.

I could smell dried blood from the thousands who died for some false god. The heat from the wax that dripped off the black candles that circled the table ran off the candles to kiss the altar beneath them. For some reason, only black candles were used. I wondered if that was because no other color could touch the table without its color being drained like the blood of an innocent being sacrificed.

Whispers filled my ears. They came from the ghosts that were trapped within the altar. They seemed to be everywhere and nowhere all at once, just like a ghost that moved slightly in the corner of a room. In the corner, the ghost would hide from the direct sight of any person that was around. But then, at the right moment, when the person wasn't really looking, it would pounce. Only out of the corner of the person's eye could the movement be seen. The multitudes of voices were in unison.

Every time I tried to focus on one particular voice, it was gone before I was actually able to understand it. It was like I was trying to catch the smoke from a bonfire with a net. The harder I tried to lock onto one voice, the harder it became. So I gave in, and let the voices pummel me like a loser in a prize fight.

The voices began to transform into a blend of emotions that could be heard and felt every time another voice was heard. The depression and loneliness droned in cries that were deep and long. It didn't matter whether it was from a man or women, the voices remained unified. The bitter and angry voices were rapid and always on the move. They reminded me of a very fast guitar solo, like Steve Vai or Joe Satriani, screaming over the top of the depressed voices. The ones that were crazed by being locked in that prison for so long then came in an unpredictable pattern. The scariest and most unpleasant sound they made was when those crazed voices came in at such a low tone that the whole room shook with the rage of an 8.0 magnitude earthquake.

19

Devin's story

On the table, I could only see the candles and their flames because thick, black smoke blanketed whatever was on the table. The smoke itself seemed to appear out of nowhere, and the only purpose of the smoke was to prevent me from seeing what was on the table. I was not blind to what was going on or to the events of that evening. I knew that death's presence was somewhere there, but I wondered if it was going to come back. I could taste the bitterness of blood. I felt the coldness of that empty stare from someone that was bound in the afterlife. From what my senses were telling me, there was a very proud emotion that sang loudly throughout the room. It was an arrogant feeling of victory filling the air with a lustful smile.

The smoke revealed that it wasn't covering up the dead. It was the victory lap of something, but why I was stuck there in between the fabrics of two worlds to see it was beyond me. The smoke grew darker as different shades of black smoke from the candles, started to roll and twist, becoming a swirling upward cloud. They seemed to drink all of the light.

The table started to reveal its true form as the smoke around it settled onto it. It was an ever-moving cloud that seemed as if it was rolling off the edges of the table, the only parts that remained untouched by the settling cloud. But the candles never stopped emitting more smoke feeding the cloud.

I was only a few inches away from the table, and I was finally able to get a good look at it. I was also close enough to feel there was a cold, damp moistness coming from the sides. There were also smells emitting from it. Within those smells, I could taste the bitterness of clay. I could also feel my skin becoming drier like when I played or worked in the dirt. With all my might, I wanted to reach out and see if it was a table or not, but I was forced to forget those thoughts by something that was mirroring my movements on the other side of the table just past the smoke cloud. I could not see it clearly, but I knew it could see me.

Every few seconds, I thought I was going crazy and that it was all in my mind. There were two oval flashes of red looking right at me. In the center of the red ovals were two perfectly-shaped, black circles that never seemed to move their gaze away from me. If the wind in the room blew a candle's flame, a reflecting glow shone on those ovals. Like a hungry dog, those eyes were locked onto me. Only the height of the eyes made me think it was not a dog but a werewolf.

I pictured myself standing alone at the altar of some heathen god from a hidden corner of the world during the Dark Ages. It was definitely a blood sacrifice to bring forth the creature that was portraying itself as a god. With the atmosphere of the room, it had to be a destructive god, demon or evil being. From its eyes, I could see that there was no rushing it. The creature was old. It waited on the other side of the earthen altar until the time was right to take what it needed without any hesitation. The eye movement reminded me of a predator waiting in the bushes for its prey to come close enough that it almost ran right into the creature's claws. The creature was looking at me with those same killer eyes. There was only the rectangular altar separating us. The table was maybe ten feet by four feet wide and just less than three feet high.

It was perhaps my fear or intuition, but I had the feeling that the wannabe god could see all of me. The creature easily changed spots. When the light reflected onto that area, somehow, just like a possessed doll, it had moved when shadows blocked me from being able to see it. Its eyes were somewhere else, but still looking at me. I couldn't help but wonder if the creature had some god-like qualities because it was able to control the lighting and reflecting when it wanted.

Oddly, there was seldom any noise during the whole time. In fact, it felt as if a glass had been placed over my entire body to block out sound and movement. I had a feeling that I would often get in a shower when washing my hair. While in my shower, my eyes would be closed, but I always feared the moment that I had to open them. Often, I would rush washing my hair and face to lessen the time my eyes were closed. I could see the monster in my mind that was waiting in the shower for me to open my eyes. Its hair would be long and knotted. It was either dark brown or light black, and there were sprinklings of red throughout it. His hair and face appeared to be wet from the spray that bounced off me as I washed completely unaware of him standing there. Most of the moisture on him was from sweat or from whatever else he had just killed.

He was not human. He was a mix of different monsters blended into one. His face had patches of hair. Down the sides of his face where sideburns would have been was a thick, almost bear-like fur that traced his outer jaw until it blended into snake-like skin on his neck. He also had the teeth and tongue of a serpent. Every tooth was razor sharp and slightly curved back so that whatever it bit into could not escape. His upper body was exposed and ready to attack at will. Through rapid-fire breaths, his chest and shoulders rocked up and down like a dog that has been running around in the heat all day. The rancid smell of a fresh kill emanated out of his mouth toward me. The smell mixed with all of my soaps to form a blend of pleasing aromas and those of the bitterness of death.

At that moment, when I finally opened my eyes, the monster melted into the water and soap until it was nothing more than another curious dream. Even though the image of the man-beast had gone, a part of me wished that what I saw in my mind and felt within my soul was real. I could prove to myself that the fear I lived with was valid.

The fear also manifested itself each and every time I walked into a dark room. There would be a ghost-like glow that outlined all of the objects that were in the room. In the corners, shapes constantly formed. As I raced to flick the switch, anxiety overwhelmed me. It always forced my hand to go faster to flip the switch.

"Click" and the light came on with such speed and power that I stood half-blinded by it, yet I had a perfectly-formed photo burned into my eyes, much like the way a camera would let light in to expose the film, creating a negative. Some of the objects in the photo had shape but not any real color, and I was never able to view it for long. Before long, they would melt away into a warped and blurry image, instead of what it was.

There was no time for me to search the dark room after switching on the light. Were those creatures the ones who forced the images to fade out? Did the images change so as to let me see those creatures? But I had to look, and just like the man-beast that plagued my thoughts during my showers, there was nothing there waiting for me. At least, I did not see any. They must have hidden when I entered.

Once again, happiness and regret filled me. They stayed with me until I had switched off the light. As I shut off the light, I could feel that Hell had released its minions behind me. I couldn't hear them, but I knew they were crawling. Their half-eaten, ripped, mangled bodies were moving toward me, and I knew that they were coming. From every corner, shadow or obscured place, I could feel them coming.

In the air, I could taste the decay of their long-rotten flesh. The taste had changed from death into a musky, deep, swamp smell with its own pungent taste to it. The musk had more properties to it than mere taste and smell. It brought with it a heat that was powerful enough to burn my mouth and tongue. The heat hit my tongue, and instantly burnt it and dried it up. The swampy part of that taste was thick and heavy. It held my tongue down and made it so I could not move it or even taste anything other than what those minions had brought with them.

My sight stretched with a will and determination that always seemed to fail me. I could see shadows within the darkness moving as rolling water in a rushing river. There was only a slight variance to the shapes and the directions of the waves. With no light, how was I to know or trust what I saw? But if I were to run back and give into the fear, would the force controlling it know the terror and horror that I lived in? By doing that, therefore, would those attacks become more frequent until they were not shadows anymore? Did my heart rate increase only to betray me, revealing to that evil one my real fear? Had I already been broken and exposed? Years later, was that the answer to my fears? Had I found a way to live with it and bury it deep inside?

The smell that those beings brought with them seemed to change with my mood. It seemed the more fearful I was, the more there was a sulfur smell mixed with the smell of the seashore after a strong storm has washed a lot of dead fish onto it. If my fear was lacking, the smell of a cocktail waitress's perfume would be present. It always seemed that as soon as I smelled it, it just disappeared. After a step or two, the smell always returned. I felt like it was some sort of baiting game just to see if I cared about the dark. But I also felt that if whatever did it was powerful enough to pull different smells out of the air and put them by me, I might have already lost the battle. So I would act as if I never smelled them, and would walk away. I knew there was something somewhere mocking me as I walked right by it.

The red eyes were free from the darkness once more, almost as a way of reminding me not to forget what was before me. Quicker than a blink of an eye, it disappeared, short enough that I even questioned my own sense of sight. The man in me tried to pull my mind away from anything that was irrational, but at that point, all logic and reason was vanquished. Only the soul, heart and every cell that carried breath in my body shouted that what I saw was real and it was time to believe and trust in my senses if I wanted to make it out of there.

The candle, the laminated darkness and the smell of clay grabbed hold of my thoughts again. Without so much as a sound, the world before me melted as if it were made of wax. Only the little pod I was in was immune to the melting and the heat. The wax world ran off my pod in the same manner as the hot wax in one of those high-pressure, car-wash machines. My thoughts were not immune to the melting, and they melted along with everything else.

It seemed as if years of my life were being erased. The dreams I had when James and I started the trip were gone, and they started shifting to the dreams I had when we first formed the band; of learning how to play together, how to respect the other's music and above all, being a friend through the awkward teen years. Then, like a glass of water being dumped onto a watercolor portrait, those dreams vanished, and I was a young child again.

I drifted into a night in my distant past. There must have been something there that I had to see again; something that lived in the partial night; something that held a memory I blocked or erased. I was still in the pod, which was physically unchanged, yet there was something about it that seemed darker and more real. The pod was made solely for me, and it was going to reveal the truth that my child mind might not have been able to comprehend.

From the look of where I was standing, it appeared that I was standing outside my neighbor's house. The world was in night's firm grasp, so it must have been late. Just outside the picture window, I stood in amazement at the reflection of the young child staring back at me. The gap in years somehow seemed to fade away like oil on top of water after soap is applied. There was always a part of me that was trying to come back to that night; to be that child again. There was always something standing between me and my memories of that day. I had to remember that night when I was a child and the fear of the night started to creep up as I stared at the window that separated me from safety. It was one of those humid nights in late July. The moisture that was in the air was so thick that I could almost feel the electrical energy that was building into a powerful storm nearby. Even the leaves on the nearby trees had turned up in order to catch as much of the rain that they could. I remembered that day and how it ended a heatwave in Wisconsin that had been extremely long, but that's all I remembered about that day and night. The heat was still very intense, and even though I was only a young child, the sweat that was pouring off me resembled that of a man in his twenties running a marathon. But I was not running, or even moving. I was just standing there. The trees that usually filled the night with their gentle tasseling of the leaves back and forth throughout most of the evening and night had become as still as stone. Their look was like they had been turned to stone by just one simple glance of Medusa.

The thick wood that lined the gravel road between our two homes always seemed to be alive at that time of the night. I had always known that something other than birds, insects and small animals watched me when I walked loudly down the gravel road. Those feelings were easily dismissed when the animals hidden in the trees and bushes sang their mating calls. Those songs from the night animals and insects and the faintest movements of the leaves always brought a reassurance to me that there was more life out there than my own.

That night, though, I felt like I was stuck in a cemetery at the moment before God released the dead to walk free finally. All of the air tasted like that clay table in the kitchen, and all I could smell was that same musk. Taste and smell blocked me from whatever was on the other side of that table, so I wasn't sure if it was a good thing to be tasting and smelling that or if it was an omen of bad things to come.

I took my first step away from the little bit of light that was trickling out into my world from the window. Inch by inch, I walked backward until the tips of my feet were still in the light. There was so much fear inside me. To confront my fear, I jumped so that my whole body was then in the shadows of the night.

A murder of crows burst out of a tree just as my feet landed on the grass. The tree was one of the older oak trees, but it was half dead. The oak tree must have been some 200 feet away, yet I could see almost every crow that burst from it. There was a crisp, sword-like sound that pierced what was otherwise a soundless night.

I wished with everything I had that I was dreaming and that I would soon wake up or be tossed into another nightmare, even if it was a nightmare in which a killer clown stood uninvited at the foot of my bed. But it was no dream, and there was no way I was going to wake up or forget about it.

The lights that illuminated the window only a moment earlier were no longer there. The house seemed as if it was hollow and that it had never had any life or light within its walls. Perhaps the residents had decided to leave, or maybe they went to sleep. But in any case, there was no turning back to step back into the safety of the light. The only path for me was further into the shadows, which would lead me past that half-dead oak to my home.

20

Luther's story

Luther anticipated the blending of his mind and spiritual power with Jacob's mind that was too spiritually sensitive. He had been building Jacob's connection to the supernatural over his entire lifespan. All of the physic powers that Jacob had gained were the results of all the gifts that Luther had been bestowing upon him. When the time came, and he took over Jacob's body, he would be much more powerful.

Luther's plan was not a complete success because Death chose to let Jacob die before Luther could take over his body. That forced Luther to alter his plan. He would have to find another way to achieve the godhood that he craved. But the part of him that was locked in a sarcophagus would have to be found and unlocked if he was to achieve his goals.

The locks were part of a preventive measure that God, angels and demons had placed in order to stop him from overthrowing Heaven and Hell and turning it all into a mirrored image of his dimension. His father was the destroyer of universes and realms. He was able to break through the defensive measures God had in place to prevent powerful beings from crossing over into his realm, and he was able to place his son in that one in the hope that his son would become a god and a ruler. It was in the back rooms and hidden passages of Hell that Luther grew in strength and might.

After his true power was taken away from him, Luther was allowed to roam the earth for thousands of years before he was finally locked in Hell. Even though his true power was taken away, he was still very powerful and was left alone to do what he wanted. Throughout that time, he portrayed himself as different gods, demons, devils and demigods. Luther always saw a way to build up his own cult following.

Luther found it comical how the two worlds collided each time he stepped into a new body. He remembered how the confusion of the blending drove his first few hosts mad, and that some of those first few, in a fit for control of their mind and body, ended up taking their own lives. One of his greatest successes was a seer, one of the first great kings of the Vikings. He told the seer he was the true god of their gods, and told him to call him Lut, the king.

Luther only spent a few months as he tried to build up the seer's strength and ability to talk with the gods. The seer was blind to the world around him. There were only one or two of his minions who were talking to him before Luther showed up. Satan was trying to teach Luther how to control the seer and to use him for his purpose, with the hope that it would benefit Satan. But the self-proclaimed god refused to listen to Satan's teaching and stole the control of that unaware man.

At first, Luther sought out the seer's attention through drug-infused sleep and lengthy meditation periods. He presented himself as an aide and guide. In nightmares that Luther used to plague the man, he would rush in and save him. Then, as soon as he was free from the threat, Luther quickly lied to him, showing him how the other 'gods' were the ones that were lashing out at him. Within a few weeks, the seer was seeking out Luther to be his only source to the world of the gods.

Again and again, he would cry out for Lut to teach him or reveal something profound to him. Lut told him that he had a large group of supernatural warriors at his call. He told the seer that his warriors traditionally were beautiful, young men that would trick young women to jump into the water where they would drown them. They were also shapeshifters that would transform into powerful horses. Then they would search out boys and let them ride on their backs back into the water to be killed and eaten like the women.

By calling himself that name, the seer both feared and loved him. Lut promised that as long as the seer worshipped him and told all the people he ran into about the Lut king, he would keep the lesser minions out of all of the waterways they used. As the attacks that were orchestrated by the demons that once controlled that area quickly faded away. The Lut king's worshippers grew very rapidly in number.

The power that the Lut king took made him untouchable throughout Hell. Not even the Devil himself was able to challenge him. So he rapidly became a god among the demons and started creating his own minions to lead as generals for his army. His power was absolute, and before he took a body and soul, the Lut king created physical monsters that could walk in both the physical and spiritual world. Their main form was a mix between a blackened werewolf, a vampire and the coastal mist.

The werewolf portion was the shape, color and predatory lust. The new form of Lut had an elongated nose and pointy ears that resembled a wolf. The nose was as wide as it was long and could withstand very powerful blows without any damage. The ears changed in size, depending on the danger that they were facing. When in battle, the monster's ears would then fold down and harden themselves into a shell-like helmet that was completely impenetrable, but it still allowed the creature to hear with the same clarity.

The claws changed instantaneously, depending on the purpose. If the Lut was running or hunting, they took the padded form of the wolf, but if it faced an opponent in battle, the creature could change its claws to that of a vampire. That was so that it could hold a weapon or use its unbreakable claws to rip through armor, shields and flesh. The Lut could also form a fist, and smash it through stone castle walls.

When complete silence was needed and only a small force was deployed, the creatures would use the form of a mist to glide through cracks, windows and doors to their target. Depending on the task, they sometimes could absorb their target so that there was nothing left of them. They could even turn a person into the same mist that they were made of and transfer them back to the human leader that deployed them. On missions, when a message needed to be sent, they would utilize that form. Behind the closed and secured castle, a bloody massacre occurred.

The seer craved complete control over the Lut king's minions, and he was told that as soon as he gave his body over to the Lut king, he would have complete control over everything. Willingly, he begged the Lut king to come in, and live inside him. The Lut king lay down on top of the naked seer and tied his presence to the seer's soul.

The emotions of the real world and of the seer flooded his mind as the two realities blended together, creating a very vivid hallucination that even powerful drugs wouldn't produce. Wildly, the Lut king started tearing at the seams of the physical world. His screams provoked his worshippers to run to the seers and see what was happening to him.

The area immediately surrounding the woods and the earthen home of the seer shook as if it was about to explode. Giant trees covered the top of the home, pushing it down and away from the home in all directions. Cracking and snapping sounds ricocheted off everything around. The sound could be heard in distant villages.

Light flashed, like strobes of different colors, from inside the house. Those flashes blew out the windows and doors. That only intensified the power of the light until it became such a blinding force that the people looking at it were permanently blinded. Those who were lucky enough to look away and cover their eyes only received powerful headaches. The light could be seen from villages that were many days' journey away. There was also a heat that accompanied the light. It instantly flash-burned the ground, like napalm, around the seer's home. The fire from the heat didn't seem to consume anything it touched. It was just there one moment, then gone the next.

Only the Lut creatures could endure the light and the shaking, and they came running with such speed that they were practically invisible. Even though it was a dark and moonless night, the explosion made it as bright as midday. The only way the people near the house knew that the creatures came was by the turbulence they caused as they ran past the people. One by one, they piled on top of each other, blocking the light from escaping. The world grew so dark that even nocturnal animals could not see anything.

Ten of the stronger Lut creatures found their king in his new body five feet off the ground. They knew that it needed to end, or else all of the work their king had completed would have been for nothing. They transcended reality in order to bring Satan out of Hell and end it. Time stopped as soon as Lucifer stepped forward and ended the craziness. He then rewound time to the moment when the Lut king took possession. Then, over and over again, he repossessed the body of the seer until there were no more issues in his possessing the body.

Luther partly wished that the events that happened all those years earlier with the seer would happen again the moment he attached his presents to Jacob's body. With his soul already gone, there was no way that it could happen. He wondered if the realities would be as blended as in the times he took over a living body. Without any love or care, Luther melted into Jacob's frozen body. From the moment he first touched the cold, dead skin, he could tell that it was different. He saw himself standing in the back of a long, narrow, black tunnel a long way from the opening on the far side of it. The opening looked like it was one that was originally made for a train. The tunnel exit was a door with a half-circle top. Even with the exit being so far away, Luther could easily tell that the height of it was close to 15 feet. The width of the tunnel was eight feet. It had to be that way so that light could flow in without too much difficulty. The block-type tunnel construction seemed to have been made to fit perfectly. Like the pyramids, each block melded into each other. It didn't look like there was any mortar holding them together. Each brick had a different look and feel as if they were all made from different molds.

There was a different feeling in there. It was one that Luther had never felt before or cared about or even knew how to react to. Power, hate, lust and fear were the feelings he dwelled upon. There was something more in there, and it was very intoxicating. A faint piano was playing a melody leading him down the tunnel. Every time he thought he had the melody in his hands, it faded away before he could wrap his thoughts around it. That made him want it even more. He started running down the tunnel in search of it, but the faster he ran, the further away the song sounded. It was as if the song was taunting him as he looked for it as he ran. He looked and sounded like a freight train roaring through a dark tunnel.

The sound of his running resounded through the tunnel and out of the entrance. The shock waves of it burst out of the tunnel, and all that somehow blew back through him. Quickly, the sound was swallowed by whatever lived in those shadows. Just as an avalanche rocketing down the side of a mountain, the sounds he created only grew in intensity until it was so massive that even the large door was too small for it to leave. The sound reached and surpassed the equilibrium so fast that the tunnel was forced to bend in order to compensate for the added pressure of the shock wave. In the distance, it took Luther all he had to run through one set of doors. The semicircle that was at the top of the door was flattened. Stress cracks ran along the sides and ceiling of the tunnel. There was a high-pitched scream. It was a blur to Luther because all he wanted was that song, but it didn't matter what was happening to the place.

Instead of reaching the end, it seemed that Luther was sinking further and further into the shadows from which he thought he had already emerged. Every step forward was a giant leap backward, or at least it appeared to be that way. That forced him to use more power and energy than he had ever used before. He could see that moment when he was going to explode out of the tunnel, and it became an uncontrollable lust. It was the same type of lust that forced Jacob out of his bed in the middle of the night to go looking for that giant face. Two more steps and he would be there. Time froze for him in between steps just before he reached that moment. He truly believed that if he reached that point, he would finally be able to get that song, but instead everything started to reverberate in pulsating waves. The pulses acted as if they were in an uncontrolled rage. The spaces between them were never the same, and the strength grew and lessened, but it was never in line from greatest to weakest or vice versa.

He was stuck in mid-air between steps, so he could not run away from the sound or even cower from it. All he could do was withstand it. It felt as if it was ripping him apart, piece by piece. It was incredible chaos. The unpredictability to it all was absolutely planned to occur. For a brief moment, Luther wondered if this was Death once again acting against him. That moment of thought was very short because of what was occurring. There was no time for anger and hatred for whatever being created this chaos. There was only time to feel what was being done to him. It was a feeling of loss that the song was completely gone.

The pulses were at that point right on top of each other. If there was a break between them, it was unnoticeable to the Lut king. It was forcing his body to move in and out, synched with the vibrating pulses. Each time his body was pulled, he felt as if his skin was about to rip apart to let his innards paint what was left of the tunnel. Every time his body was squeezed, it felt as though everything inside of him was about to whistle out through his nostrils. But as abruptly as it started, it ended, locking him still in the floating position, unable to move or to free himself. All sound had gone. There was not even ringing in his ears to hear; nothing.

21

Devin's story

The adult in me was fighting angrily to see what the child in me was seeing and feeling. Something was preventing me from seeing the truth, or maybe I was not ready to see or understand it. In any case, I pushed out to face it with the fears and imagination of a child. It only took ten steps to reach the gravel road. But then the forest would be next. The forest encased the gravel road like a living tomb. When I got to the road, I thought about stopping, sitting down, and waiting until my mother, father or one of my older brothers would come for me. Fear over knowing what they would do to me because I made them wait and then come and get me was far worse than what I imagined was waiting for me in the forest.

It was hard to tell if it was bravery or fear that drove me, but with that first step I took, a rock shot out from under my shoe. It sounded like it went into the forest. I thought that announced my arrival. I could faintly hear that it hit something not wood, stone or metal but more like something that was alive and quite large.

The entire forest became dead silent; not the sound of a cricket or toad or a chirp of any sort, nor any movement. It felt as if I walked into a museum. It was like the creatures were waiting for the right moment to pounce like a black panther on me. Just like a symphony conductor, the wood's sounds were directed. None of the other pieces could make a sound without the say-so of the conductor. Even with the horrible outcome that was almost certain to happen, the beauty and the perfection of the pure music held by the world drew me, one foot at a time into the forest.

A vivid feeling of being watched from an open window on those hot, summer nights creeped like a hunting beast stalking me as I got closer to the forest. Over and over, I studied the outer edges like those dark nights when I looked endlessly out the window in search of anything that stood out. The black world that lay beyond dared me to try and find its secrets.

One night, I remembered sitting on a couch watching TV, but there was a red glow from the other side of the window; little more than a quick, cigarette-sized, red glow, then nothing; not even a bird or a sound of wind. There was only the chilling sound of emptiness and my rising heartbeat. My fear was growing like a wildfire inside me. For the rest of that night, I continued watching for that red glow, but it never again appeared.

In just a few more steps, I hoped to hear the song that the conductor had seemingly written for me. The absence of sound was perhaps a song in its own right. It seemed as if it was the end of something. I recalled the old tales of sailors being lured to their deaths by the beautiful songs of the mermaids. In a small way, I then understood craving. Being serenaded, even if it was the last thing I heard, seemed beautiful. Even if the true intention of the serenade was predatory in nature, the desire to be needed in that way was powerful enough to become an obsession that I couldn't shake.

Step after step, I walked until I entered the overgrown forest. The smell of clay infused with musk got stronger and stronger until that was all I could smell or think about. The smell became so strong that it started to extinguish my ability to focus. I started to forget where I was even going.

I couldn't tell if I was being pulled or led, or if I was running to where I was going. All I could tell was that I was in a hurry and it seemed like I was moving faster than the speed I could physically travel on my own. My eyes were forcefully closed by all of the branches that started hitting me in the face. Even with my arms up, it seemed like I couldn't block them. This had to be what a prize fighter felt when the opponent never stopped connecting with his punches. Each branch dug in like razor wire, and I could feel my skin being ripped open from every one that touched me.

Then, as quickly as it began, the branches stopped hitting me. It seemed that I broke through an opening, and I could then finally see how I got to where I was. As one would do with an unwanted sack of potatoes or laundry, I was thrown to the ground without making a sound. Instantly, my body landed partly on the ground and partly against something made of stone and earth. My breath was forced out of my lungs, and I couldn't reclaim it. It confirmed my realization that I was not placed but thrown here by something very powerful. All I could think about was this unstoppable quest and ache for air. I didn't even care if it had that foul, horrid, musty, clay taste to it. I have had my breath knocked out of me numerous times before leading up to that day, but it was far more powerful.

My vision was also blurry after the throw, so I wasn't able to see who or what did it to me. Because my main goal was to breathe, I didn't even notice if whatever threw me was walking around me, talking to me, or interacting with others. I was somehow able to make it to my hands and knees. My lungs and stomach lurched, and I almost forced myself to vomit. Slowly, I crawled away from the hard thing I hit by pulling at the grass and weeds on the moist ground. I wasn't aware that I was doing that, because my sight was only getting worse. It wasn't until a massive, doglike leg stepped right in front of me, stopping me from going any further. As soon as that dirty and sharp hair touched me, fear rushed over me, and sent a deep breath of fresh air into my lungs.

I was an addict who went for what seemed like a lifetime without the drug I needed to make me whole again. With the drug having been given to me, I felt as if every part of me was on fire. There was nothing that I would not take on, given that I was complete again. The fresh breath that was my drug somehow made my sight more powerful than before.

At first, it was just the aching in my lungs that vanished so quickly that I couldn't even remember what the pain really felt like. Then all of the scrapes and cuts I got from the rush through the forest vanished. The shock of seeing it happen erased the gravity of what was happening all around me and to me. The pain from being thrown onto the ground and into the stone object was gone as well. Finally, my sight came back. All of that happened before I was able to exhale.

The animal that pressed itself against me was a black wolf that was abnormally large. It had white strips running wildly all over its body. It had a low growl it used to talk to me. It let me know that I should back off, and that I should do it sooner rather than later. Slowly, I scooted away. All around me, different things, animals or whatever else was there started to move. I could hear their movements, but not see them. Even with my heightened sight, it was impossible to make out what else was out in the tall grass all around me. I knew the place, but it was not real. I only saw it in my nightmares. It was not somewhere I'd physically been. Even with all of my years playing in those woods with my friends, I never saw that place.

I was in a large grassy area perhaps outside of the forest. The tall grass took the place of trees, bushes and shrubs. It also stretched from the outer rim of the trees to a landing area just on the banks of a bend in a stream. The stream did not exist in the forest. There were no waterways anywhere in the forest. The stream was around 30 feet across, and the rushing water almost gave it away as a river. There would have been no way any of us children around there could have missed it. It would have become a haven on those hot and sticky dog days of summer. Fog rolled off the rushing water and into the humid night and to show the relief that such a stream would have provided while escaping the heat of the sun.

I could also picture all of us children camping along its banks. I could see us huddled tightly together around a fire, making sure to stay close to one another as we took turns telling tales of the native tribes that might or might not have lived in the forest hundreds of years earlier or how they learned to live with some of their pagan gods. But this was no camping trip, and it appeared that I was living through one of the tales that rushed through my thoughts. I wished that I had made it all up.

The stream curved around the grassy area, and I was sitting at the point it curved. At the tip of the point to the curve and on the same side of the water as me stood a massive tree only a few feet inland. The tree looked half alive and half dead, but the dead part was not death like I had grown to know. From the dead half, darkness poured out like black ink floating and then dissolving within the gentle waves of a lake that was almost placid. There was a calming solitude in the movements of the ink. But there was something else beside the peaceful ink coming from that half. There were claws that were ripping a hole into the darkness that death had over the tree. The strength of the ink must somehow have fueled the death-keeper and was able to keep whatever was behind the darkness at bay for the time being. I had the feeling that I was brought there to see the opening of that darkness. I knew there was more to it than a tiny rip of a claw that I was to witness.

Just under the dead half of the tree was the stone object that I landed upon. It was a massive stone sarcophagus reminding me of the ones I had seen at museums and on TV. It appeared that the water from the stream must have washed it up because it was perfectly clean, yet the smell of clay and musk pouring out of it was stronger than the smell of waste while walking onto a pig farm on a humid day. It was the source of the smell that I had been smelling. There was something that seemed unusual about the sarcophagus. I walked up to it and pushed the top aside.

I had expected a mummified body to jump up and grab me, but the moonlight revealed that there was no mummy.

Initially, all I saw was more stone and clay that filled almost all of the sarcophagus. Then, just as the quiet light was refocused to the center, an object began to emerge out of the shadows made by the lid. The object that was entombed in the stone jail was a book of the same material.

22

Nine months before Victoria was born

Luther floated silently in absolute solitude in a place where time had no meaning. Every time he tried to focus his mind on how long he had been there, his efforts dissolved into empty thoughts and ideas. That happened to him repeatedly until he no longer cared about how long he had been there. Memories of Jacob's life flooded his thoughts, but they weren't just thoughts. Luther relived those moments, but not through his own eyes; they were through Jacob's eyes. All the feelings and emotions that were interlocked with those memories became his as well as Jacob's.

Luther found himself standing in a moonlit bedroom. He was looking down onto a beauty he could not imagine. He was lost in that thought. A part of him wanted to reach inside of himself and rip his evil heart out so he could escape, but he couldn't move. It was her beauty that held him there. The light bled so gently onto her yellowish-white skin so as not to wake her up or disturb her dreams. He wondered what she was dreaming and if it could possibly be about him. With all his might, he tried to see into her dreams, but something inside him stopped his efforts. Jacob's love began to overwhelm him.

Luther began to hear the song he was chasing again, but he didn't care about it any longer. All he wanted to do was sit there and look at her as long as he could. If it was just a memory, he never again wanted to wake up. All he wanted was right there lying fast asleep. The song was getting louder and louder until it was wrapping itself around him, but he ignored it. The line between stalker and lover was quickly blurring, but he couldn't look away from her. He wondered how her warm, naked skin would feel pressed against his, if only for warmth. The song was roaring as loudly as a group of fighter jets flying circles around him. The song shook him, and tore at his clothes and skin. Tiny pieces of his clothes were torn off. Then larger pieces followed. Piece by piece, his clothes were ripped off until he was completely naked and bitterly cold. He was standing beside Nina, who was still fast asleep. The song forced itself into Luther's soul via Jacob's body. From every note, a new part of him was growing stronger. It was the human part inside of him that was stepping forth and taking control. It was new to him. Never before had any of the bodies he possessed been able to radiate their old feelings to him. It was always his will and desires that took center stage. Jacob was not even there anymore, but his love for Nina somehow created the same feelings in Luther.

Luther wanted to feel and remember the first time Jacob looked at her. Was it an accident or a set up? He wanted to feel the desire to talk to her finally after whatever long, drawn-out hesitation Jacob used to build up the courage that was needed. He desired that moment just before Jacob held her hand, but he could not take his eyes off her lying there in perfect sleep. Glimpses of those first encounters flashed wildly behind his eyes so that every time he blinked, those images were all he could see. Every time he blinked, it became harder and harder for him to open his eyes, but knowing that she was right there, he couldn't keep his eyes closed. The tingling butterflies that Jacob locked away in his stomach during those first few times were reborn inside Luther. Through one of Jacob's memories he saw her from across the street walking with a friend. It was midwinter, and the freezing cold tightened its grip on the world. Everywhere there was heat escaping, looking like steam. Lines of people were moving like cattle from one place of warmth to another. Most were covered from head to toe in the latest winter gear. Some wore stocking hats. Others used their long hair and a scarf wrapped tightly around their necks and face. Chapped lips were easily seen from those who thought they were too cool to wear anything over their faces. Hands were either tucked safely inside deep pockets or else they were covered by gloves. Most of the gloves were thin, leather, driving ones, but some of the younger ladies had knitted mittens instead of gloves.

A strong wind was blowing off the Michigan lake that was almost completely frozen over. The narrow Milwaukee streets only seemed to help funnel the 30-mile-an-hour wind onto everyone that was still on the streets. There was a homeless man nestled tightly on the side of one of the buildings. His makeshift home was shaking and almost blowing away. He looked like a man that was fighting to free his sinking rowboat from the rising tide. Every time he caught something, another piece just out of his reach peeled off and almost flew away. People here and there would help him secure some part of it before they waved and said "Goodbye". A young, dark-haired woman stopped five feet from the man fighting the wind. She had on a long, tan coat that came down to her knees. It looked warm and well-constructed. She also had on a knitted hat, scarf and mittens. Only her hair was allowed to escape, resting over the top of her narrow shoulders. As she stood looking at the man, the wind thrust itself into her and sent her hair wildly around her head. Her coat was also being pushed against one side of her body, dislodging itself from her other side. She seemed to be completely oblivious to the wind, the cold and all the people that were walking past her as quickly as they could.

Luther, who was then in Jacob's body, was staring at her from the coffee shop across the street. Cars, buses and working trucks drove by, but that never forced him to break his gaze at her. There was a pull that drove him to get lost in just looking at her. He didn't need to see the rest of her, because to him, there was something about her that perfectly sang of a quiet beauty, only for his ears.

She stepped closer to the man who looked as if he had given up trying to save his house. An absolute look of defeat was plastered on his face. He had his hands and arms wrapped around his chest as he fought back the tears of defeat that were building up in his eyes. Luther couldn't tell if she was talking to him or not, but if she was, he was ignoring her, just as those people that walked past him did. The closer she got, he still refused to look at her. Then, in one swooping motion she ripped her long jacket off and wrapped it around him. She then undid her scarf and tied it around his unwashed hair and beard. Next was the hat that did not fit him, but with a pull, it stretched with ease. She offered her gloves, but there was no way they would fit.

Some people stopped to see if she was OK, but they ignored him. The cold wind gave them an excuse to walk away. Jacob's body forced Luther to run out of the warm building toward the girl that was then standing there in a light blouse and dress pants. The wind easily ripped through those pieces of clothes, so by the time he got close to her, he was able to see that she was shivering, and the parts of her skin that were exposed were starting to change into a pinkish red.

Before Luther knew what was happening, his coat was off and he was wrapping it around her. She didn't notice anything other than the man sitting on the frozen concrete. Not even the placement of a stranger's jacket around her could snap her out of the trance. The man on the ground pointed up toward Luther, and with a look of shock, she turned her head and her blackish-brown eyes locked onto his. Luther felt the explosion of love that overtook Jacob's heart and soul.

The blink was over, and he was once again standing next to Nina, who was asleep on the bed. He must have taken a few steps during that blink because she was so close he could almost feel the warmth for her uncovered skin. Her breathing tickled the hairs on his arm. Even that tickle was something new to him. All of the bodies he had ever possessed were mostly numb. Her breath was warm at first, but then the warmth faded away into a cool breeze. The cold, mixed with the tickling sensation, made it almost unbearable. The growing need to be close to her was undeniable; stronger than he could have imagined.

Every few times Nina breathed, a half-mute snort rang out of her mouth. Luther thought it was adorable, and he could hardly wait for the next one. He wanted to stand above her, and watch her for the rest of the night, but the newfound body was growing tired from standing naked in the cold, dark room. His heart and soul protested the move away from Nina's side of the bed, but knowing that he would be lying next to her made it easier to move. The blankets on his side of the bed were still folded open in a triangular form from when Jacob got up to chase after Luther's face. It made getting in and under the blankets very easy.

His side of the bed was the same temperature as the rest of room. He lay frozen in place for minutes while he waited for his dead body to warm up. With the covers on top of him, Nina's hot side of the bed started running together with his cold temperature. A few soft moans escaped from her lips as she turned away from him and onto her side.

It took all the power he could muster not to roll over onto her and place his naked body against hers for warmth. He didn't want to wake her up and force himself upon her. He couldn't hold back his entire body, though. He had to touch her, even if it meant that only one of his hands would. Unaware of what was going to happen, he guided his arm closer to her. The warmth from her body embraced his hand and aided in placing it just above her hip. She moved at first because of the temperature difference, but then gave in to his touch. A mainly inaudible group of words escaped under her breath to him. Luther couldn't understand what she said, and he remained unmoved until she grabbed his arm and pulled him tightly until their bodies were pressed together. For the first time ever, Luther finally felt what it's like to love someone and what it feels like to be loved. They made love well into the morning, and even called in sick for work the next day so that they never had to leave each other's side.

23

Devin's story

The book that was lying in the sarcophagus was almost as long as the sarcophagus's width inside. It was close to three feet wide, and the book was the same distance in width. It formed a perfect square. There were locks in place that held the book tightly imbedded half in and half out of the stone, and refused to let it out without the proper key. There were no keyholes, so whatever held it there, it was a lock that only words and actions could unlock. It gave the illusion that the locks themselves were intelligent. The locks looked to be hands holding it down. The hands did not look dead but alive. Different veins inside of the hands pulsed up and down with their own rhythm. They showed that none of them were from the same creature. I somehow knew that only a human sacrifice would allow those hands to open and release the book. I was not afraid that the sacrifice was me, because I felt that if it wasn't me, I would have never been allowed to see the book. A voice deep inside me told me that it was the other part of the creature, and if they were connected, it would have the power to take over Hell and Earth.

A deep, sadistic growl started humming out of the half-dead tree. The growl was powerful enough to shake everything around. The stream vibrated so much that tiny tidal waves formed. The air itself shook with a rage that made it almost impossible to breath. I couldn't sit there any longer. I had to fall down and lie on my back. Only the wolf was unaffected, but it turned to see if I was OK, and then, with a twist of one of its ears, it looked away from me. The growl morphed into an evil laugh that ranged in pitch and depth. It felt as if my ears were going to explode from the laughing. It shook my head in and out with such speed that I didn't think there was any way I would be able to live through it. A loud ringing started taking the place of the laugh until there was no more laughing, only the ringing.

The creature that was trying to claw its way through the crack in the tree stopped clawing and laughing to look through the crack, and stared directly at me. Its pair of large, red eyes somehow was able to stare through the crack together. I felt cold as soon as I locked eyes with it. I could feel the anger of that creature as it wanted to taste my blood, and somewhere within me, I wanted to give in to it. Without even knowing why or how, I was walking toward the tree. Patiently, it waited for me as I walked into the ink. Initially, I felt cold when the ink touched me, but then there was a strange peace. It was like I had finally found a place of true acceptance without pain. I was somehow changing and becoming that ink; flowing peacefully with the tides, but never fully mixing into it. While lost within that wave of peace, an arm was reaching for me even though I fought it with everything I had so as not to let go of the ink. The hand was always able to find me. I was somehow able to find a way to drift away from the arm without letting it grab me. It appeared that I was one step ahead of it. With a strength I never knew existed, I was ripped away from the tree and out of the ink.

The arm placed me beside the large wolf that had stopped me from wandering off earlier. The crack in the tree closed before my eyes. Both the ink and the crack were gone, leaving nothing physically left to prove that it was real, only a fading memory or a distant nightmare.

The large, humanlike person that closed the crack turned to me, and pointed to my left. There I saw an area where the grass was cleared away to make an altar of sorts. There was also a very large bonfire there. The stone sarcophagus was at that point beside the fire, but the top was closed, and there was a young woman tied to the top of it in the form of an X.

Around the fire, men and women chanted, and were dressed according to their religious views of the god they were hoping to resurrect or please. She was awake and aware of what was being done to her. In a language that appeared to be that of the Norse people, the ritual began. I was somehow able to understand what was being spoken. She begged them not to do it to her; to let her live. But her pleas were ignored. It was as if her killers were lost in a trance themselves. As the cuts began to slice her skin slowly, she screamed for relief. The first cuts were not to kill, but to torture her. Then the torturers placed some powder or salt over the cuts either to stop the bleeding or inflict more pain.

They would take breaks every 10 to 15 minutes. Then they would open the top of the sarcophagus. They did that in order to see if any or all of the hands had loosened up. By the looks on their faces, matched with obscenities they screamed when they opened it, I could tell that the locks remained in place. The tormenters let their anger fuel them, and it forced them to take it out on their sacrificial offering. One of them smashed a finger, toe, arm or leg bone with a large hammer.

When she passed out from the pain, they blew some sort of drug onto her face, which seemed to wake her up and energized her. She awakened with such a fury that she broke the ties that held her arms back numerous times. It forced the officiants — the five men and two women helping the one who led the sacrifice — to hold her down by placing new ropes on her. They broke her legs at the knees the one and only time she broke the ropes that held them. They must have broken her legs in other spots at the same time, because they were beating all over her legs with what looked like a stone-and-wood version of a sledgehammer.

A group of monks was leading the worshippers around the fire. The worship consisted of song, dance and prayer. The fire was as bright as the sun during those midday hours, but the light from the fire was only powerful enough to penetrate the first few rows of the people that gathered around it.

There was no possible way I could tell how many people were there. At three opposite corners of the fire, there were three women standing almost six feet away. They all had some sort of cup in their hands. All the people started to count down from six. As soon as everyone got to zero, the women holding the cups threw some type of liquid into the fire. Just before the liquid hit the flames, the head monk chanted a prayer, "Let my fire both burn you out and give you light."

An explosion shot flames and a fireball almost a hundred feet into the air immediately after his words stopped. It lit up the entire grassy area. I was able to see rows upon uneven rows of Norse people dressed in what appeared to be their finest handwoven leathers, animal hides and dark feathers that depicted the raven. The raven feathers had a darkness that give birth to new ominous darkness until the light of the fire struck them as just right. Then a purplish-blue color sparkled out from the dark feathers in the same way a finely-cut diamond would refract light off it when it rolled loosely on the hand, neck or earring.

None of the people were leaving from around the fire. Even when the explosion shot the summer's afternoon heat onto their faces and bodies of the first few rows, not one of them flinched. It seemed as though the rows of people were specifically seated in a certain way, which did not appear to be by rank. Those that needed the fire for heat and light were closer than the mightier ones, who watched over the sacrifice. The warriors in the back seemed to be watching the forest with a stronger intensity as the ritual was going on longer and longer.

A loud woman's scream pierced through all of the music, drumming and repetitive chanting. Instantaneously, all the other noises faded into nothing. I could see that they were still making those noises, but my hearing had then become fixed on the woman, who had become little more than a series of small cuts and large breaks. I could hear everything that was happening to her. Her heartbeat, almost as fast as a rabid rabbit, whispered prayers to her own version of Thor for a quick death, hoping that that was enough to welcome her to his table. I could hear her ribs crack with every labored breath she took. Her lungs burned when they blew the drug into her face. It also caused her heart to race faster. That caused her to breathe harder until she almost passed out. That would start the cycle all over again.

This time, when they came up to blow the drug into her face, someone or something whispered into her ear saying, "Breathe deeply, and your pain will be gone, but theirs will now begin."

The voice was so quiet that her own heartbeat could have covered it up, yet she heard it. Her heart rate slowed as the hand with the drug was raised once again, but this time, instead of closing her eyes and trying not to breathe, she opened her mouth and eyes wide. She raised her head to meet the hand that had the drug in it. Even before the monk could stop from the shock from her new reaction, he had already begun to blow it into her face. She inhaled every last bit. Her blood ran extra fast. First, it spread the drug to her heart and then to her mind. The drug invaded every cell in her body. Initially, the world around her changed in color and texture. Everything that was solid started to melt into a fluid figure. Then there was a tightness that was building inside her chest. It was different from the tightness she already felt as they hit and beat her. This one was powerful enough to take the breath right out from her lungs. Taking in air did nothing to help her. Her muscles contracting and releasing forced her head to turn and rest on her right check.

As soon as her head finally rested, a voice spoke to her saying, "It is time for you to come home."

Her heart instantly stopped pumping. A look of peace came over her face as she lay there half smiling.

24

Nine months before Victoria was born

"Jacob, I guess it's time for us to get up," Nina said while looking up at Luther.

She had her head resting on his chest. Luther, not knowing what to say or do, just continued to lie there with her in his arm.

"Come on. I'm hungry and I know you are by the sounds of your stomach," she said while laughing and patting him on his empty stomach.

He never had to eat before, so that too was a new feeling for him, but he took her word for it and motioned for her to get up. She didn't move.

"It is hard to get up when you are lying on top of me," he finally answered with a teasing look waxed on his face.

"But I don't want to move. You go, and I'll just wait here naked in bed for you to return," Nina said.

She gave him puppy-dog eyes. She made sure to blink a few times as a way of flirting with him. That was always the one thing Jacob could not turn down. That part of Jacob was still locked away inside, and Luther could not have turned it down if he wanted to. With an extra-long stretch, he drew out longer than needed with the hope that she would not move from off his chest. Nina took that movement as an invitation to roll off him so he could get up.

"You're going to be the death of me. You do know that?" he said while sliding to the corner of the bed.

"Yeah, I know," she answered with a wide smile glued on her face.

Her hair was wild from the time they had spent making love. Luther thought that there was no other hair in the world that was as beautiful as hers was at that moment. Her skin glowed so powerfully that even the human eyes that he was looking through could easily see that. It was almost like her body produced more blood out for the outermost layer of cells that formed her skin. She was even more breathtaking then than that first time he looked at her through Jacob's eyes. The walk out of the bedroom and down to the kitchen felt eerily similar to the walk that Jacob did less than ten hours earlier. Luther could see the image of the husband and wife that Jacob saw all those times before. Only he knew that it was his work behind the shadows that forced both deaths.

The newfound emotions intertwined with his every thought were taking him to places he never thought he would be able to go. For the first time, he wondered why he orchestrated it, and if he had left them alone to live, what their lives then would be like; whether they would have children and still be together, or whether life would have led them to that same ending, only to have it happen in a different place and different time than there in that house.

The remorse he felt reminded him of what some people feel the first time they take a life. Whether it was animal or a human, it didn't matter. The feelings were always the same. The sickness that they felt, he then felt. He ran down the stairs as quickly as he could, hoping that if he rushed through it, the feelings would disappear. He was wrong. It only reassured his guilt, and brought him to the point that he ran as fast as he could into the bathroom, not the kitchen. During his run down the stairs, his mouth began to fill with saliva, and his stomach began to twist and turn. He could not stop the violence that was building inside from coming out. He could almost taste the acidic stomach acid that was clawing its way up. He didn't waste any time turning on any of the lights; just a straight shot to the bathroom. He hoped that the seat was up because there was no way he had that kind of time. In one fluid moment, he threw himself onto the floor, wrapped his arms around the cold bowl, and let whatever was inside of his stomach out with a loud scream. Over and over, he kept throwing up. It felt like it was never going to end. Even when there was nothing left, his stomach forced him to hold on and lean into the toilet just in case. Every time he was forced to hover over the top of the toilet, the smell was enough to send his stomach into fits all over again. Hoping to end the cycle, he flushed and lay to the side of it. The combination of cold, vinyl flooring and the toilet itself felt very good. Luther was then able to endure the halfhearted gags that his body was making. Tears were streaming down the side of his face and nose caused by both the act of getting sick, and then more so, by what he did to that family all those years before.

"You are right, Luther, to feel that way. That was cold, but it is not even close to the many other ruthless things you have done," a voice hiding in the shadows sang out from behind the open door.

The voice was deeper than the best baritone singers and higher than the beautiful soprano opera singers. He knew that voice, but it had been at least three millennia since he had heard it, and with his thoughts then on the family, he could not picture whose voice it was.

Behind the door, the shadow started to move like some blood that was dropped into a bowl of water. The more he looked at it, the deeper and thicker the color grew. It wasn't just the one talking that moved; all of the shadows that encased the hidden side of the door moved together. When the thing took a breath, the area grew in mass. When it moved its head, the shadows took on the life of a flashlight. Everywhere it looked, a darker beam pushed out to encase everything and everywhere it looked. It could not see whatever it was looking at without those dark flashlights shining onto it first.

Luther's demon eyes allowed him to peek a little into the shadows. His human eyes needed time to adjust to the absence of light, and it was too dark for those eyes to see past the outermost parts, as if there was a wall to the shadows that prevented him from looking into it. Through his immortal eyes, he saw something that didn't make any sense. What he saw had no true solid form. It just kept moving in and out, up and down and larger and smaller all at once. It reminded him of one of the gas giants that glided through the dark space of that universe. Everything that came into contact with the thing instantly faded from the well-manicured form that it once was and into something that decay had eaten away for decades. It was hard to see that, even with his demon eyes, but Jacob's psychic eyes saw nothing. Luther couldn't even use Jacob's soul to feel into the shadow cloud and find out what was there and what it wanted.

"It's not that hard. All you have to do is ask me, and I will gladly tell you, old friend," the thing in the shadow said after taking a few labored breaths.

It was more annoyed that Luther was trying to see who or what it was, rather than simply ask or remember. It sat down onto the white, enamel-covered, cast-iron tub. The tub refused to give in to the decay, even though it was then covered by the shadow cloud.

"They really don't make them like this anymore," it said, while slapping the inner side of the tub.

Luther was sitting with his head against the wall furthest from that thing, and was looking for anything that would show him what he was dealing with and how to destroy it if a battle between them occurred. He knew it was not an angel, because they never traveled as a shadow cloud, and there was no one crying out for one. There was too much power pouring out of that thing to be a demon. The king of Hell, Satan, was too proud to portray himself in that fashion. Then again, the power Luther could feel and see that radiated out of that thing had felt stronger and older than Satan's power.

The cloud continued to wave as if it was water and someone had just thrown a handful of stones into it. Ripples formed from each one of those stones. As soon as one of the circular waves hit another ripple, it formed newer and stronger waves

Then it looked like another handful of stones was tossed in to start it all over again. The only part to the thing that the waves had no effect upon were the two black flashlights that continued to move wherever it was looking. Those two dark lights were fixed firmly at the floor where its feet would have been if it had feet.

"So, tell me, Luther, how does it feel to be locked inside a body that forces you to feel?" the creator asked while turning its sight directly at him.

Like a rapid-firing gun, memories of what it was started to play across his eyes. He remembered it being there the day that he crossed over into that dimension, and how he was always there, reminding him that everything had a beginning and an end. It was the reaper of souls; the destroyer of gods and demons.

"This is not my time, because you hold no power over me," Luther finally said, just as the strength that he had always had started to come to life again. "So, tell me why you are here."

With a laugh, the reaper replied, saying, "All this time you have existed, and yet you are still too cocky to realize that I do not answer to you." It paused for effect. "My orders come from above. But I am more than delighted to tell you why I am here. After all, I did this to you. I don't know if you remember, but I told you that you had to wait to possess this body. Then, after I took the soul out of it and plugged you into it, I put you in that tunnel," it stated, still looking at Luther, who had stood up. "That song you heard was Jacob's death song. I wrote it just for him, like I do everyone else that I claim."

All that had transpired to him over the last half day and night started to revive itself inside Luther, including the anger he felt when he had to wait to take over that body and the absolute vulnerability that took hold of him while in the tunnel, then the purest feelings of love and the passion when he finally looked at Nina lying fast asleep in their bed.

"I'm sick of cleaning up your messes, Luther. So now you will feel what it is to live, love, and lose as a human. Oh, and if you choose to make your own exit, well, I will be more than happy to end your existence permanently."

"You can only control me until I am finally made whole again, and that will happen," Luther said while taking a step closer.

"Ha ha! Good luck at making that happen. You do remember what happened the last time you attempted to release your book from that sarcophagus. Until that time, I truly hope you learn something about living," Death said as it stepped backward into the shadow that it had emerged from just a few moments earlier.

25

Devin's story

At first, the monks did not know what had happened. They had planned it to be the moment they were going to kill her. The leader, who oversaw the sacrifice, observed that she was dead, and before anyone else could tell, he cut across her neck. It was not, however, the blood of a living person. It was a blood offering from a dead body, but the blood didn't look like it was from someone that had just died. It looked like it had begun to coagulate. Her blood came out in thick dump-like sacs that pushed out of her cuts in the same way a bug would push dirt out of its underground home. Her blood had also changed to the same color as the raven feathers they were wearing. The other monks ran their blades down the inside of her wrist in order to assist the draining. They did not see what had happened when she was cut across her neck, so all of them were shocked when they saw what happened to her blood. When the first clump-like masses fell out of the long incisions, all of the monks gasped.

"What trickery is this?" one of them demanded an answer from the leader.

A few of them were convinced that it was the work of Loki, and asked, "Why would Loki choose to do this to us now when so much is at stake?"

The rest cried to their god to comfort them.

"Our fate has been sealed by a whisper I felt but did not hear," the leader said as he took off his robe, which was made of what appeared to be a bear's hide that had large raven features sewn onto it.

The monks around him looked shocked, and almost terrified, by his actions.

"I know I am not pure, like this young girl of 19 years was, but please, if only to quiet your anger, accept my blood tonight."

His words were so shaky, that I didn't see how his fellow monks would believe he was freely giving his body as an offering. By the way he presented himself, not even a vengeful god would accept that offering. The monks rushed him toward the table. Someone had just turned the lid 90 degrees in order to funnel as much of the girl's blood toward the hands that were holding the book in place. They were hoping that the god or demon they were trying to please would accept the blood.

"Quickly! No one noticed yet," one of the monks closest to the leader said quietly in a way to show urgency.

It appeared as if at least four of the monks had to push and pull the leader at one point or another to get him to the sarcophagus. His quick decision to give himself without thinking started to sink in, and the desire to live made him fight back with everything he had. He fought the other monks just like the girl did. He then understood how and why she continued to fight, even after they broke almost every bone in her body. Within less than an arm's length, the leader's legs gave out on him, and the four had to carry him the remaining distance.

Just as the monks finally got back to the sarcophagus, a prayer was whispered to the god or demon locked within the book. The leader looked for a way to escape until his eyes stopped at the head of the young girl lying dead next to him. He then remembered her begging him for mercy and to be released when it was decided that she was the one to be sacrificed. The bribes he took from families that had money just so he would look the other way and not choose their daughters burned like magma deep inside of him. He could feel how cold his words were when he told her she had been chosen by the god himself to die and live in paradise with him. He could then see himself lying there tied to the table, pleading to be set free, as those monks cut and broke his bones while laughing to themselves.

The six hands that lay flat on top of the book, locking it down, began to pull the book into the stone and clay so that the book was barely visible anymore. Only a faint shadow of the indentations made by the cover could be seen by the way the clay reflected the images that formed and molded it. The monks were less worried about the leader and about how they were going to kill him. Their attention was drawn to the book, and they started to pull at the hands, hoping they would stop the sinking of the book, and possibly, even bring it back to where it was when the night started.

One of the elders saw that they were reaching into the sarcophagus, pulling at something, and that the girl was dead. That elder started praising the one they were seeking, while making sure the others around her saw what was going on. As fast as a fire burning dried leaves, the entire crowd started cheering and chanting. Not a single person noticed that the leader's robes were stripped from him and that he was standing naked on the opposite side of the sarcophagus. Some of the warriors, who were supposed to be watching the forest, turned their attention to the monks to witness what they had done. Their actions left all of the people exposed, vulnerable to all the evils that waited deep within the tall, blacked-out grass that the light from the fire refused to shine on.

"Please be patient; we are not yet done," one of the stronger and more forceful monks said as he stepped in front of the sarcophagus.

He raised his hands, but the cheering, praise and chanting was so loud that no one could hear him. Over and over, he tried to silence them, but his words fell short every time. He knew he needed to stop trying to silence the crowd, and help sacrifice the leader, because there was more work for each of the monks due to being short one person.

He looked back at all the monks, and simultaneously they all asked if they were ready to proceed. As soon as they reached for their knives, a force blew all of the monks off their feet. They flew more than ten feet away from the sarcophagus. The force was so powerful that it also blew out the fire, sending a chill in the air that only the cold breezes in January and February could equal. The blackness did more than blind everyone. It quietened everyone to the point that I could even hear the furthest people away from me breathing until the slow sound of a stone rubbing against another stone could be heard. The sound echoed everywhere; never stopping; repeating itself. The echoes were just as loud as the initial sound, and that made it impossible to find out what had originally made the sound. The moon decided to end the stalemate. Like a spotlight, the moon focused on one spot and one spot only. That one spot was the sarcophagus, and it was closing without any help.

The eeriness of the solemn sound marched throughout the hushed group of people in the same flowing manner of the ink that moved through the wavy water. But the marching of the sound was thicker, bringing certainty of evil, not a welcoming of possible glory and peace. The sound also brought with it the same feeling as creasing a paper or scratching a plate with a fork or running knives across the chalkboard. I could see and feel the shivers that were running up and down all of their backs, yet I had not one shiver myself. I only felt their pain and torment.

The exact moment the sarcophagus closed, the moon that shone down on it blinked out of sight until it was nothing. Complete darkness engulfed the prairie. When blackness retook the night sky, thunder exploded with a force I had never known or heard before. The thunder never stopped; it was one after another. There wasn't, however, a single bit of lightning anywhere in the sky. All around us all that could be heard was a nonstop ringing of thunder. I thought maybe it was God thundering his fury onto the people who had turned away from him. Just when I thought I could not take it anymore, the sky finally lit up as a fireball as lightning fell from the sky, sealing the sarcophagus with heat and electricity

The lightning continued for what seemed to be an hour of nonstop strikes from all angles. It seemed to be hitting pinpoint spots everywhere on it in a clockwise manner. I was amazed how the lightning only hit the sarcophagus. I thought that with all the electricity that was buzzing in the air, some of those bolts would have hit the ground and people. The lightning didn't even raise the hair on any of the people standing less than ten feet away from it. There was nothing. It was as though whatever was in control guided it directly at it. The sarcophagus withstood all of the energy that was being rained down onto it, absorbing it.

Without warning or slowing down, the thundering and lightning ended. There was nothing; not even a single hissing sound of heat coming from the sarcophagus. I expected to hear the same sound as that of a sizzling piece of meat, but it lay there as if nothing had even happened. The only thing that was different was that the young girl was nowhere to be seen. Not even an ash as a reminder of her was left.

"What did you do?" one of the warriors yelled to the monks as he raised his axe and shield. "You told us that it would make us gods and we would conquer the world."

"They killed us, dooming us to the underworld I warned you about," a blind and half-crippled seer shouted as he stepped out of the shadow of people. "Now accept your fate and lay down your arms. Or you can take up your arms and shields with courage to face the shapeshifting Lut warriors who have come out of these waters in their hundreds to face you. They will not wear the faces of the young men they typically appear as. No, they will be in their truest form — a black, ever-shifting werewolf, vampire and mist that once fought with us. If you fight, you may make it to the halls of Valhalla."

He stopped talking as he somehow found his way without help to where the leader of the monks was standing, still naked. Without so much as a word, he took a short sword from the inside of his robes, and plunged it through the back of the leader. Carefully, he placed the blade through his lungs so that he could not scream, and then slowly and skillfully, he pushed the blade into the leader's heart. The seer held the leader up as he was dying to ensure as much pain as possible would be inflicted.

"You do not get the chance to right your wrong," the seer said just before the leader passed out and died.

Movement all around in the grass could be heard, but there was so much it was hard to hear just where the sound was coming from. If I was an owl, flying overhead, intertwined with the thicket of the blackness that made up the night sky, I would have been able to see just where those shapeshifting monsters were, as they were closing in on the encampment of Viking warriors and people. The night sky that always seemed to hold such mystery and transparency to my eyes, my dreams and even my soul on those moonless nights then became hollow. The world I used to dream about unendingly faded. Forgotten gods and lost worlds had become a thick, soupy substance that seemed to swallow dreams and sight. The new substance that was thickening the night sky became impregnated with the shapeshifters, and the two began working together. Each one fed off the chaos the other brought. The noises were getting more animalistic and crazed as they got closer to the group. Shield maidens and older children grabbed their swords and axes, while some of the braver men, who must have believed this was to be their death, stripped naked with only their boots on, an axe in one hand and a sword in the other.

"I will not hide from my death, and I will dine in the halls of Valhalla before dawn breaks!" one of the warriors screamed to a cheering crowd. There were many other hardened warriors who joined in with him.

"You are weak Lut creatures and fools to step on our land! This is not your watery home, so we give you this one warning. Run and we might spare you," the one who looked to be the chieftain of the tribe roared, and only stopped to let it sink in. "But make no mistake. Many of you monsters will not make it back to the water if you do not retreat." He stopped, as he raised his sword above his head, and then, like a machine, he lowered it, and pointed with it toward the thick darkness. "And you will be first."

To the sound of swords and axes banging against each other as a cadence for the chieftain, he ran into the darkness. With each step, the banging got louder, as the chieftain grew closer to the edge. He was determined to be the first to face the threat which was sneaking in on all sides. The chieftain towered above the rest of his men that were standing tall and strong to show strength and respect for their leader. None of them reached above the top of his shoulders in height. I could not see much detail, but his shaved head was covered in black tattoos and scars from the many battles he was in. His naked arms and chest revealed a man of great physical strength, which would have made wielding the large double-sided axe he carried an easy task. I could see the places where swords, axes and other instruments of war tore through his flesh in the attempt to end his life or torture him. His tribe of people parted for him to pass through. It was so perfectly timed that it felt natural; without ever needing to be rehearsed. Everyone was chanting a word that I was not permitted to understand. It almost felt like a battle cry.

Their chanting and hollering was so loud that I was the only person who could hear the Nokken closing in on the camp. They did not stop moving. In fact, they appeared to use the extra noise as a way of hiding their movements while all getting into position. I had a feeling that those monsters were not answering the call for single battle, but were making their final preparations to end the battle without letting any of the Vikings have a chance to fight and earn their way out of Hell's fire and torment.

The chieftain's heart beat loudly with a mix of rage, fear and excitement. His face had the look of a man betting in a card game when he didn't even have a single pair, only his bluff. Getting closer to the edge, he did not alter his facial expression or body language. Even his walk stayed the same throughout his march to the outer rim of his people. He matched his steps with that of the beating of axes, swords and shields in the way a marching band marches in proper cadence. By the time he was only a few feet from the rim, I could feel his heart wanted to explode out of his chest, but for some reason, he didn't stop. He took that last running step out from his people into the shadowy mix of monsters and the spiritual world of the thick darkness. A few steps out of his camp into the darkness, all the cheering faded into a sound that was more like listening to someone talking under water. The clarity of it was gone; all he could make out was that there was noise there. I watched as he turned his head to listen, and I knew it was not for the monsters but for his people.

He just kept running, and then stopped briefly, hoping to find the one whom he challenged, but there was nothing out there. All he found was the thick blackness. It felt like he had to swim through it to get anywhere. It was at that moment, he realized the blackness was a water-like substance and that he and his tribe were not facing an enemy on their land, but in its water grave. I watched as he turned back to find his way back, but all he saw was the blackness. His own breath began to choke him, and he started to drown. With each breath, it became harder and harder for him to breath. The chieftain looked like a swimmer caught underwater, panicking to reach air again, but within moments, he just slowly floated down to the ground.

All sounds of the Lut monsters had stopped; they were then in position. Every so often, I would see a blade of grass move or a purplish-black object in the shadows, but then, when I looked back to get a better view, it was gone. I tried my hardest to watch the group of people who were still cheering for their chieftain. I don't think they were able to see him, and they were not able to tell that he was already dead. Perhaps, because those things were shapeshifters, there were two of them in view, fighting each other; one posing as the chieftain and the other in one of the Lut shapes.

The monsters took over the battle. Moving in between and quieter than a single breath, they weaved throughout the tribe. They appeared to be a black mass that could and would change its appearance with every moment. Sometimes, they would move close to the ground, and reaching only one arm-like tentacle up to drain the life effortlessly out of as many as six people at a time. Men, women and children — those monsters didn't care. They wanted the old, the young and the strong. All that mattered was the life that was drained. Others stood tall, stepping over the top of their prey. Just as the person would look up to the sudden darkness that swallowed them, a hand or tentacle would shoot through their open mouths, impaling the person to the ground. They seemed to take a great deal of pleasure in the life they were taking. They sought out the warriors first, but they would kill up to three people at one time if they had to. The most agile ones were lower hunters, hugging the ground with a serpent-like grip. I couldn't make out the true height of those because they were always low. All I saw were the ten or more snake-like tentacles shooting out in all directions, killing anything that they touched. Those versions would disappear right after a kill. There would only be a glimpse of a shadow moving in the night.

In the time it took me to take a few deep breaths, more than half of the tribe had been wiped out without a single word, battle cry or manmade weapon swung. The monks were the first slaughtered, and the monsters seemed to enjoy killing them enormously. They made a cheering sound. As the tribe grew smaller, the shouting for their dead chieftain stayed the same. In a way of continuing their stealth attack, some of the Lut warriors changed their voices to match the fallen Vikings, and proceeded to shout and cheer loudly. Even with the tribe's size dwindled down to only 12, the Vikings were completely unaware of the attack because of the cheering.

The seer had been blocked out by the black cloud where the monsters were, because of how they surrounded and gathered around him. He found the sarcophagus and sat peacefully upon it, as if he was waiting for the battle to be over.

The 12 Viking warriors left still cheered and shouted out to their chieftain. They became the stalking prey. 12 of the largest Lut warriors were only a few steps behind the Vikings. Those 12 Vikings were some of the first that stripped off their clothing and welcomed the fight. They were easily 12 of the fiercest warriors in the tribe. Their bodies were all covered in scars, tattoos and scaly areas where they must have been burnt once.

All of the other Lut warriors filled in behind. There was a bloodcurdling scream that rivaled the thunder that had encased the heavens earlier. Partly by the deafening scream but mainly out of surprise, the Viking warriors fell silent. The biggest reason they stopped screaming and cheering was they knew what was behind them and what wasn't. Only the monsters remained.

"For my father's fathers!" all 12 shouted together, as they spun around and thrust their swords or axes into the towering black monsters that stood behind them.

Deafening screams came from the Lut warriors as the blades pierced their skin. In a reflex, they plunged their long, dark arms into the naked warriors and lifted them high into the air like they were children's toys.

"Victory!" is all I could understand the monsters shouting, while still holding the dying warriors in the air.

With little to no effort, they turned, and threw the Viking warriors into the dark mass of the Lut warriors. Rather quickly, they gathered the dead and dragged them into the stream, which seemed to have changed into the ocean. The seer, who was still sitting on top of the sarcophagus, was smiling and laughing to himself.

The battle had only lasted a few minutes. Not one of the monsters had been killed. Only the 12 that revealed themselves were even injured, but to what extent, I will never know. They did not look very injured when they threw the warriors into the Lut warriors. The only remembrance that there ever was a Viking tribe there was the firepit, the weapons of war, the tools of sacrifice and the sealed sarcophagus.

The seer was standing before me. He stood with the confidence and determination of a concurring king. He wasn't just the seer of a tribe that has just been completely erased from history. He was not a tall man, but I felt as if I was standing in the shadow of a great giant. Even though his height was somewhere between 5'5" and 5'9", there was something that was standing with him, making him appear taller, stronger and wiser. His eyes were sewn shut with the same thick leather that was used to make their leather armor and rugged clothing. His face was worn as though he had spent his entire life in the sun, not in the cold land of the Vikings. To cover most of the age marks on his face, he grew a thick beard, and wore a large cloak that he could use to shield his skin from any more damage from the sun. In many ways, he looked and appeared like a living, breathing, walking scarecrow. His mouth had a black, ink-like slime oozing out from the corners. When he opened his mouth to breathe, I could see that the ink outlined the few teeth he had left. The smell of rot came from his mouth and nose every time he exhaled.

"What you just saw here tonight was the first of many failed attempts at raising Luther."

He stopped to catch his breath and look toward the half-dead tree. Never once did he look down toward me, even though he appeared to be talking directly to me. I was merely a passing note in his life. With a force stronger than my father had ever thrown upon me at that stage in my life, the seer grabbed my right shoulder and pulled me closer to the rotten smell pouring out of him.

"You will see the last time as well when you are a grown man, and it will be the rising of his strength not his body. Luther will already be living in another human's body for some time at that moment. He will guide the followers of his cult. You will forget this night until that night is upon you," the seer said solemnly as he let go of my arm and started to walk toward the tree.

I knew he couldn't physically see the tree, but I knew he knew where it was and what he was doing. Then, within a few steps of the tree, the dead half came to life again. The ink squirted out into the thick night's air, and this time, it was harder for the ink to find a rhythm like before. The two red eyes that were looking hungrily at me earlier were nowhere to be seen and neither were the claws that had been trying to rip a hole in the tree. At first, I thought more ink was pouring out to try to find a way to harmonize with the surrounding nature, but as I watched, I could see that the hole had become bigger and that that had let more of the ink escape. The red-eyed monster was not there, the Vikings were all gone, and the Lut warriors had retired to the water. So what could possibly be the reason it was opening up wider? Hidden in the black ink all this time was the truth, and with a single fireball at the base of the tree, I could see that the seer was walking into the dead half of the tree. That single moment when the smallest part of his body crossed the threshold, another explosion erupted, and continued to erupt, until his whole body was gone. I did not want to watch the end, so I covered my eyes and turned away.

It felt like an eternity had passed since I closed my eyes and looked away, so when I opened them, I expected to find myself lost in the middle of the woods, but my eyes adjusted a little bit to the light that was there, and I saw that I was no longer where I thought I was. I was back in my capsule, returning to the room with those two reflecting eyes waiting for me. The only difference between the red eyes then and before was that there was no break from their shining reflection. They penetrated easily through the capsule and into my blue eyes. I don't know what it saw, but there was something buried beneath my eyes that it must not have liked.

With a snort-like growl, it said, "What is it you think you can do here? The deed is done, and will be whole again."

As it spoke, the candle started to burn all the smoke and fog in the room, revealing what I already knew. I did not care for the beast or what it wanted; all I cared about was what was on the table. I also wanted to know who those men and women were that were standing around the table. Part of me wanted to look away as the black smoke thinned into a transcendent cloud, but my heart wouldn't permit me. I could tell there was a person, but who was it.

"Look, Devin. I know that your heart wants to know what your mind already knows," the beast said with a grinning laugh. "But will you let this defeat you or will this be what makes you a man? I believe you are weak and that it will crush you. You will never see me coming when I come for your soul!" the beast screamed as it ripped a hole through the side of the diner, pulling with him the rest of the smoke and fog, while shattering my capsule.

My heart stopped in disbelief as I stared down at the pale and drained body of James. It seemed that all color had been sucked out of him and onto the table he lay on. The table remained obscured under the cover of smoke, fog and darkness, but there was no mistaking what he was lying upon. It was the sarcophagus. His skin appeared to have been vacuumed tightly against the rest of his body in an attempt to squeeze or suck the last bit of life that was still within it. I could make out every muscle in his arms and he looked like a smaller version of a bodybuilder because of how defined each muscle was. I wondered if that would have happened to me; if my skin would squeeze me that tight to reveal muscles I never knew I had.

The veins in his arms were gone, flattened by the process of taking his life force while transferring it to the sarcophagus. The same was true for his neck; I could not find any vein or artery anywhere. The color of his skin had faded into some soft, white, marble statue the Greeks carved and polished to portray one of their gods. His skin and muscle were fluid, blending with the part next to it. Looking over his arms, neck and the lower parts of his face brought destruction that my heart did not know it could feel. I felt myself slipping away quicker than I could even think, but there was a voice inside me telling that maybe, just maybe, it wasn't him, and that I had to continue to force my eyes to meet his lifeless gaze. The last look he took before finally meeting death was the same look that I saw plastered upon the faces of others when they saw a friend or loved one they had not seen in a long time. Perhaps it was one of his family members that death had brought to take him to peace or to damnation.

At his lips, my sight found rest for a moment. I could hear and see the words he used to say. Whether they were good or bad, encouraging or filled with obstruction, I could hear them all. The jokes and laughter that we shared throughout the years rang out loudly, but I also imagined the jokes we would no longer share. I wished that I did not have to look anymore, because what good would it do to see the eyes of my friend staring off into the afterlife, all the while knowing the only place I would ever find him again was in my heart. There was a force pushing me to look longer and deeper at James. It became so powerful that it overwhelmed my ability to close my eyes and look away. My heart broke, weakened with grief and disbelief at the loss of James. I was forced to look past James's nose and into his eyes. Fear took hold of me, but it was not in his eyes. It was in mine. James always had such bright, sky-blue eyes. They were so bright they would light up the darkness within any room he entered. The blue that was in his eyes was taken, and in its place was the same blackness that I saw coming out of the tree with living flames burning all the edges of that ink-like substance.

Swirling around in a tiny circle where the blues of his eyes used to be was the ink, trapped by some unending flame. Both were spinning in opposite directions, coming down the inside of the face, out toward the ears and up again. It felt like a trap, and it was trying to pull me into it. I wanted to pull away, if only to grieve for my friend and possibly to find a way to join him, but his eyes stopped me from doing anything. My eyes grew tired, and dreams started to crowd my focus as the world around me faded into those dreams.

That was the last time I ever saw James, that diner or anything in that part of the world. When I came to, I was standing at the beginning of the driveway to the house.

A man in a blue, four-door pickup truck pulled up, and asked out of dark windows, "Are you Devin Bradley?"

Not really sure what to say at first, because I didn't know where I was or who the guy was, I just stared at him with a dumb look on my face.

"Look, kid. I don't have all day, so if you are him, this is the deed to the home. The truck is in the garage; cable and electricity's on," he said as he leaned out the window.

He was a middle-aged man who had the look of someone who was sick of doing those stupid jobs and just wanted a break once in his life. Unlike most men going bald, who shaved their hair off, he did not. Instead, he chose a comb-over.

"Yes. I am Devin Bradley," I said as I reached up and took the yellow, manila folder from the real-estate agent.

26

Devin and Victoria

Vic sat back, pressing heavily into the back cushions of the couch. Her eyes were locked onto the fire. The reflection was easily seen in her eyes and what looked to be some small half tears. I wanted her to look at me and show me through a look that she believed me, but then again that would mean I had to face her. After bearing all that I had locked away inside me, I didn't want to answer questions as to why I had never said anything. Had I told that to his mother and family? What did the police say? Those were questions I had no answer for. I told her more than I should have, but I did not tell her everything. I held back maybe the most important part.

That monster did not just leave through a hole in the wall. It first took its time to crawl over the top of James, inching closer and closer with such fluidity of motion that it never looked like any part of his body stopped moving. At first, only a shadow of his body crawled toward me, but as the candles lit up his underneath and sides, it appeared that a thick fur was melting away into dust, revealing a sweaty, dirty and blood-covered, whitish-red skin.

His head was in the shape of a bear-wolf hybrid. It was thick like a bear, but his nose was longer and more defined. With every inch he came closer to me, he took a deep breath from James's corpse and showed his teeth while also growling at me. His two red eyes never left my sight. If this was a stare down, he was winning.

I wanted to challenge him for what he did to James, but I was frozen. The only movement I could complete was blinking. With every blink, he seemed to move a foot closer until he was halfway over James's body and stopped. I couldn't help but blink, and as soon as I opened my eyes, I was hit in the face by its breath. It was so hot that my entire face, neck and upper chest was covered in sunburn-like damage.

"Devin, your time to die at my hands is not tonight. In fact, I will leave you alone until our predetermined time comes. If, however, you so much as even mention this night to anyone, I will be able to come to you," he said in a deep, rasping voice. It reminded me of a hard- rock singer's voice. He took another deep breath off James and added, "One of my many generals will always be around you. In every dark corner or alleyway or standing beside you, there will always be one. So don't think you will be able to hide from me. Even in a church, one of them will be there. If you do tell someone, you will have to witness another one of your friends dying all over again."

As soon as he was done threatening me, he stepped off the table and walked smoothly out of the hole in the wall. He must have done me a favor in a way when he sent that dream to me and moved me 3,000 miles away and months later. That way, I had no one to answer to.

When I searched for any information about the diner, I saw that there was a shooting that happened there. The person responsible for it burned the place to the ground and that there was only one recognizable body, and it was James! The newspaper article somehow inferred that both of us were killed that night. The person responsible for the shooting and the fire was killed by the police when they got to the diner. There were a few photos from James's funeral that were of his mother and mine embracing each other. The mournful rain hid their tears.

I knew that I had to tell Vic the whole story, but how could I? I knew what the creature was going to do. Maybe that time had come anyway, because it had already pursued both of us, just hours earlier.

"Vic, there is more, and you really need to know this," I said distantly while staring off into the fire.

The warmth from it was alluring and gentle.

"No," Vic added softly. "I don't need to know anymore." She turned to me, placing her cold hand on my cheek. She waited until I looked up at her and said, "I mean, all we have is right now, and even if this is our last moment or mine, I couldn't ask for anyone better to spend it with."

We made love.

Want to get in the mood?

Grab your free copy of
A Mix of Love, Lust and Pain.

Go to **matthewyard.com** now!

www.ingramcontent.com/pod-product-compliance
Lightning Source LLC
LaVergne TN
LVHW041315080426
835513LV00008B/465